**An Inside Look
at External Affairs
during the Trudeau Years**

An Inside Look at External Affairs during the Trudeau Years

The Memoirs of Mark MacGuigan

Edited by
P. Whitney Lackenbauer

Foreword by
Paul C. Martin

UNIVERSITY OF
CALGARY
PRESS

University of Calgary Press
2500 University Drive NW
Calgary, Alberta
Canada T2N 1N4
www.uofcpress.com

National Library of Canada Cataloguing in Publication Data

MacGuigan, Mark
An inside look at External Affairs during the Trudeau years

　　　Includes bibliographical references and index.
　　　ISBN 1-55238-076-9

　　　1. MacGuigan, Mark, 1931- 2. Canada—Foreign relations—1945-
　　　3. Politicians—Canada—Biography. I. Lackenbauer, P. Whitney. II. Title.

　　　FC626.M323A3 2002　　　　　327.71'0092　　　　　C2002-910895-0
　　　F1034.3.M323A3 2002

The University of Calgary Press gratefully acknowledges the financial assistance of the Donner
Canadian Foundation, the Court Martial Appeal Court, and the following individuals for the
publication of this book: Mike Brogan, Kevin Coon, Robert Daudlin, Brian Ducharme, John
English, David Fleet, Alfio Golini, W. C. Graham, Sharon Gray, John Haviland, Darrel V.
Heald, C. M. Huddart, J. K. Hugessen, Frank Iacobucci, Julius A. Isaac, A. M. Linden, Clare
Lowery, Kenneth Lysyk, Paul Martin, Francis C. Muldoon, Ken Ouellette, Terry Patterson,
Camille Quenneville, Carl T. Quenneville, Fred and Lisa Quenneville, Fred Quenneville Sr.,
James C. Quenneville, A. J. Stone, B. L. Strayer, and Margaretha G. Zonjic.

Canada　We acknowledge the financial support of the Government of Canada through
the Book Publishing Industry Development Program (BPIDIP) for our
publishing activities.

The Canada Council for the Arts
Le Conseil des Arts du Canada

Printed and bound in Canada by AGMV Marquis.
∞ This book is printed on acid-free paper.

For the women and men
of the Department of External Affairs,
for whom I was for a short time
privileged to be the spokesperson.

Contents

Mark R. MacGuigan,
P.C., M.A., Ph.D., LL.B., LL.M., J.S.D., LL.D.

Foreword

Between these covers, you will read about the life of an individual – Mark MacGuigan – who dedicated his life to bettering Canada in a wide variety of ways.

From his fascination with the law to his interest in politics and international affairs, Mark made a lasting mark on virtually every area to which he turned his efforts. You will make your own judgment of that legacy after reading what follows, but my purpose here is to simply remark upon the Mark MacGuigan who was a great friend to my family and to me over decades.

I first came to know Mark MacGuigan in the early 1960s at St. Michael's College. He was a graduate student in philosophy, and I was an undergraduate in the same discipline. As the old saying goes, his reputation preceded him – even back then. Around St. Mike's, Mark was renowned as a rigorous and careful thinker – but also as someone who was very generous with his time. He was the kind person to whom others – undergraduates such as myself – might turn to second-guess their own logic and work. He was always willing to share an insight and suggest an improvement – and he was asked often.

These qualities were ones that I would come to rely upon substantially during my next period of time with Mark – as his student in bankruptcy law at the University of Toronto law school. What I remember most clearly about this course is that Mark – while perhaps not entirely fascinated with the detail of bankruptcy law – was clearly at home in academia. He loved the surroundings. He enjoyed the room to think. And he was good at it. Mark was a scholar born. Moreover, he was a superb administrator – as became evident with his appointment as dean of the University of Windsor Law School.

Mark's presence had an immediate impact on the law school and the community. With his methodical and meticulous standards, he set about immediately and successfully building the law school that we know today.

The unique experience known now as "Windsor Law" is one that had its very roots in Mark's stewardship. He lent the school the full dint of his energies, but, more importantly, he instilled it with his personality: an eager thirst for the freedom of ideas and the places they lead.

It was also during this time that Mark's deep and lasting friendship with my family took hold. My father and he made an instant connection based on mutual interests and shared enthusiasms. He became a regular visitor to my parents' home, and, over a remarkably short period of time, Mark became one of my father's favoured confidants. More than once, I was witness to – and when I found it possible to interject, a participant in – conversations that stretched from historical debate to contemporary disagreements and which lasted long into the night.

The full impact of this relationship was borne out a few years later when Mark agreed to contest the Liberal nomination in Windsor-Walkerville and ultimately succeeded my father as that riding's member of Parliament. For decades, my father had served as that riding's representative, and, for all his achievements in public life, I can say with certainty that it was his proudest accomplishment. The pride with which he watched Mark take his place, therefore, tells you all that you need to know about the depth of respect the two men held for one another.

Throughout this period, I had stayed in irregular contact with Mark, but with his new entry into the field of politics – and as the MP for Windsor-Walkerville, no less – I again became more closely aware of his career. Almost immediately as a parliamentarian, Mark showed a strong facility for and interest in international affairs. Also a passion of my father's, this interest – steadfastly maintained during his distinguished tenure as justice minister – always suggested to me that Mark's appointment as Secretary of State for External Affairs was simply a matter of time.

This was, beyond doubt, the pinnacle of his career and his most cherished accomplishment in public life. Those two years, while short in duration, were significant in impact. He would be thrilled to know that, years later, his efforts in that office would be the subject of debate and discussion among students of politics and international relations.

That Mark would one day choose to contest the party leadership also came as little surprise. He believed that ideas had to be debated, and he saw no greater position from which to do so than that of prime minister. Moreover, he understood that even an unsuccessful bid for the position of leader could present one with the opportunity to propose and present such ideas. While his contest for the leadership fell short, his challenge to the party and the nation in the field of discourse did not.

In 1992, when my father passed away, Mark was quick to express his deep regret and condolences. Too few years later, I found myself in the same position when I learned of Mark's passing. Mark's loss was huge for the federal bench – where he had sat since 1984 – for federal politics, and for public affairs more broadly. But for all the impact he had on these fields, it was Mark's kindness and humanity that was the greatest loss.

In delivering the eulogy at Mark's memorial service, I spoke on this point. I told those present of the habit that Mark developed in the last few years before my father passed away of paying regular visits, phone calls, and conversations with my dad. Sharing a mutual enthusiasm for politics, international affairs, and the law, they would spend hours doing what each loved best – discussing, debating, and exchanging anecdotes.

In my opinion, this provided a critical insight to the personality and character of Mark MacGuigan. Not only did it display the kind of loyal and thoughtful friend that he was, it revealed that other fundamental quality of his: a limitless passion for debating public and political affairs.

That is why I am so pleased about the publication of this book. It will serve as an immutable testament to Mark's legacy. It guarantees that the Mark MacGuigan who was such a great friend and influence on my family, on Windsor, on the Liberal party, and on the nation will rest forever on bookshelves and desktops. It will ensure he remains in those places he most enjoyed – where people come to debate and discuss ideas. Please enjoy.

Paul Martin
Ottawa, Ontario

Background

A few months before his death on 12 January 1998, Mark MacGuigan spoke to us about two projects that he knew he could not complete. One dealt with his career as minister of justice in the government of Pierre Trudeau between 1982 and 1984, the other with his tenure as Secretary of State for External Affairs between March 1981 and September 1982. The former was little more than a series of rough drafts of chapters. The latter, however, was in the final stages of revision, but Mark knew that he did not have time to complete it. He asked for our help.

Although Mark's tenure was brief, the period was historic. Ronald Reagan won the U.S. presidential election in 1980, and the so-called Reagan revolution began with its direct challenge to the "evil empire" of Soviet communism and its assertive economic policy that appeared to threaten Canadian interests. Reagan was conservative; Pierre Trudeau, who returned to office in the Canadian general election of 1980, was not. The two began to joust regularly, and the task of the Canadian external affairs minister became difficult. The economic nationalism of the Trudeau government rankled American officials who demanded explanation and complained about numerous specific policies, especially in the energy field.

After the Quebec referendum on sovereignty-association in 1980, Trudeau announced that he would repatriate the constitution and develop a charter of rights and freedoms for Canada. This repatriation attempt meant that Canada would have to deal with the British Parliament, since the British North America Act was a British statute that had to be amended for repatriation to occur. Margaret Thatcher, the British prime minister, was no admirer of Trudeau. Moreover, some British parliamentarians were troubled by the initial opposition of Canadian provinces and aboriginals to the proposed constitution act. Mark MacGuigan was a specialist in constitutional law and was superbly placed and trained to deal with these momentous questions. He took responsibility for dealing with the British and played a major part in planning strategy in caucus and cabinet.

There were, too, myriad bilateral and multilateral problems that faced Canada's foreign minister during this period. Canada was seeking to diversify its trade and gave special attention to Japan and booming East Asia. Maintaining ties with Cuba and other communist regimes became more complicated with the increased hostility between the west and the communist world. Morale in the Department of External Affairs was poor, and Trudeau even appointed a royal commission to study the department's low morale. The commission pointed to several specific problems, notably the age profile of the department and the increasing difficulty of finding postings where spouses who wanted to work could do so. A major reason for the lack of confidence within the department was the attitude of the prime minister. Trudeau was no admirer of the Canadian diplomatic corps, as Lester Pearson had been. He once said that he learned more from *The New York Times* than he did from the diplomatic despatches that landed on his desk.

Trudeau often took an issue from MacGuigan on very short notice and made it his own. He even intervened to make certain that he determined the architect of the new Canadian embassy in Washington. In this study, one glimpses the peculiar prime ministerial style of Trudeau. Attention was intermittent in the area of foreign affairs, but once he noticed an issue he could pursue it relentlessly. Established patterns of foreign policy were broken, and allies needed to be reassured. That job fell to his foreign minister and departmental officials.

This detailed memoir is one of the finest descriptions of the operations of the last Trudeau government and of the Department of External Affairs. The full draft of the memoir will be available for consultation. We believe that Mark would have shortened his volume considerably and would have probably added some more personal detail. Unfortunately, his early death prevented this work. We were fortunate that a brilliant graduate student in Canadian history, Whitney Lackenbauer of the University of Calgary, was able to edit the book for publication. He has done a superb job for which we and the MacGuigan family are most grateful.

We miss Mark, his quiet wit, his shrewd judgment, and his personal compassion. This book reminds us of the wonderful friendship we shared.

John English, Waterloo, Ontario
Allen Linden, Ottawa, Ontario

Biographical Note

Mark R. MacGuigan, P.C., M.A., Ph.D., LL.B., LL.M., J.S.D., LL.D., was born on February 17, 1931, son of the late Agnes Violet Trainer and the late Hon. Mark R. McGuigan, Prince Edward Island, both Canadians of Irish descent. Mark's father was a Minister of Education and Public Health, Attorney General and Judge on the Supreme Court of Prince Edward Island. Mark had one sister, Roberta (1938–1991).

Mark was educated at St. Dunston's University, Charlottetown (B.A.), University of Toronto (M.A., Ph.D.), Osgoode Hall Law School, York University (LL.B.), and Columbia University (LL.M., J.S.D.) and held five honorary doctorates of law.

Mark was admitted to three Canadian law societies and the Queen's Counsel, Ontario, Canada.

One of his most fulfilling career paths was as a teacher. He was an Assistant Professor (1960–63) and Associate Professor (1963–66) of Law at the University of Toronto. He also was a visiting Associate Professor of Criminal Law, New York University (summer, 1966); Professor of Law at Osgoode Hall Law School, York University (1966–67), and Founding Dean of the Faculty of Law, University of Windsor (1967–68).

Elected to the House of Commons for the constituency of Windsor-Walkerville in 1968, Mark served for sixteen years in the House of Commons. He served as Parliamentary Secretary to two ministers, chairing three Parliamentary Committees and one Joint Committee. In 1980, Mark was appointed to the cabinet as Secretary of State for External Affairs and was also appointed Minister of Justice and Attorney General of Canada in 1982. He became a Judge of the Federal Court of Appeal on June 29, 1984 and held that position until his death on January 12, 1998.

Mark wrote and published extensively on such subjects as law, philosophy, and social policy. His most recent book, *Abortion, Conscience, and Democracy,* was published in 1994.

One of his proudest accomplishments was being awarded the Tarnapolsky Medal for Human Rights in 1995 by the Canadian Section of the International Commission of Jurists. Mark was a staunch advocate of individual human rights his whole life. While I am sure my viewpoint may be somewhat prejudiced, I believe he was the best human being I have ever known. He possessed unwavering integrity and was such a warm, kind, and gentle man, but he was always willing to fight for the less fortunate. I loved his generous, renaissance spirit and our children and I miss his inspiration and warmth terribly. We especially miss his exuberant laughter. He had a passion for books, music (both classical and jazz) and travelling, and thoroughly enjoyed our children and grandchildren. Our combined family includes five wonderful children (Ellen, Mark, Tom, Beth, and Buddy) and six sweet (most of the time) grandchildren: Tashina and Tecumseh MacGuigan; Jessica, Jack, Abby, and Charles Maye; and Lily and William Robinson. I was honoured to be his wife and soulmate.

I am confident Mark would be pleased and most grateful that his considerable work on this book has been rewarded with this publication. It could not have been accomplished without the efforts and financial contributions made by so many friends and colleagues (especially Justice Al Linden and John English), and I deeply and gratefully appreciate their caring and thoughtfulness.

Patricia D. MacGuigan

Editor's Note

The Honourable Mark MacGuigan (1931–1998) passed away before he had the opportunity to submit a final, polished manuscript to a publisher. Recognizing the fundamental importance of Mr. MacGuigan's memories as Secretary of State for External Affairs to the historical record, his literary executors asked that I edit the manuscript for publication. The following is a brief note of the changes I have made to his final draft, and it introduces the major themes, issues, and events that are examined in this volume.

MacGuigan explicitly states in the introduction that the book was not meant to explore every aspect of Canadian foreign policy under Pierre Trudeau, but rather to serve as a personal chronicle of his experiences as Secretary of State for External Affairs – a political autobiography focused on foreign affairs. Much of the material contained in these pages was gleaned from External Affairs files, which MacGuigan has presented in the context of his own experiences, and his insights into the personalities and issues that marked the period are clearly those of a man of sharp intellect. The content spans a wide range of bilateral and multilateral issues, weaves together an intriguing cast of national and international characters, and offers important insights into the making of foreign policy from a ministerial perspective. MacGuigan placed a premium on making his observations and reflections accessible to the general reader, avoiding the convoluted jargon that clouds much current scholarship. I have significantly shortened and edited his final draft of some five hundred typed pages, while retaining primary respect for his express wishes and designs.

MacGuigan adopted some scholarly apparatus akin to academic work, but this is still largely a memoir – albeit an unconventional one. That this manuscript lies somewhere between the "normal" scholarly and autobiographical realms reflects both the author's background as a lawyer, academic, and politician and the complex foreign affairs of the early 1980s. MacGuigan's death short-circuited other versions that he might have furnished so the material in this volume will not emerge as in more traditional memoirs. But this book draws upon the version the author wanted to produce. To rewrite the manuscript as a traditional autobiography would change the essence of this study and would raise significant issues of voice, given that the author is deceased. I have gone to great lengths to retain as much of the author's original language as possible, so as to ensure that I did not distort his impressions or impose my own understanding of events (apart from correcting obvious errors).

I have taken the liberty of reorganizing and severing substantial portions of the original manuscript, while at the same time avoiding as much as possible rewriting the text. MacGuigan recounts the context of decisions and the unfolding of diplomatic relationships in tremendous detail. I have condensed much of this detail where it concerns activities in which Mr. MacGuigan had a limited personal role, but I have endeavoured to retain his important descriptions of personal relationships and of the character of decision-making in Canadian foreign policy. The Cold War context that shaped the author's world view is crucial to understanding the international milieu of the time and, accordingly, Canada's responses to developments as both a sovereign country and as a member of alliances. I have therefore retained more contextual detail in the chapters on the East-West divide and on arms control and disarmament than in other sections.

***

The first part of the book introduces the personalities and structures integral to the making of Canadian foreign policy. MacGuigan begins his memoirs by describing how and why Trudeau made him Secretary of State for External Affairs (SSEA) – a post coveted by several key individuals (including Jean Chrétien, who seemed to take the appointment personally). Despite previous claims that Trudeau appointed MacGuigan so as to secure personal control of external affairs, the latter argues that the prime minister did not unduly interfere with the conduct of foreign policy, even when he and his SSEA expressed divergent views. The author explains Trudeau's relationship with his ministers, cabinet, and senior bureaucrats; his intellectualism; and also how Ivan Head's departure from the Prime Minister's Office provided MacGuigan with more freedom than his predecessors at External Affairs. MacGuigan explains his own background in and outlook on international issues: his intellectual pluralism and aversion to bipolarism in a "multipolar world," as well as his rejection of totalitarian Soviet communism and general belief in supporting the "vibrant and imperfect democracy" of the United States in East-West issues.

Chapter 2 explores Trudeau's principles in foreign policy, identifying various "stages" of self-interest and altruism and a leadership style driven by a "Canada First" policy, rather than moral zeal. MacGuigan compares and contrasts his own views and beliefs with those of Trudeau, especially vis-à-vis the United States and East-West relations. While Trudeau loved to "thumb his nose" at the United States (and President Ronald Reagan, in particular), MacGuigan harboured no animosity towards Americans and saw them as the obvious leaders of the Western Alliance. It was Canada's duty, he suggests, to point out the folly of American ways only on occasions where they genuinely conflicted with Canadian interests (he called this "responsible nationalism"), rather than intellectually sparring with the United States over international initiatives that broadly served our national interests. Trudeau's combative style could be dangerous, and only respect for his tremendous ability spared him domestic and international disfavour.

Next, MacGuigan turns to explaining the personalities in and influences on the Department of External Affairs in the Trudeau years. He describes the major changes that took place in External Affairs during his tenure, including a more realist foreign policy by concentrating on particular bilateral relationships with dominant trading interests. Allan Gotlieb and others played key roles in educating and advising the new SSEA, and the author's complimentary appraisal of key public servants stands in sharp contrast to his predecessor Flora MacDonald's depictions of bureaucratic "entrapment" and excessive power. Intra- and interdepartmental bargaining was an accepted reality at External Affairs, and MacGuigan stresses that confrontations between ministers and senior bureaucrats are foolish and indicative of faulty leadership, rather than systemic flaws. MacGuigan also describes how combining his diverse responsibilities as SSEA with his duties as an MP could be onerous.

***

The second part of the memoirs examines general themes of the period. The fourth chapter provides a detailed examination of U.S. president Jimmy Carter's proposed boycott of the Moscow Olympics over the Soviet invasion of Afghanistan. MacGuigan explains how politics, public opinion, and personalities influenced the decision to boycott the games and how unanticipated developments almost "upset the applecart." The Australian prime minister committed the taboo of revealing Canadian intentions to the press, and a delay in West Germany's official commitment derailed MacGuigan's plans to make reference to that country when announcing Canada's adherence to the Olympic boycott. In the end, the boycott was only partially successful, at least denying the Soviets a chance to showcase purported communist supremacy, and MacGuigan's first foray into external politics was self-avowedly somewhat disappointing.

The author identifies the East-West divide as "the overriding international problem" during his tenure as SSEA. The superpower conflict cast an ominous shadow across the entire globe, and MacGuigan stresses that he always appreciated that our most profound differences remained with the Soviets and not the Americans. MacGuigan interprets East-West relations through observations on various international personalities and the meetings that brought them together. Jimmy Carter emerges as a "thoroughly decent human being" with capable advisers. Ronald Reagan comes across as lacking Trudeau's capacity for abstract thought, merely delivering lines penned by lamentable advisers who shunned a nuanced approach to international relations. Al Haig emerges as a more sensitive and attentive individual. Despite Margaret Thatcher's impressiveness, MacGuigan suggests that she lacked a social conscience. Helmut Schmidt's balance endeared him to Trudeau but not to the Reagan administration, and the wisdom of his foreign minister "Dieter" Genscher made him MacGuigan's favourite. Given international realities (the end of détente and Soviet aggression in Afghanistan), MacGuigan argues that the West had no choice but to take a hard line against the East. The "two-track policy" of weapons modernization and arms control negotiations became core to both Western and Canadian policy. The narrative focuses on various gatherings of NATO and the Council for Security and Cooperation in Europe, where international – and domestic – consensus proved elusive because of crises over martial law in Poland (an issue on which MacGuigan and Trudeau differed) and pipeline sanctions.

Chapter 6 looks specifically at arms control and disarmament – an issue that elicited significant popular interest during the period. MacGuigan assesses Canadian and international perceptions of security and the disarmament movement, focusing on negotiations at the United Nations and explaining why the international situation inhibited agreement until after he departed from External Affairs. He also discusses bilateral and multilateral dimensions of Canada's nuclear policy (in terms of both armament and export) and his government's strong commitment to nuclear safeguards. Finally, MacGuigan assesses the contentious issue of cruise missile testing, placing external criticisms and government decision-making within the context of NATO's deterrence strategy.

Trudeau's preoccupation with Third World issues made the North-South dialogue an area of priority during MacGuigan's tenure as SSEA. In Chapter 7, the author describes his efforts to augment Canada's official development assistance levels, explains how the government determined which countries should receive Canadian aid, and chronicles international meetings in which he and Trudeau tried in vain to create the basis for a comprehensive global negotiations process. In hindsight, MacGuigan is critical of both his and the government's actions on human rights issues, rationalizing why the government's course was taken but suggesting that Canada should have made the human rights agenda a more explicit, and more public, foreign policy objective.

***

The third part of the memoirs examines particular themes and regional relationships. In chapter 8, MacGuigan places Trudeau's constitutional initiative in the context of British-Canadian relations. He describes visits and negotiations with the Queen, British politicians, and their senior advisers to illuminate how patriation (and more specifically the Charter of Rights and Freedoms) caused division and posed difficulties. MacGuigan recounts episodes of intrigue and tension that demanded measured responses and careful posturing, such as Sir John Ford's "unseemly actions" as British High Commissioner to Canada and massive leaks of Canadian diplomatic cables to London eventually attributed to a foreign service officer with separatist allegiances. He describes how proponents and critics of the patriation process lobbied from outside of Canada to try to influence the process, and also notes reactions to the resolution of constitutional matters within the Liberal party and the country.

The author then examines the most important and most challenging foreign relationship for any Canadian government to manage – the relationship with the United States. MacGuigan discusses the principal bilateral issues during his time in office. Disputes over maritime boundaries and fisheries (the Gulf of Maine and West Coast crises) brought to the fore sovereignty and economic issues that led to adjudication and arbitration. Discussions on transboundary air pollution (acid rain) began during this time, although substantive agreement remained elusive. The Garrison Water Diversion Project, which threatened to pollute Canadian waters, precipitated intense lobbying in Washington and persistent concerns. MacGuigan shows how the management of these issues represented a move towards a "new diplomacy" of direct intervention in American politics and illustrates the enlargement of foreign policy to include new areas (e.g., the environment), and federal-provincial relations regarding external policy. He explains how the National Energy Program upset domestic producer provinces and elicited predictable complaints from the Reagan administration. The government took American concerns seriously, MacGuigan argues, and did concede some reasonable modifications (although not for legal reasons). The chapter concludes with an appraisal of how the personalities of Trudeau and Reagan clashed and the role of a distorted media diatribe in exacerbating American suspicions about the prime minister. Trudeau's indifference to the personal aspect of foreign policy, the author suggests, inhibited the building of relationships and affected the conduct of foreign policy and politics.

Chapter 10 shifts the focus further south in the western hemisphere. MacGuigan examines Canada's official developmental assistance for the Commonwealth Caribbean and why the government continued to give aid to Grenada after the Marxist coup, but withdrew all aid to Cuba in 1980. Nowhere did the bipolar extremists of both superpowers battle more in this period than in the Caribbean and Central America, he laments, and both were misguided. In office, MacGuigan had to grapple with the revolution in El Salvador and balance somewhat divergent American and Canadian interests through "quiet diplomacy." Of note is the interplay between MacGuigan and the Conference of Canadian Bishops, which illustrates not only the author's views as a Catholic but the range of pressures he faced. Most Canadian policy towards Latin America was, however, based on economic self-interest expressed through bilateral trade relationships. MacGuigan explains why he was in favour of Canadian membership in the Organization of American States (OAS) and received Trudeau's consent to act in that direction. His successor, Allan MacEachen, did not pursue it, and it was left to the Conservatives to join in 1990.

The following three chapters look across the Atlantic and Pacific to Canadian relationships with African and Asian states. MacGuigan explains the government's policies towards South Africa, and how negotiations over Namibian independence, linked to Cold War considerations, led to divergent Canadian and American approaches. He then shifts focus to discuss Canada's interest in trade with the Pacific community and the multifaceted diplomatic benefits that accrued from Canadian participation in Association of South East Asian Nations (ASEAN) foreign ministers' meetings. He reflects on the bilateral relationship with Japan and his meetings with Chinese leaders. The Vietnamese invasion of Cambodia in 1979 dominated dialogue amongst ASEAN states, and MacGuigan discusses the Western response and Canadian aid. In chapter 13, the author focuses on the Arab-Israeli conflict, setting Canadian positions in historical context. He is critical of the preceding Conservative government's decisions over the issue of the Israeli capital and explains his personal pro-Israeli tendencies. Nevertheless, the author is "far from uncritical" of Israeli behaviour, such as the attack on an Iraqi reactor in 1981. MacGuigan traces the ups and downs of the Camp David peace process, of which Canada was a strong proponent but avowedly not a major player, and he describes the impacts on Canadian policy decisions of contentious issues such as Palestine and the PLO, and the invasion of Lebanon in 1981. MacGuigan and Trudeau seemed to hold some of their most divergent views in the realm of Israeli policy, with the prime minister (and members of the Liberal caucus from Quebec) desiring to "lash out at Israel," while the SSEA favoured a more balanced foreign policy.

Few of the international crises and initiatives that began during or continued into the early 1980s found resolution during the two years MacGuigan was SSEA, and he explains throughout this book why this was the case. In the conclusion, the author recounts his final days in the portfolio and then provides an insightful overview of his life and times as external affairs minister. In his final impression, the era was "close to the worst of times, short of war." Détente had given way to renewed Cold War aggression, and Canada found itself divided internally and its difficulties with the United States "had seldom been so widespread and deep-seated." Bipolar "extremism," conflicting personalities, and economic realities heightened tensions and made MacGuigan's "multipolar liberal policy of supporting the middle against the extremes" all the more difficult to implement. By placing Canadian foreign policy within the context of the larger federal and prime ministerial agendas, MacGuigan identifies the limitations and delimitations of Canadian options and actions at the time. Finally, he reflects on the post-Cold War period and the new challenges facing his successors.

* * *

Several editorial decisions warrant particular mention. MacGuigan devoted an entire chapter to the "Problems of the Sea," focussed on the Law of the Sea negotiations. His role in these discussions, however, was self-avowedly very small and, as a result, the chapter has been removed. Portions dealing with the important bilateral fisheries problems with the United States have been incorporated into chapter 10. I have dismantled a former chapter on La Francophonie and the Commonwealth for similar reasons, and sections that dealt with MacGuigan's personal involvement have been incorporated into other chapters. Chapter 8 is a combination of two formerly separate chapters on constitutional questions and resolution. Alas, I have also found it necessary to abbreviate or remove many of the personal anecdotes and reflections on jogging, sleeping habits, ill-fated flights, lost luggage, and numerous other unique and daily experiences that MacGuigan interspersed throughout the text. Hopefully those that remain afford the reader a glimpse of the author's travails as SSEA, and his sense of humour.

The photographs were graciously provided by the National Archives of Canada and Mr. MacGuigan's family, as selected by the literary executors and myself. To help the reader navigate the sometimes bewildering array of acronyms that accompany any such study of foreign affairs, I have added a list of those used in this book. At the request of the Press, I have added a brief note to sources by Mark MacGuigan and on Canadian foreign policy during the period of his tenure as SSEA.

The comments of various anonymous reviewers were helpful in determining the scope of structural changes required and in suggesting those portions that should be retained. Judith Pond offered sage editorial advice and was instrumental in suggesting ways to prune the manuscript down to its present length. The scrutinizing eyes of Jennifer Arthur were similarly indispensable. The patience, guidance, and investment of resources by the University of Calgary Press, and particularly by its director, Walter Hildebrandt, are sincerely appreciated.

P. Whitney Lackenbauer
Calgary, Alberta

Preface

This book is based on my personal reminiscences and diaries, the hundreds of departmental files I read in the course of its preparation,[1] Hansard,[2] and Canadian newspaper articles. It is intended as a subjective account of Canadian foreign policy from 3 March 1980 to 10 September 1982. It is at the same time the objective truth, as far as I was, and am, personally able to discern it. I have held nothing back, but have tried to describe the actors and events exactly as I saw them. Except where noted, I have not described any incidents in which I was not a participant.

During my period of office I was always aware that, in the medieval phrase of Bernard of Chartres, I was comparable to a dwarf perched on the shoulders of giants, seeing perhaps more and farther than they, but only because of the vantage point inherited from them. I was conscious of giants such as Louis St. Laurent, Lester B. Pearson, Paul Martin, O. D. Skelton, Hume Wrong, and Norman Robertson. I was also so well served by countless dozens of foreign service officers that I have been moved to dedicate this book to them. My accomplishments, if any, were theirs.

I am also profoundly grateful to those who kept me in politics long enough to serve in External Affairs and the electors of Windsor-Walkerville and my campaign team over the five elections that I had to win to make it to the Cabinet (with apologies to any whose names I may have inadvertently omitted): Dan and Cathy Ashe; Stan and Majda Bah; Charlie Banich; Jane Barlow; Marsha Bartlet; Alan Bauer; Michael Benziger; Norma Brockenshire; Mike and Mary Brogan; Pero Bulat; Faye Campbell; A.J. and Sandy Campeau; Dominic Cantagallo; Pat Carroll; Charlie Clark; Don Clarke; Luther Clarke; Brian Clements; Alice Comartin; John Comisso Sr. and Jr.; Pat D'Amore; Audrey Da Sousa; Edwin and Blanche Da Sousa; Elio Danelon; Frank Dattilo; Frank Deangelis; Luigi DiFazio; Betty Doyle; Nick Dunlop; Huntley Farrow; Frank Fazio; Bohdan and Frances Fedchun; Frankie Fernandez; Pat Fiorino; Dee Fontaine; Brian Furlong; Hugh Geddes; Jake Geller; Alfio Golini; Robert and Monique Goyeau; Robert Grondin; Bill and Jocelyn Gutteridge; Pam, Kim and Pat Gutteridge; Jim and Lee Ann Halpin;

John Haviland; Chris Holder; Isabelle Holder; Fred Holmes; Ron Ianni; Andy Iannocello; Amedée and Rita Janisse; Mike Joyce; Shirley Kasenberg; Todd Kasenberg; Jack Kerwin; Fred Knight; Fred and Irene Kushnir; Bruce Laird; Senator Keith Laird; Lorne Lanthier; Don Lappan; Joe Lawler; Doug Lawson; Ellen Lawson; Bea LePage; Gerard Levesque; Albert Mady; Sandra Manzig; Jerome and Pauline Marcotte; Jerry and Donna Marcotte; Gino and Liz Marcus; Don Martin; Jack Martin; Lucille and Mary Ellen McAndrews; Mike and Mary MacDougall; Rod McDowell; Elaine McMahon; George Jr., Ian and Steve McMahon; Margaret McSweeney; Tulio Meconi; Louis Mele; Gerry Meloche; Leo Miernicke; Joe Miljan; Bob Millson; Joe Mlacak; Carolyn Momotiuk; Mary Montsch; Mike Moore; Tom and Peggy Moore; Camille Watson Mueller; Tom Muldoon; John Naccorato; Vivien Nall; Bernard Newman, M.P.P.; Gary Newman; Don Nesbitt; Jack Norris; Ron and Shirley Oleynik; Clarence Ouellette; Ken and Doreen Ouellette; Ray Ouellette; Vic and Gail Ouellette; Bill and Mickey Parker; Terry Patterson; Wayne Patterson; Charlotte Perry; Frank Petrcich; Joan Phillips; Janis Pouyez; Fred and Barbara Quenneville; Fred Jr., Carl, Camille and Jamie Quenneville; Isabelle Quenneville; Ramona Quenneville; Joe Rainelli; Fedor Rajic; Tess Richards; Dick Rosenthal; Ed Ryan; Marthe St-Louis; Marie Sanderson; Tony Sassine; Germaine Schiller; Monroe Schooley; Betty Sinasac; Trevor Stott; Pat Sullens; Bill Sytsma; Frank Tedesco; Ann, Katie and Diane Thomas; Eddie Thomas; John Thomas; Anne Thornton-Hill; Juliette Trudel; Tony Wachna; Walter Wachna; John and Rita Weatherby; Doug Williamson; Tim Williamson; Zoran and Margaret Zonjic.

I was also well served by my staff during my years in office: Catherine Anderson, Karl Feige, John Haviland, Jim McDonald, Derek MacLean, Carolyn Momotiuk, Jim Moore, Marthe St-Louis, Janis Thordarson, Anne Thornton-Hill, Zoran Zonjic. I am most grateful to them for helping me to look as good as possible in the circumstances.

For this book, my principal indebtedness is to my judicial assistant, Patricia Holland, who laboured for hours in transcribing and retranscribing my words. Without her efficiency and unfailing good spirits my task would have been impossible. I am grateful to Allan Gotlieb, John Halstead, R. Douglas Sirrs, Larry Smith, and Si Taylor, who took the time to read and comment on portions of the typescript, as well as to John Hilliker, Ted Kelly and Mary Halloran of the Historical Section of the Department of Foreign Affairs and International Trade, and to Paulette Dozois of the National Archives and her associates for facilitating my access to the files of the Department of External Affairs. Thanks also to the reference service of the Library of Parliament for answering countless minute inquiries with great dispatch.

I am also indebted to my wife, Patty, for her encouragement and helpful criticism.

Mark MacGuigan

**Part One
Introduction**

Chapter 1
The Beginning

It was a long day, that Friday, 29 February 1980, when I waited in my office on Parliament Hill all day for the expected call from the prime minister. By dint of burning the midnight oil earlier in the week, I had cleared up all of my current work, and when I returned to the office I lay down on my couch and napped. I was awakened by my aide Marthe St-Louis about 5:00 with the news that the Prime Minister's Office had called with the request that I present myself at about 5:30 – no purpose stated. Since I had been seeking an appointment with the prime minister during the week, I was not entirely sure whether I was being summoned because the prime minister wanted to tell me that I was in, or whether he was merely doing me the courtesy of satisfying my request for an appointment and telling me that I had not made it again. However, my inclination was to the former hypothesis.

In my own mind at least I had good reason to expect a cabinet position, having been spoken about as "cabinet material" since my first election as member of Parliament for Windsor-Walkerville in 1968 when I was still dean of law at the University of Windsor. But I was cursed by geography, having as my neighbours two longer-serving and capable members of Parliament, Herb Gray and Gene Whelan, both of whom had served in the cabinet at various times during the seventies – to say nothing of the Honourable Paul Martin, to whose seat of Essex East I had succeeded under its new name, who was Government Leader in the Senate from 1968 to 1974. Having been passed over for promotion repeatedly in the past,[3] I felt my day had come in 1980.

I had to wait a few minutes before seeing the prime minister; it was about 6:00 when I got in. The PM began by apologizing for keeping me until so late in the day, then, speaking in a very matter-of-fact tone, shuffling his papers and not looking at me, he said "well, it's External Affairs."

All in all, the meeting lasted about thirty minutes. I then went back to my office and broke the news to my incredulous staff.

* * *

I had never for a moment expected to be Secretary of State for External Affairs (SSEA). The days when I was awaiting the selection of the new cabinet in the aftermath of Prime Minister Pierre Elliott Trudeau's return to power on 18 February 1980 after nine months in opposition were anxious ones, and much given to speculations, imaginings and forebodings on my part. [4] It was not only that External Affairs was a senior cabinet position, which I felt would be beyond my reasonable expectations as a first-time minister, but also that I had chosen an entirely different path in my parliamentary career. I had specialized in constitutional and legal affairs,[5] and I had twice in the past decided against confining my life to international affairs, even though it had always held a considerable fascination for me. Though I had followed world events with a passionate interest from childhood, I had decided not to specialize in international affairs, since it always appeared to me to be an all-consuming world, one that demanded total dedication from its subjects. My interests in law were much broader than that, and indeed focussed particularly on constitutional law and a possible charter of human rights.

Upon entering Parliament, I had to decide upon my primary parliamentary committee, since the whip gave us to understand that he would do his best to accommodate our first choices. The External Affairs committee was certainly a temptation, both because of my strong interest in the field and because of its travel perks. Nevertheless, I made as my first selection the justice committee, for the same reasons as I had passed up total dedication to international affairs as an academic.

I did, however, manage to have a certain number of international contacts during my time in Parliament. I was active in the Canadian World Federalists and particularly in the parliamentary branch. In the latter capacity, I attended international conferences near Oslo (1971), in Brussels (1972), and in Paris (1977). I regarded a world federal state as a future aspiration and direction, not as a realistic goal in the present. With Canadian colleagues Warren Allmand, David MacDonald, Walter McLean, and Doug Roche, and Ross Smyth of the Canadian World Federalists, I founded an offshoot international organization, Parliamentarians for World Order, in 1977, a movement that has developed into the current Parliamentarians for Global Action. I was a member of the Canadian delegation to the United Nations for two-week stints in 1969, 1976 and 1978. As parliamentary secretary to the Minister of Manpower and Immigration Bob Andras, I travelled to Tokyo, Hong Kong, Canberra and Sydney, Singapore, New Delhi, Islamabad, and Beirut to view immigration problems first-hand and to talk with officials of the various foreign governments. As parliamentary secretary to the Minister of Labour John Munro, I was on the Canadian delegation to the International Labour Organization (ILO) in Geneva in 1975. I spent a month at Westminster on a Commonwealth Parliamentary Association seminar in 1972, and went on a Management and Members' Services Committee visit to London and Washington in 1977. I also got to attend an Inter-Parliamentary Union Congress in Bonn in 1978, where I first met Chancellor Helmut Schmidt, and Canada/U.S. meetings in New Orleans in 1978 and Yukon/Alaska in 1979.

These were helpful experiences, as it turned out, but hardly ones to project me to the international forefront. My expectation therefore was that I would be named Solicitor General, or when I was being optimistic, that I might make it to the Justice portfolio. Paul Martin, my close friend and neighbour in Windsor, had apparently spoken during "cabinet-making" with Jim Coutts, the PM's closest adviser. When Paul told me guardedly that things might come out better than I imagined, it never occurred to me that he meant anything more than my ending up in Justice. In retrospect, given Paul's preoccupation with foreign policy, it is easy to understand that for him "doing well" meant being in External Affairs.

* * *

During my meeting with the prime minister, he stated that the reasons he chose me were: first, my coolness and rationality – he was particularly anxious not to abandon détente, and he wanted a cool head to deal with the issues; second, my familiarity with and understanding of the United States from my vantage point in Windsor since our relationship with the U.S. was at a crucial stage; third, my bilingualism – I was, and am, far from perfect in French, but at my first international conference I was described by the correspondent for *La Presse* as being very acceptably bilingual;[6] and fourth, my acceptability to the department – they had been very worried about whom they might get, and he knew they would be delighted with me.

In the course of our meeting, the PM explained that the post had been much sought after, that a lot of people would be surprised at my appointment, and no doubt some who wanted it would be displeased for a short time. No fewer than four senior francophone ministers (Jean Chrétien, Marc Lalonde, Romeo LeBlanc, and André Ouellet) had expressed interest in foreign affairs, and the PM had left me to the end to be sure that he would be able to stave off all the other claimants.

Marc Lalonde could easily have handled any portfolio, but the prime minister wanted him in Energy, Mines and Resources, where he had been Liberal critic during our time in opposition and where major challenges were expected. Romeo Leblanc went to the logical position for a New Brunswicker of Fisheries and Oceans, where I worked easily with him on problems of the sea. André Ouellet was returned to the Ministry of Consumer and Corporate Affairs, where he had been earlier a passionate consumer advocate, to which was added the position of postmaster general. My relationship with them was not altered in the slightest by the cabinet-selection process.

It was otherwise with Jean Chrétien, whom the prime minister named Minister of Justice. No doubt the PM saw him as indispensable in Quebec and for the constitutional dossier generally, but Chrétien himself may have been of a different mind. In any event, soon after the new cabinet was formed, I realized he was not speaking to me. As the situation continued, I came to the conclusion I should do something to break the ice. So in a telephone call one evening, I shamelessly gilded his lily. I said, "Jean, I've been meaning to express my gratitude to you for letting me have external affairs. I know you could have had either External or Justice, and it was exceedingly generous of you to allow External to go to me. Of course, you are in the critical portfolio to deal with the Quebec problem, one nobody else could handle so well. [I sincerely believed that assertion to be true.] Anyhow, thank you very much." He made no comment, but from then on our relationship was a normal one.[7]

* * *

At the time, some commentators alleged that the PM had appointed me as SSEA so that, as a neophyte, I would abandon foreign policy to him. This proved unfounded. Indeed, the prime minister allowed me free rein in running Canada's foreign policy except at the summit level, with no instructions or interference whatsoever, save on some peripheral matters such as "patronage" appointments. It was, of course, always his option to intervene if he desired to, but he never did. I had the impression that he preferred to be judgmental rather than executive. He enjoyed being, in the phrase of Granatstein and Bothwell in their outstanding book *Pirouette: Pierre Trudeau and Canadian Foreign Policy,* "an adventurer in ideas."[8] Several times he expressed displeasure with something I had done, but accepted it as a *fait accompli*. He also sometimes expressed himself publicly in a way inconsistent with our foreign policy as formulated by me, most notably over Poland. Such incidents led to lots of explanations, but to no change in our foreign policy. On only one occasion did the PM and I ever have a face-to-face disagreement over a matter of fundamental importance. Otherwise, our disagreements were expressed by indirection, by a simple lack of congruence. Unlike the halcyon days in 1968–69, when the PM intervened decisively in foreign policy, he no longer seemed to possess any desire to go back to first principles. For the most part, I was left to run foreign policy as I saw fit.

It was my observation that most matters of real moment in Trudeau's time were decided, not by cabinet, but by the prime minister alone with the minister or ministers responsible. The classic example was the annual budget. The PM and the Minister of Finance alone decided the budget – or in the fall of 1980, with the help of Marc Lalonde, because of the inclusion of the National Energy Program (NEP). For the rest of the cabinet, there was merely an information session on the day of the budget.

Cabinet met in plenary session once a week and was chaired by the prime minister, or in his absence by Allan MacEachen as senior minister. The principal cabinet committee, on priorities and planning (P and P), was also chaired by the PM and also met about once a week. It consisted of about twelve senior ministers and dealt with the most urgent and the most fundamental matters. Initiatives passed by P and P were not raised in full cabinet, so that it was in essence a substitute and smaller cabinet. During my time in External, I was a member of P and P by virtue of being chair of the Cabinet Committee on Foreign Affairs and Defence Policy.

The PM ran cabinet and P and P meetings with a light hand. For the most part, he let ministers take the positions they preferred, without comment or even guidance; although no doubt he had had discussions beforehand, where he deemed it necessary, with the ministers involved. But except for some economic issues on which we did not have a collective sense of how to proceed,[9] I am not sure how much cabinet decisions really mattered. I always felt that the matters discussed had been, or would be, settled by the PM with a small group.

In my experience, in these small groups, senior civil servants from the relevant departments had enormous influence. This was where Michael Pitfield, the clerk of the Privy Council, exercised strong guidance. With Pitfield, I never knew for sure whether he was protecting the PM's interests or his own. In the corridors of power, Pitfield's convoluted *modus operandi* was often described as byzantine. His playing field was, of course, the bureaucracy. He rarely dealt with ministers – or even spoke with them. His world was an officially non-political one.

* * *

For the most part, during my time in External, the prime minister and I worked amicably. He included me in every foreign policy matter, and I reciprocated. But in general the prime minister was a remote presence. He was not interested in ministers' day-to-day lives or decisions, except insofar as they impinged upon him at Question Period, and he was a remote presence in the party: though there with less fortunate consequences than with cabinet. Parties are mostly volunteer organizations, and people in such circumstances usually need a lot of stroking to produce their best. They want to know that they are observed and appreciated. Trudeau either could not or would not play the role of backslapper, and the party suffered because of it. That it functioned as well as it did was because of many people within the organization who were prepared, unheralded and unsung, to perform a leader-like role towards those in lower offices. There was also constant frustration on the part of organizers who put, for example, business leaders in a position to be influenced by the PM, only to find that he reacted negatively in such situations, "putting off" those he was supposed to influence positively.

Caucus, too, missed a more involved leader, but the PM's intellectual dominance of the weekly caucus meetings – and of the other party leaders in their House exchanges – constantly reassured caucus members that they were being led by someone who knew supremely what he was doing, even if he did not know what they were doing.

Trudeau always focused on intellectual challenges, not on people. Ideas engaged him. People did not. Nor did their problems, unless presented as intellectual challenges.

The prime minister was essentially a lone gunslinger, totally absorbed by his own mission, and involved in society only to the minimal extent necessary to achieve his goals.

* * *

Granatstein and Bothwell have written that Trudeau "had little long-term, consistent interest in foreign policy."[10] I entirely agree, with one qualification. His primary focus was on politics within Canada, since he had entered political life in order to augment and cement the role of French-speaking Canadians in Canada. Then again, it is hard to imagine any democratic leader, except perhaps occasionally a president of the United States, whose fundamental preoccupation is not the domestic scene.

Trudeau's own involvement with foreign policy was accordingly highly interstitial, but he made up for that lack in his first ten years as prime minister by his symbiotic relationship with Ivan Head. Head became closer to the PM than Henry Kissinger ever was to either Richard Nixon or Gerald Ford, since Head aimed to be Trudeau's confidant and completion, not his alter ego. As Head and Trudeau have recently written, "there evolved a relationship that ensured no major foreign- or defence-policy decision or initiative would be taken, conference attended, or speech delivered by the prime minister without Head's involvement."[11] Trudeau thus extended himself into a full-time foreign policy role through the persona of Head from about 1970 until the latter left the Prime Minister's Office (PMO) in 1978 to become the president of the International Development Research Centre (IDRC).

As a result of Head's departure, I had more freedom of action than Trudeau's earlier foreign ministers, since I was the first and only one not to have had him at the PM's side during at least part of his time in office. After Head's separation from the PMO, his policy advisory position had been transformed into a purely bureaucratic role carried out in the Privy Council Office (PCO) by the secretary to the Cabinet Committee on Foreign and Defence Policy.

In the beginning, of course, I needed tutelage, which I was grateful to receive from my Undersecretary (USSEA), Allan Gotlieb. Well before the time Gotlieb effectively ceased to be USSEA in the spring of 1981, I was feathered and already aloft. In fact, I would date my coming of age to the summer of 1980, after my first round of international meetings, to that July day on which I rejected the first draft of the aid strategy developed by the Canadian International Development Agency (CIDA), because it did not tie aid policy in sufficiently with our foreign policy. From that day on, I determined the policy of the department and of CIDA, so that from that point on Canadian foreign policy became effectively my foreign policy.[12]

Still, Trudeau let me know that he had a few initiatives he would want to take himself. I soon came to understand that the areas he considered his private preserve were his personal relationships with other leaders and also with the Soviet ambassador to Canada, Aleksander Yakovlev, the periodic meetings of the Commonwealth Heads of Government (CHOGM), his occasional ceremonial visits to various countries (for example, on the way to or from economic summit meetings), and generally all contacts among leaders.

* * *

Although in March, 1980, I did not possess a fully formulated foreign policy, I was far from being a *tabula rasa*. I grew up during the Second World War, which engaged my interest from the outset. The first newspaper headline I can remember is "Franco Wins Spanish Civil War," which would have appeared in the first half of 1939. Curiously enough, it was not the sad fate of Poland, attacked from both sides, that aroused my first passion, but that of Finland, which had to engage the Soviet bear on its own, and in the early stages gained some successes. My young friends and I played Finns with our toy soldiers: no one wanted to be on the Soviet side.

From that early experience of Soviet aggression grew my rejection of Soviet totalitarianism in all its forms, and as the war progressed with the Nazi invasion of the Soviet Union, I childishly hoped that the two sides would destroy each other. By adulthood, I had become convinced that the Soviet system was the most persistent menace to human freedom in the twentieth century, surpassing the Nazi threat, if not in virulence, then at least in staying power.

The prime minister appeared to take a different view than I of the Soviet system, particularly in its manifestations such as Castroism; or perhaps it might be more accurate to say that he was equally persuaded of the evils of American militaristic capitalism, so that he found it hard to draw a strong moral distinction between the two systems. As I saw it, with communists we were dealing with people who were in bad faith both as to their objectives and as to their means of attaining them; whereas, even at their worst, the Americans were for the most part in good faith in their goals but willing to do almost anything to achieve their good ends. To my mind, this made for a clear moral differential in the Americans' favour, even if we had to admonish them from time to time. Moreover, the Americans always had strong voices with which to articulate the other side (sometimes even a Robert McNamara to recant publicly), whereas the communists allowed no free public opinion within their domain. The United States was, after all, a vibrant though imperfect democracy, whereas the Soviet Union and its satellites were absolutist and totalitarian states.

It might well have made a difference to the prime minister's choice of me as SSEA if he had known about my policy preferences. During the recently completed election campaign, his instinctive response to the policy announced by President Carter of boycotting the Olympic Games in Moscow in retaliation for the Soviet invasion of Afghanistan had been a negative one. But campaigning in an other-ethnic riding where anti-Soviet feeling ran high, I was under great pressure to have the party take a more responsive position to the American initiative. I also strongly agreed with adopting the same position as the United States, vis-à-vis communism.

My inclination in dealing with the U.S. was always that, with all the difficult bilateral – and some multilateral – issues between us, we should as a normal policy make a point of assuring the Americans of our reliable co-operation and support on East-West issues. After all, Canada's interests, as members of the same alliance, were fundamentally similar to those of the United States. In my view, we had nothing to lose and everything to gain from prompt acceptance of most American East-West initiatives. Soothed by our reliability in that respect, American leaders might find it easier to be less bloody-minded on bilateral matters. This was not at all a matter of toadying to the U.S. in a manner later adopted. In fact, my strategy was precisely the reverse: to keep our powder dry for contentious bilateral issues. Of course, this was the Carter era. Once Reagan was president we had to become more guarded in our response even to direct East-West initiatives, let alone in the rest of the world spectrum.

* * *

When I refer to assuring the Americans of our reliability on East-West issues, I have in mind not *their* perception of such questions, but *our own*. Americans, particularly Republicans as in the Reagan Administration, tended to see almost all world problems in an East-West perspective. For them, the world was divided into two, between what Reagan called "the evil empire" and the forces of truth and righteousness.

I was a political liberal, an intellectual position by no means equivalent to membership in the Liberal party, which I arrived at in the early 1950s under the influence of the American Catholic weekly, *The Commonweal.* I did not see the world as "cleft in twain." I perceived almost an infinite variety of in-between positions, and thought it no service to the truth – or to enlightened democratic policymaking – to merge the in-betweens with the extremes. In the words of the Irish poet Louis MacNeice, the world is "incorrigibly plural."

Intellectual bipolarism has been the besetting American sin in foreign policy at least since the Second World War. Indeed, Jimmy Carter has made the same point: "For some reason, Americans tend to see conflicts in terms of friend/enemy, angel/devil. This view is one of the major impediments to realizing our global potential as a champion of peace."[13] There was, of course, a sound reason for a hard-line policy against real Soviet-inspired communism, as I would be the first to urge: this was the solid rationale for the Marshall Plan, the Truman Doctrine, the resistance to the communist invasion in Korea and to Soviet threats to the viability of the Western portion of Berlin. But non-aligned countries like India could not be approached in the same light. They had in mind a third way, one between communism and capitalism. Their position might be from the Western point of view naive, but it was by no stretch of the imagination Soviet-dominated. In consequence, the Third World could not be treated as merely another forum of the Cold War.

The world, when I became foreign minister, was one that required a hard-line answer to communist aggression when it occurred or was threatened, and a soft-line response to the attitudes and initiatives of the rest of the non-Western world. I saw, in short, a multipolar world that necessitated highly nuanced rather than automatic reactions.

This book is an account of what I personally experienced in my development of foreign policy under Pierre Elliott Trudeau, a chronicle of the events in which I participated, along with my motivations and reactions – in other words, a highly personal chronicle. In that sense, it is a mélange of autobiography and foreign policy. It may be said to be history *from the inside*. I think it can rightly be regarded primarily as a political autobiography focussed on foreign affairs.

Chapter 2
Trudeau

As far as I am aware, I had – and have – no fundamental foreign policy differences with Pierre Trudeau – although I have to admit that it is not easy to divine his fundamental orientation in foreign policy. Ivan Head has written with Trudeau's authorization that the PM intended that "Canada should function as an 'effective power'" and that "moral principle has become the defining element in effective policy."[14] I agree with the former statement, but I do not believe that the latter statement as to moral principle is sustainable for Trudeau, even if it is for Head.

On the one hand, I have no doubt that moral principle was for the prime minister a defining element in foreign policy, as it is for me, and, I suspect, for most Canadians. On the other hand, the thrust of *Foreign Policy for Canadians*, published in 1970 by authority of Mitchell Sharp, Trudeau's first SSEA, was taken at the time to be Trudeau's assertion of the primal role of national interest in foreign policy, and thus a departure from the earlier and more high-minded Pearsonian policy. In fact, it may be that *Foreign Policy for Canadians* reflected his Gotlieb stage, as opposed to a later and more altruistic Head stage, depending on whether Allan Gotlieb or Ivan Head[15] exercised greater influence on him.

However, there is never found in Trudeau anything like the ethical foreign policy announced by Labour Foreign Secretary Robin Cook for the Blair Government in the United Kingdom in July 1997. Cook's declaration was one of intent to make concern for human rights a central factor in British dealings with foreign governments, and an invitation to the world to judge the success of British foreign policy in part by the degree to which it improves the lot of people in states where human rights are currently being violated. To my mind, all of this is completely alien to the Trudeau worldview.

On the contrary, there was a hard-boiled side to Trudeau's nature which was not easily associated with moral inspiration. I am thinking of the extension of Canadian pollution-prevention jurisdiction over Arctic waters in 1970 beyond what was internationally accepted, necessitating a reservation to Canada's acceptance of the compulsory jurisdiction of the International Court of Justice; a reservation which Paul Martin, for one, regarded as a shocking reversal of traditional Canadian policy. I have in mind also the work of the Communications Security Establishment (CSE) in electronically intercepting, analyzing and passing on to the Government of Canada reports of the contents of communications traffic of foreign states and corporations.[16]

Foreign Policy for Canadians outlined the six main themes of national policy which were said to form the broad framework of Canadian foreign policy, since foreign policy was said to be the extension abroad of national policy. These foreign policy goals were: first, to foster economic growth for Canada; second, to promote social justice both in Canada and the world; third, to enhance the quality of life in Canada; fourth, to ensure a harmonious natural environment in Canada and in the world; fifth, to work for peace and security in the world; and sixth, to safeguard Canadian sovereignty and independence. Three of these goals – economic growth, the quality of life, and sovereignty and independence – were clear manifestations of national self-interest. Economic growth was explicitly ranked as the highest goal, ahead of social justice, which was expressly stated to be the next priority. It seemed intended that the overall ranking was the order I have utilized above.

Foreign Policy, of course, recognized that these goals were not absolutes, and that hard choices would require trade-offs among them. It stated succinctly:[17]

> Foreign policy can be shaped, and is shaped, mainly by the value judgments of the Government at any given time. But it is also shaped by the possibilities that are open to Canada at any given time – basically by the constraints or opportunities presented by the prevailing international situation. It is shaped too by domestic considerations, by the internal pressures exerted by the Government, by the amount of resources which the Government can afford to deploy.

There is nothing here of explicitly moral redolence nor is an approach to foreign policy in terms of morality true to the Trudeau I knew. His instinctive avoidance of human rights issues in his contacts with other countries – one might say his subordination of them to Canada's commercial interests – did not bespeak a leader charged primarily with moral zeal. Moreover, the policy of bilateralism (discussed in detail later), which I sponsored but which was adopted by Trudeau and the cabinet, also embodied an approach to foreign policy in terms of Canadian national interest. Trudeau's whole approach to foreign policy was a "Canada First" policy.

As I interpret Trudeau's position on morality in international affairs, it was essentially the same as my own – except that I gave a higher priority than he to human rights questions. My view is that, although foreign policy, like all human behaviour, must not transgress moral principles, it does not for the most part arise out of morality *per se*. In the case of foreign policy, moral principles are to be found in traditional international law, the *jus gentium*, or the natural law as applied to nations. But this, like all natural law, does not take us very far. For the most part, we live, not in the realm of the *per se* (intrinsically) good or bad, but in the arena of what is intrinsically morally neutral.[18] This is where national interest always holds sway with every country, whether it admits it or not. Americans are particularly prone to clothing their actions with a moral patina, but that would fool no one who has negotiated with them, especially on trade matters, for an instant.

Canadians are also given to analyzing international problems in moral terms. We came to a consciousness of our national identity largely during and after the Second World War, when issues tended to be expressed altruistically by our great international figures, Louis St. Laurent, Mike Pearson and Paul Martin. But justification of Canadian action in moral terms should not be taken as defining our international perspective. Moral terminology was perhaps particularly appropriate in the East-West arena, where the contention was at bottom over human freedom. It was also *a propos*, in the sense of social justice, in the North-South sphere. But even in those two multilateral areas, what was morally right was also in my view very much in Canada's national interest. We benefited politically from restraining the Soviet Union. We created new markets for our goods by helping the Third World. Reliance on moral terminology should not thus obscure our self-interest entirely. I suppose the ideal international situation is one where morality and self-interest coincide, but, for the most part, especially in our bilateral relationships with countries or regions, we had to make foreign policy decisions without the advantage of moral guidance, and enlightened solely by our own self-interest.

For me, therefore, foreign policy is for the most part a matter of the national interest, restrained by morality where there is conflict. As I put it in the House in June 1982, our foreign policy "is the expression abroad of the nature of our country."[19] I am inclined to think that was also true of Trudeau, who was frequently given to speaking, especially in private conversation, in terms of great-power spheres of influence. On balance, I believe there was general congruence between our views of foreign policy. I endorsed his opening to China, his decision to reduce our NATO commitments and to retire from a nuclear-strike role, our Arctic environmental initiatives, his crusade for nuclear disarmament and disengagement, and the National Energy Program, which had special consequences vis-à-vis the United States. I think we were of one mind in our desire to contain Soviet communist expansion, to manage the American relationship advantageously for Canada, and, above all, to encourage development in the Third World.

On the other hand, I was totally lacking in sympathy for the revisionist and neutralist views apparently endorsed by Donald Macdonald, then president of the Privy Council, during the first Trudeau government. To my mind, Canada's traditional foreign-policy posture was dictated by our geography, history, and national interest and could not be fundamentally altered. Indeed, the NATO policy ultimately established by the prime minister and cabinet at that time was not withdrawal from NATO but rather a planned and phased reduction in our contribution. I agreed with this change, because I did not think our earlier level of contribution was in our national interest. The Americans were willy-nilly going to dominate Western defence policy, and should accordingly pay for the privilege.

By way of exception, however, I did not agree with Trudeau's establishing diplomatic relations with the Vatican in 1970. In fact, I was the only MP to speak against it in caucus. My opposition was based on the idea that, as a liberal Catholic, I thought the Church should not be recognized as a temporal power beyond the necessary minimum to guarantee its independence within Italy. It was perhaps ironic, therefore, that I was the first Canadian minister to make an official visit to the Holy See, including a papal audience with John Paul II, on 8 May 1981. I did so for reasons of national self-interest, particularly to explore Vatican perceptions on Eastern Europe, rather than for moral or religious reasons.

* * *

Since the end of World War II, the chief authority figure in the Western world has been the government of the United States. In common with many left-leaning Western intellectuals (that was about all he had in common with them!), Trudeau was always ready to thumb his nose at the U.S. Hence he first reacted negatively to the U.S.-led Olympic Boycott in 1980, and then wanted to delay the decision as much as possible. He cultivated a personal friendship with Fidel Castro and also liked to think of himself as an interlocutor between the Soviets and the Americans. He delighted in the way the National Energy Program cut American interests down to size. He took a pro-development position toward the Third World and tried to manoeuvre the Americans in the same direction. In the Polish Crisis of 1981–82, he appeared to express more sympathy for the Polish communist government's campaign against Lech Walesa and Solidarity than for the latter's U.S.-supported struggle for democracy. Later, after I had left External for Justice, he conducted a world peace initiative that the Americans found barely sufferable; though in that instance his crusade was a valiant, if quixotic, one.

And he lost no opportunity to tweak Reagan's nose. At the communal picture-taking at the end of the Bonn Summit in May 1982, when Reagan, besieged by reporters, was vainly attempting to respond to their questions about the Israeli invasion of Lebanon on that day, Trudeau shouted out, "Ask Al [Haig]. He knows." Reagan may have been too absorbed at the time by his own difficulties to take this in, but his entourage was not, and the comment did no good to either Haig or Trudeau. Haig fell out of office as secretary of state within two weeks.

Trudeau's apparent ill will towards Reagan was soon reciprocated. Reagan, never long on subtlety, came to regard Trudeau as a communist dupe or worse. In this, he was aided and abetted by others in Washington who were always alert to the supposed communist menace. Accordingly, after the Bonn Summit a crisis developed in the Reagan-Trudeau relationship. We had to launch a rescue operation led by Ambassador Gotlieb in Washington to try to save Trudeau's hide, as it were, since it would not be in Canada's interest to face a gratuitously hostile administration in the United States.

* * *

The expression of my own views was largely identical with the prime minister's on all matters apart from East-West issues. But on East-West questions I believed it was folly for us to play at opposing American policy when it was against our own interests to do so.

First of all, I had absolutely no animosity towards Americans or the United States. While I regarded much in U.S. public life as either mistaken or meretricious, I felt no need to lecture Americans on their shortcomings, and still less to lash out at them in resentment of their leadership.

The United States was, plainly and simply, the leader of the Western Alliance. They protected us and other Western states from Soviet expansionism. Sometimes, as in the Vietnam conflict, they mistook indigenous communist-inspired nationalist movements for Moscow-inspired imperialism. In Korea, on the other hand, they were right in taking a stand at the outset against North Korean aggression, though less than adept in their handling of the Chinese factor.

The Americans were not always capable of intellectual discrimination. They tended to see Soviet-led hegemonism in many places where it was not present and were even suspicious of the genuineness of the split between an independent-minded Beijing and a Comintern-inspired Moscow. It was our duty, as their allies, to try to show them the error of their ways, when in our view they were wrong. I tried to do just that with respect to Namibia, the Caribbean and Central America, and generally as to the lack of adequate consultation within the Western Alliance before U.S. decision-making.

But with respect to the heart of the East-West divide, on matters such as Afghanistan and Poland, in my belief there could be no difference of opinion between the Americans and us. Afghanistan was a case of open aggression, Poland of masked aggression. Not only were our interests perceived as identical with those of the United States by the cabinet as a whole and by our foreign service, but also I believe the Canadian public massively supported the American view – which was in effect the common Western reaction. To me, it seemed pettifoggery to accept the shelter of American defensive capability and at the same time to quibble over international initiatives in which our own interests were being adequately served.

Canadians tolerated, nay embraced, a certain ambiguity towards our American big brothers. It was seen as good to be friendly with the Americans, but not too friendly. The trick was to draw the line in the right place, both for Canada's real interests and for the public's satisfaction, which were not always identical (such as the case of El Salvador, described in chapter 11). In my view, Trudeau drew the line in the wrong place from both points of view. He projected more anti-Americanism to Americans in the Reagan era than was tolerable to them, and more than was palatable to most Canadians. In this respect, he served neither Canadian interests nor Canadian preferences.

Canadians had lots of genuine conflicts of interest with the United States: energy, trade, environment, and fishing being prominent examples. In my opinion, we needed to keep our powder dry for these issues, not to squander goodwill by appearing to lack resolution in the East-West arena. We needed to put ourselves in a position to receive the benefit of the doubt on bilateral issues – although I must admit that such an eventuality, such as the Auto Pact, was more likely to come to pass under a Democratic administration than under the flinty-eyed Reaganites.

The prime minister was by no means truly anti-American. He knew ultimately on what side our bread was buttered and was prepared to concede in the long run. But he liked to tilt at the American windmill, jabbing it whenever he felt like it. On the other hand, I took the view that we should scream bloody murder only when the Yankee elephant was about to step on our own Canadian toes. I saw this as being responsible nationalism, very different from the fawning servility that came to mark the Canadian approach later in the decade, or, for that matter, that had prevailed during the Mackenzie King era – though in the earlier period it served also as a tool against British imperialism.

For Trudeau, the matter was not really one of winning or losing. In my perspective, I ultimately got my way when there was a difference of emphasis. Perhaps I should rather say that the prime minister allowed me to win. Had he wanted to be victorious, he could have simply ordered me to implement particular policies or replaced me as foreign minister at any time. But I believe that what he wanted was rather to maintain an independent sphere of action from within which he could personally survey events and pronounce judgment as he wished, without any consequences flowing save his own intellectual satisfaction and the corresponding discomfiture of his enemies. But what to him was perhaps an intellectual game in which he pricked the Americans and the bourgeoisie was not regarded so lightly by the Canadian public or by our allies, particularly the one immediately to the south. The game was for them a real-life struggle. There were therefore public consequences to Trudeau's approach.

* * *

The impact of the prime minister's intellectualism was exaggerated by his style. He has rightly been recognized throughout his life as a person of overpowering intellect. His fame preceded him when I was first associated with him in the work of the Special Committee on Hate Propaganda (Cohen Committee) in 1965, and I found it richly justified.

But I remarked something else about him when I first saw him campaigning in Dieppe Park in Windsor in 1968. He displayed a fine talent for invective and scorn in taking on the heckling post office workers in the audience. His gift for political one-upmanship was visceral. He was not only combative, but also contemptuous.

Trudeau's style was also dangerous. His instinct, it always seemed to me, was not just to establish objectively that he was right by demolishing his opponents' arguments, but also to destroy their self-respect, to hurt them in the deepest recesses he could reach with his words. He wanted to demean them, to rub their noses in their deficiencies.

His style, in short, was to bring, not peace, but a sword. The effect was to set teeth on edge, and to inspire his opponents with an overpowering passion for revenge. He had a rare talent for turning opponents into enemies, who would dedicate their lives to getting even.

The resulting bad feeling in the Canadian body politic spilled over from the "nobodies" in the parliamentary opposition to the general public, many of whom were also members of groups who felt themselves spurned by the PM. Trudeau's political success was therefore very mixed: *voted in*, with enthusiasm, in 1968; *in* with a minority government, but with a plurality of only one seat in 1972, after the public had experienced him in office; *in* with some enthusiasm, again in 1974, after the public reacted against opposition policies during the minority government; *out*, in 1979, with a Progressive Conservative minority government; *in*, decisively, in 1980. For completion, I assume he would have lost badly in 1984; in fact, his successor, John Turner, failed in that campaign because he could not establish a sufficient distance between himself and Trudeau. The public found Trudeau in office too much to bear, I think more because of his style than his policies, but its respect for his enormous ability (and also his newsworthiness) kept bringing him back into favour.

His effect on his international co-equals in major states was very much the same as on the Canadian public: respect for his ability but no great liking for his person.

Chapter 3
The Department of External Affairs

The Department of External Affairs was in my day a superb institution, staffed with outstanding officers. Competition for admission was keen, and for the most part advancement was relatively slow, since there were many senior officers who were not quick to depart. For quicker results, a good many middle-ranking officers jumped ship, moving to other departments. External had a long memory for such "traitors," and it was almost impossible for them to be reinstated in the foreign service.

I was extraordinarily fortunate in my first Undersecretary of State for External Affairs (USSEA), Allan Gotlieb, with whom I had happily been acquainted for some fifteen years. I had a lot to learn of the detail of foreign policy, which I picked up as quickly as possible from Gotlieb and his associates. But I had already a definite *Weltanschauung*, which I might describe as anti-Soviet, pro-American where our interests coincided, strongly nationalist where our own interests diverged, pro-Third World, pro-human rights, and pro-Israel. Gotlieb had a similar orientation, and we never had a serious disagreement during our association, either during his time as USSEA or afterwards as ambassador to the United States. In addition, he had been well schooled by his mentor Marcel Cadieux, by reputation one of the ablest USSEAs ever, in the exacting detail and nuance of foreign policy. He was rigorous in his thinking and imposed his own high standards on everyone below him. It was therefore an impressive department, and Gotlieb was the ablest public servant I had the opportunity to associate with during my sixteen years in Parliament.

Gotlieb had a lengthy transition period to his successor role as ambassador to the United States, a post to which he was appointed in October 1981. However, he effectively ceased to be USSEA before the Ottawa Summit in 1981, to which he was the prime minister's personal representative. With Trudeau's role as chair, this position required a great deal of advance preparation. Gotlieb was succeeded as USSEA by Gordon Osbaldeston, as part of the departmental reorganization in 1982. I had a highly satisfactory working relationship with Osbaldeston, but he was for the most part absorbed by problems of reorganization and personnel management and had little to do with foreign policy as such, where my advice continued to come from de Montigny Marchand,[20] as deputy minister for political affairs, Bob Johnstone, the deputy for economic affairs, and, with respect to CIDA, from Marcel Massé. I did, however, find Osbaldeston particularly helpful on economic matters, even after I moved to Justice.

* * *

I was also fortunate in the two senior departmental assistants I had during my time in External.

The department's original choice for me was Vern Turner, a senior officer who subsequently became a highly successful ambassador to the Soviet Union. Turner served me for a month until I was able to spring Alan Sullivan free from the prime minister. It became clear in that time that Turner was a highly competent foreign service officer who would have met my needs well, and I parted from him with a genuine sense of regret.

Sullivan and I had become friends in 1974 when, as parliamentary secretary to labour minister John Munro, I was in Geneva for two weeks to attend the annual meeting of the International Labour Organization. Because of his great interest in music and things cultural, we became friends in short order. I saw him from time to time over the years, and it was natural that I should think of him when I assumed office. In fact, he, Gotlieb, and Larry Smith were the only people I knew in External before becoming SSEA.

Joe Clark had appointed Sullivan to the Privy Council Office as his senior departmental adviser on external affairs in 1979. Sullivan had served Clark effectively during his prime ministership, but he wanted to return to External if Trudeau would release him. The PM agreed to do so, since Gotlieb was offering to make his own executive assistant, Bob Fowler, available to him. In the result, I was able to capture Sullivan, who had an immense knowledge both of the department and of foreign affairs and was able to advise me sagely on all my decisions. His position was in a sense ambiguous in that he owed fealty both to External and to me. As far as I could see, he bore the burden of two loyalties without trauma, and I never felt deprived of his best advice. In fact, he would frankly tell me what the department's view was and what he thought himself.

Sullivan had so much promise that I thought of him as a future USSEA, and after a year of profitable association I felt I could no longer stand in the way of his career development. I offered him the ambassadorship to Ireland, a position which he happily filled until I had to ask him to move to Austria to make way for Edgar "Ben" Benson, the former minister of finance, whom the prime minister wanted to send to Ireland.

I met Mike Phillips, Sullivan's successor in my office, when I spent two days in Kenya (where he was number two) in July 1980. I was immediately attracted by his keen sense of humour and by his competence. When Sullivan was departing in 1981, Phillips was back in Ottawa in External's legal bureau. He was considered vital there and the department did not want to transfer him to my office. I persisted, however, and he was with me to my last day as SSEA. In the meantime, we tackled a world of problems, which I handled better as a result of his counsel, assistance, and funny bone.

I was also well served by my press officers, André Simard, F. M. "Chips" Filleul, who succeeded Simard, and their associate, Gilliane Lapointe, and was also helped for some months by Lorne Green who had earlier served Paul Martin effectively in London.

* * *

No other foreign minister of the Group of Seven laboured under my disadvantage of having to represent a constituency of voters and to participate on an almost daily basis in an elected legislature. Lord Carrington, the foreign secretary of the other parliamentary democracy, Britain, did not have the same problem, since he was a member of the Upper House and had a spokesperson in the House of Commons.

Despite its occasional inconveniences, however, I was never unhappy with that aspect of my lot. It was our system, and by and large I found it fulfilling. What I did somewhat resent was that I was required, on my return from diplomatic missions, to make up for the ministerial "duty days" I had missed in the House. In order to ensure that there were always at least two ministers in the House in the event a motion had suddenly to be moved, ministers except for the prime minister had to be in the chamber one and a half days each sitting week. When absent, they had to secure colleagues to sit for them, and to make up the time to those colleagues on their return. This system provided a surplus number of ministers in the House at all times and could easily have been interpreted to make an exception for the SSEA, when away on official business.

The prime minister refused to exempt me from this onerous duty, and, even though I tried to make all of my longer trips when the House was in recess, I was frequently out of the country during sittings. One result was that, when I was in Ottawa, I had to spend most of my days sitting in the chamber. It was not required that I listen to the debates, however, and I was usually surrounded with a huge pile of memoranda and signature books. Fortunately, the whip, Tom Lefebvre, was a very understanding man and would allow myself and others to absent ourselves for cabinet committee meetings elsewhere in the Centre Block – with the understanding that we would rush back if called by him.

Another result of the requirement to make up House duty was that, when in Ottawa, I had usually to work in my office until one or two in the morning to catch up on all my work. On such occasions, I would release my chauffeur so that he would be fresh in the morning and I would return home by taxi. My driver, Robert Plouffe, was the champion bowler in the Hull league, and I tried to accommodate his hours on Thursdays, his bowling night. On one such occasion, I was at dinner at an ambassador's residence – it was usual for the SSEA to accept the hospitality of the ambassador for a country he was soon to visit – and I knew Bob would not be around for me before 11:15 p.m. It was the custom for diplomatic dinners to end by eleven o'clock, but I deliberately delayed my departure. Finally, one exasperated ambassador snapped at me, "Why don't you leave? Don't you realize that none of the rest of us can go before you do?" Obligingly, I went outside and walked around until Bob arrived.

Regardless of my hour of retiring, I ran every morning in good weather along the Ottawa River near my condominium and during the winter months at the Ottawa Athletic Club. To this end, I issued standard instructions for the posts I visited that I wished to run every morning, preferably in a park, and that, if possible, I should like someone who knew the city to run with. I had some interesting experiences. In Beijing, the route I was taken on by a Canadian military attaché was partly on city streets, where I had to contend with what seemed like tens of thousands of locals scurrying to work by foot, by bicycle, and by motor vehicle. It seemed to me that they all stopped what they were doing to watch these two "round eyes" running in the sun with no utilitarian object in view.

My greatest running challenge was at a seven-thousand-foot elevation in Kenya, where it had been arranged that I should run on a track with a half dozen Kenyans, some of whom I was told were members of the Kenyan national team. Somehow, I found myself on the outside lane where I tried to keep up. Though I manfully did my best for Canada, I decided that four miles was enough exercise that day!

I remember also running on Bowen Avenue, high above the city's heart in Hong Kong, among hundreds of joss sticks and as many practitioners of Tai Chi. In the sweltering heat of Singapore, just above the equator, I had to go out to the gardens of the Mandarin Hotel at six in the morning in order to be able to run at all. Even at that, I could literally wring the water from my shirt afterwards. In Bulawayo, the capital of Botswana, I recall early morning in the wide dirt streets, passing by low-rise buildings of a uniformly dusty sameness of mediocrity.

In every city where I had occasion to run in populated areas, my early morning jaunts helped to give me some impression of the people and the country, a sense I could not have gained from my official program. It was sometimes a very useful supplement to my diplomatic knowledge and experience.

* * *

Although I did not often become involved in matters concerning office and staff accommodation abroad, there was one problem that recurred from time to time in various countries in which I had to take a hand. Treasury Board, as monitored by the Auditor General and Parliament, had strict guidelines as to the kind of payments that might be made for leases of diplomatic premises, especially in that they were not to involve any bribes or other illegal payments. However, in a number of countries, it was impossible to lease premises, as we were not permitted by these countries to purchase land except by making double payments, often in a combination of domestic (i.e., to the country) and offshore payments. Some of these countries were valuable export markets for Canada. Yet, we were able to maintain our diplomatic presence there only by double leasing or other irregular payment arrangements: arrangements which were insisted upon by local landlords. Though we entered into them only with Treasury Board approval on every occasion, they were not thought to meet the Board guidelines for commercial propriety.

Our other plans for accommodation having failed for want of co-operation from the local government, we were then faced with renewing leases with landlords who were subject to nearly confiscatory taxation and who accordingly sought payments that would not be caught as income. Other foreign missions, including the Vatican, complied without complaint with such practices in various countries, an acquiescence which made Canada's "ultra-moral" position more difficult to sustain.

I was prepared to take on the Treasury Board guidelines in a frontal assault, since I regarded it as absurd to force us to effectively sever diplomatic relations with friendly countries because we were not permitted to enter into the contractual relations necessary to continue there. Canadian pseudo-moralism had to know some limits. However, that necessity was avoided when I managed to persuade Department of Justice lawyers to conclude that the unconventional payments we would be forced to make to enter into lease arrangements were not, after all, contrary to the laws of the country in question. We were thus deemed to come within the Treasury Board guidelines.

* * *

Language was not normally a barrier at international meetings. Organizers were always equipped to interpret and translate in all major languages, and interpretation was invariably simultaneous at large meetings. At bilateral meetings and in smaller international forums, interpretation might be either simultaneous or subsequent. Speakers of less prominent languages had to utilize one of the major languages to be recorded and interpreted.

English was by far the predominant language internationally, and many foreign leaders spoke in English for the sake of clarity and immediateness. Andrei Gromyko, for instance, spoke English brilliantly, and at the bilaterals I had with him always engaged in some preliminary banter in colloquial English. However, once a meeting was considered by him to have begun formally, he immediately switched to Russian, reverting to English only when he found it necessary to correct his interpreters.

Highly formal bilateral meetings, such as those between heads of state or government, could often be tedious in the extreme, because of the use of subsequent rather than simultaneous interpretation. The usual pattern was for one leader to speak for fifteen to twenty minutes in his or her own language, followed by an interpretation session of the same length. Then the other leader would reply for about the same number of minutes, with interpretation to follow. Thus, there was often a period of some thirty to forty minutes following his or her opening remarks when the first speaker would understand nothing. The story is told that Brezhnev, during his meetings with Nixon and Kissinger, used to leave the room entirely during such blank periods, but I never saw anyone behave with such discourtesy. Usually one remained impassively at the table, with perhaps a frozen smile, thinking one's own thoughts.

* * *

Major changes occurred to the external affairs department during my tenure. Trudeau informed me during my initial interview that he had decided on a consolidation of all Canadian officers serving abroad so that there would be a single foreign service under the Department of External

Affairs, comprised of traditional foreign-service officers, members of the Trade Commissioner Service, and officers of the Department of Manpower and Immigration who were posted abroad. This consolidation affected only personnel, not policy and program, which continued to be determined by Industry, Trade and Commerce and Manpower and Immigration respectively.

This fit in well with a policy of concentration of our efforts in foreign policy. In an address to the Empire Club in Toronto on 22 January 1981, I announced a new Canadian policy of bilateralism, which expressed a more self-interested, more nationally assertive, foreign policy, in response to the changes in the world in the previous decade, particularly the rise in importance of petroleum-producing countries. I stated that Canada would henceforth be guided by a new and more hard-nosed realism. It was not enough for us to be merely the world's leading internationalists. We would concentrate our resources to achieve the necessary political relationships with a limited number of key countries. As I put it on 2 April 1981, "bilateralism is not a policy of just having bilateral relations: it is a policy of having certain kinds of bilateral relations. It is a policy of concentration in our bilateral relations...."[21]

The way had been prepared for this address by my memorandum to cabinet of 11 December 1980 by which cabinet agreed that we would henceforth give the highest priority to those countries with which it was in our interest to deal: the United States, Mexico, Brazil, Venezuela, and the Commonwealth Caribbean in the Americas; the United Kingdom, France, West Germany, Spain, Italy, and generally the European Community in Western Europe; Poland, Romania, and Yugoslavia in Eastern Europe; Japan, China, India, Australia, Korea, and the five countries of the Association of South East Asian Nations (ASEAN) in the Pacific; Saudi Arabia, Algeria, Nigeria, Francophone West Africa, and Zimbabwe in the Middle East and Africa. Generally speaking, these countries of concentration represented our trading interests.

The heart of my Empire Club address was an announcement of a new policy for Canada, and a new role for the department as its central policy manager, applying "the key consideration of credibility, coherence and planning" to the process in its relations with the countries of concentration.

It should not then have been a great surprise that the creation in 1980 of an executive-level foreign service pool, and the new policy of bilateralism with an enlarged role for External in 1981, was followed by a departmental reorganization announced by the prime minister on 12 January 1982. Export promotion and trade policy were transferred to External Affairs, effectively making it a super-ministry in order to effectively pursue export markets. Ed Lumley, the Minister for International Trade, would henceforth report to me rather than to Herb Gray, who became the new Minister of Regional Industrial Expansion. Pierre De Bané, who had been the Minister Responsible for Regional Economic Expansion, also moved to External, to become a sub-minister responsible for external relations, with special responsibility for francophone countries (a role he was already filling in fact) and for humanitarian concerns like refugees.

I explained the reason for the change on 24 March 1982:

> The roots of the reorganization for economic development lie in the *Economic Strategy for the '80s* – that document which was published with the budget last November. In setting out our objective of national economic renewal, we identified the promotion of Canadian exports as one of the five priority areas for action.... [O]ur exports currently account for nearly 31 per cent of our GNP.... In effect, the reorganization will bring under one roof the policy planning and management of all aspects of our foreign relations – trade, and economic, political, cultural and social aspects, et cetera.[22]

The opposition parties tried to make capital out of the reorganization, claiming that it was out of keeping with the Royal Commission of Inquiry on Conditions of Foreign Service, headed by Pamela McDougall, which had reported in mid-December 1981 on personnel problems in the foreign service. That attempt failed, however, when Ms McDougall stated that the reorganization was a move in the right direction and should have come even earlier, at the same time as consolidation.[23]

* * *

The SSEA's office was at the northeast corner of the top floor of the Pearson Building, with a dramatic view of the Ottawa and Rideau rivers and of the city. The whole of the ninth floor immediately below was the hospitality suite, the site of official receptions and dinners, with a sizeable art collection on display and an exterior terrace that could be used in good weather. External laid an exceptional table. Paul Bournillat, the chef, was a master of the culinary arts, and the wine cellar was also unusually well supplied with fine Bordeaux and Bourgognes. The waiters were trained with military precision and were especially eye-catching when they raised in unison all the ornamental dish covers for head table guests.

As SSEA, I had only to walk down a flight of stairs to be with guests, which meant that I could work until the last minute. It did not do, however, to be late. Diplomats were punctilious about the timing of official events.

I tried to make the guests feel as much at home as possible, largely by circulating freely beforehand, by shortening speeches, and by arranging as far as possible for congenial guests beyond the official parties. I always made a point of inviting members of the public, if possible with some connection to the official guests' country. I also always included a brace of MPs, chosen from the various parties.

Another of the congenial aspects of my role was External's cultural mission. Each year, the department put up several million dollars as a contribution towards sending symphony orchestras, ballet companies, and theatre companies on international tours. We also helped to facilitate sending individual artists abroad, and, when possible, I attended such events. During my visit to Hungary, I opened Tom Forrestall's art exhibition in Budapest in March 1981. The same month in New York, I presided at the official opening of the Canadian Arts Centre, the 49th Parallel, intended as an avant-garde gallery that would attract sophisticated Manhattanites. In April 1981, I flew to New York for a performance of *Manon Lescaut* at the Metropolitan Opera that was sponsored by the Canadian Society of New York. In addition, I was able to attend a concert by Canadian pianist André Gagnon in Caracas in January 1982, and had the opportunity of visiting the Canadian Cultural Centre in Paris in early June 1980. Government funding for Canadian arts groups and artists to tour abroad was a sound investment, with a return both in prestige and in dollars.

* * *

My immediate predecessor, Flora MacDonald, SSEA for nine months in the short-lived Joe Clark Government, devoted an address to the Canadian Political Science Association on 3 June 1980 to an attack on attempted bureaucratic domination of government, particularly on the bureaucrats who had served her in the Department of External Affairs.[24] She identified four "entrapment devices" used by the department: first, the unnecessarily numerous crisis corridor decisions; second, the unnecessarily long and numerous memos; third, the late delivery to her of her own submissions to cabinet, sometimes just a couple of hours or less before a meeting took place; and, fourth, the one-dimensional opinions put forward in memos. She also criticized the senior mandarins' attempt to set up committees of deputy ministers to parallel cabinet committees with a view to resolving as many difficulties as possible beforehand.

Far be it from me to impugn the veracity of MacDonald's experiences. Indeed, I believe she could have made such allegations only on a factual foundation. But I do dispute, on the basis of my own longer experience with the same public servants, her interpretation of the events that occurred. There could be and were differences of viewpoint between ministers and public servants, but these were not hidden. The department made attempts to persuade me to their point of view but certainly not to conceal the positions they espoused or to have me adopt them unawares. When I had made a decision, I invariably found a ready acceptance of that fact.

It is true that there were, from time to time, crisis decisions in "corridors," usually over votes at the United Nations that came up more quickly than expected. I cannot recall any occasion on which such a decision came at me without some advance notice so that I could be turning it over in my mind and with my advisers in the interval. But the point is that such crisis calls were not invented by bureaucratic demons to bedevil the minister. They were always a response to extrinsic exigencies.

With respect to the number and length of departmental memoranda, every minister, I suppose, had to make a choice. MacDonald records that "in the wake of an abject plea for mercy, the senior rewrite personnel agreed to reduce their verbiage by half." Personally, I have always felt that it is better to be fully informed.

As for departmental delay, I never had the experience of late delivery to me of my submissions to cabinet. It is true that there could be a lengthy route from the pen of the desk officer who authored a memorandum, and a disagreement or questions by a director or assistant deputy minister or the deputy himself could lead to a document's return several times to the desk officer for reconsideration. But we always had lots of lead time, and I cannot remember any instance in which I brought a document to cabinet where I had not seen a draft well in advance.

I continued the policy which I was told was instituted by MacDonald of having the author of any document identified in its heading. More than once, I called desk officers for further enlightenment on some point. Normally, on any important matter, I had an oral meeting with the deputy, lower departmental officials, and my own staff, and I always insisted on the attendance of the desk officer responsible. I held such meetings very frequently while in Ottawa.

I was greatly aided in my cabinet presentation by the "mirror committee" of deputies corresponding to the Cabinet Committee on Foreign and Defence Policy which I chaired. This was the parallel committee system of which MacDonald disapproved, sight unseen, during the Clark period, and which was actually established by Trudeau on his return to office in 1980. The principal reason in the minds of the prime minister and Pitfield for establishing the mirror-committee system was to help them contour ministerial initiatives rather than to smooth ministerial pathways. In this sense, MacDonald was right in noting the infringement on traditional ministerial prerogatives, though the focal point of her anger ought to have been her prime minister rather than the bureaucracy. But the fact is that a minister cannot prevail in any event over a determined prime minister, and, if there is going to be trouble, in my opinion it is better that it come as early as possible in the life of an initiative. When a PM goes further and establishes a new system to give his office earlier and more systematic input into decision-making, through the control of the Privy Council Office over the agendas and procedures of committees of public servants, there is nothing a minister can do but to accept the system as a *fait accompli*. It is a prime minister's government, and it is his/her prerogative to make such an organizational decision.

In fact, the new system proved to be helpful. It ironed out differences between interested ministries, in my memory usually petty ones, but which often involved "turf wars" between, say, Finance and External. It was crucial to have these problems resolved before reaching cabinet, where the agenda was overloaded, and a minister's small disagreement with a memorandum, at the behest of his officials, could result in serious delay. Often such matters, small as they were, took weeks of bargaining to resolve.

One such problem that was particularly knotty involved the role of External in legal matters, where the opposing department was Justice, which in my view rightly asserted a monopoly over all governmental legal advice. Nevertheless, there was a valid subordinate role for External. This controversy lasted so long that I was able to approve its resolution from External's side while I was still SSEA and subsequently as minister of justice to accept the compromise from the viewpoint of that department. The wording that was agreed upon gave External, logically enough, the right to "foster the development of international law and its application in Canada's external relations."[25]

MacDonald also mentioned her independent role as chair of the Foreign and Defence Policy Committee, in which position the incumbent was advised, not by External, but by the Privy Council Office. This was not, by and large, a complicated role, since External (including CIDA and International Trade) and National Defence were the only departments reporting to the committee. I cannot recall ever being placed in a compromising position as a result of having to chair decisions on my own memoranda, since the advice I received from the Privy Council was always very gentle and never counselled me against one of my own recommendations. Of course, the author of the Privy Council memoranda was none other than Bob Fowler, himself a career foreign service officer on secondment. I have no knowledge of whether his memoranda found their way beforehand to the USSEA as MacDonald alleged, but, if they did, no harm was done in my time.

I have not attempted to deal generally with the role of the Privy Council Office, because I was largely unaware of its functioning. That its role could be byzantine I well knew, but usually the prime minister would bring anything of importance to the minister's attention. If it were not, then possibly it was the top public servant, the clerk of the Privy Council, who was riding his own hobbyhorse. The minister, if s/he felt threatened, could always take the matter to the prime minister. My experience was that, given time, officials of my own department could usually straighten out any disagreement with the Privy Council Office without the need of any intervention by myself or the prime minister.

I see an attitude of confrontation between ministers and their own public servants as foolish, particularly for the ministers involved. They stand only to benefit from the advice of their public servants. If they agree, they are provided with detailed substantiation of their point of view. If they disagree, they are alerted to the arguments that many others will make, and which they will be required to refute.

The relationship between minister and department is not one of entrapment but one which is open for the participants – though not, of course, to the public. Ministers know what is going on, and they can play it, as they will. In my opinion, if they cannot get along with their departmental officials, the fault is usually theirs.

**Part Two
General Themes**

Chapter 4
The Olympic Boycott

My first serious problem after the swearing-in of the Trudeau cabinet on 3 March 1980 was the boycott of the Olympic Games in Moscow proposed by President Jimmy Carter shortly after the Soviet invasion of Afghanistan.

As the first incursion of Soviet combat forces outside Eastern Europe, the West took the Soviet invasion of Afghanistan very seriously, and the common resolve was to make sure that Moscow paid a price for its aggression. Much of the Third World joined in the denunciation, and 100 states voted for a condemnatory resolution in January 1980 at the United Nations, with a demand for immediate Soviet withdrawal. For its part, the previous Clark government had withheld recognition from the Afghan government and discontinued Canadian aid. Moreover, vis-à-vis the Soviet government, it postponed all visits of ministers or senior officials, all scientific or technical exchanges, all cultural exchanges beyond existing commitments, as well as sports and educational exchanges. The Trudeau government continued these sanctions and also decided to maintain only our traditional levels of grain supplies, with no increase to relieve the Soviet shortage.

The targeting of the 1980 Olympic Games by the U.S. arose both because of proximity in time with Afghanistan and because the USSR itself staged the Games as a propaganda event, portraying them as a symbol of the international acceptance of Soviet policies. This Soviet politicization of the Games was at least an effective *ad hominem* argument for the boycott. Prime Minister Joe Clark announced on 26 January 1980 that Canada would boycott the Games if Soviet troops were not withdrawn from Afghanistan by 20 February – the same date set by President Jimmy Carter.

During the election period Trudeau's immediate reaction to a boycott was negative and he was completely opposed to the deadline set by Clark. However, in the later stages of the election campaign, he said that Canada would accept a boycott if there was massive participation from both the West and the Third World. The U.S. had also been attempting to find agreement on alternative sites for summer games, and a small meeting to that end was held in Geneva in mid-March, which Canada attended as an observer. These summer games were not intended as a Counter-Olympics, but merely to provide some outlet for otherwise frustrated athletic competitors.

* * *

The Zimbabwe independence celebrations, for a reason which will shortly become apparent, had an Olympic connection.

I had not taken seriously the prime minister's suggestion that I try to bargain with the Americans for a *quid pro quo* for our joining the boycott. The Americans, in fact, were not asking us to do anything beyond what they were urging on all members of the Alliance. They were obviously hoping that the force of their example would influence other Western countries, and, on 15 April 1980, President Carter had written to the prime minister, along with other leaders, requesting our participation in the boycott. The Americans were not in the habit of directly asking us to take any particular action on multilateral issues, and still less of pressuring us to do so.

Although I did not take the PM's advice as to striking a bargain with the U.S. as a command, I did take seriously his desire to announce Canada's accession to the boycott only as part of a respectably large group of states, including Third World and Muslim countries. Perhaps I should have been less forward in what was after all my first decision-making in foreign affairs if I had not thought that he understood and accepted the depth of my feeling about the boycott. More than forty states were thought to be leaning toward a boycott, with the United States, the United Kingdom, Australia, and the Netherlands being strongly committed to it. France was equally strongly opposed. The Federal Republic of Germany was seen by many to be the key to its success.

By the time of the Zimbabwe celebrations, I was casting around for inspiration as to how best to present the decision I had already arrived at to follow the U.S. boycott of the Olympic Games. Happily for me, we were being driven by vocal sectors of the Canadian public, which was arguably in a mood to punish the Soviets for their intervention in Afghanistan. My colleague Gerry Regan, the minister of state for sports, was in accord with my decision for the greater political good, and the prime minister was reluctantly on board, even though it soon became apparent that there was nothing to get out of the Americans in return for our decision. What counted for me was that we were acting in our own self-interest. On 2 April, I met with Dick Pound and Jim Worrall, the president and vice-president of the Canadian Olympic Association, who accepted our likely decision as politically inevitable, though undesirable from their point of view.

Indeed, no one who was closely associated with sports could enthusiastically welcome a decision to subject sporting considerations to political ones, and in the past the Western world had for the most part tried to discourage various Commonwealth countries from boycotting international games because of South Africa's presence. Afghanistan, however, was seen as a special case, since it involved not merely Soviet participation in the Games but also their playing host to all the Olympic nations. Public opinion, or at least the interplay of governmental and sporting forces, was not uniform across the whole Western world. Some governments were not able to compel their Olympic committees not to send participating athletes, while others did not care to try. These governmental failures principally limited the effectiveness of the boycott. While the Canadian Olympic Committee voted 137–35 not to participate in the Games, the committees in the United Kingdom and Australia – both countries that were among the leading political supporters of the boycott – defied their governments and voted to go to Moscow. Undoubtedly, Canadian public opinion was highly influenced by that in the United States.

The Zimbabwe event, which I had to attend for Commonwealth reasons, turned out to be very helpful in the planning of an Olympic scenario. So as to be sure not to slight the Commonwealth aspect, I asked Arnold Smith, the outstanding Canadian diplomat who had for ten years served as secretary-general of the Commonwealth, to accompany me as part of our delegation. The day I arrived, 17 April, I had bilateral meetings with Hans-Dietrich Genscher, the West German Foreign Minister, Lord Carrington of the United Kingdom, and Prime Minister Malcolm Fraser of Australia, among others. It was the encounter with Genscher that proved the most helpful in relation to the Olympics. I learned from him that he intended to announce the adherence of the Federal Republic of Germany (FRG) to the boycott in Bonn at the beginning of the following week. Given the FRG's bellwether status, I immediately saw it as an advantage to fall in with West German timing, and I then and there decided to proceed in that fashion.

Malcolm Fraser almost upset the applecart. We had a full and frank discussion of the difficulties confronting our two governments with respect to the Games, and I told him in confidence what I expected we would do. Perhaps driven by his desire to find support for the Australian position, but in gross breach of diplomatic protocol, he immediately went out and revealed our intentions to the press. My officials were horrified since such revelations of what other states had said or would do, resulting from private conversations, were strictly taboo. They let the Australians know in no uncertain terms what we thought of this behaviour and also did their best to diminish the effect of Fraser's revelation by presenting it merely as a possible scenario. That the Australians had taken our rebuke to heart was evidenced when I met Andrew Peacock, the Australian foreign minister, several months later. In an attempt to offset their blunder, he felt it incumbent on him to provide what seemed to me and the Canadians present to be a patently exaggerated account of how much I had impressed Prime Minister Fraser. Tom Delworth, the effective and outspoken assistant undersecretary of state for the Pacific, remarked afterwards that "if B.S. were coral, Peacock would be the Great Barrier Reef."

In any event, I returned to Ottawa determined to make full use of the German parallel and on 21 April quickly obtained the agreement of the prime minister and cabinet that our boycott announcement should be made the following afternoon. There was one hitch beforehand in that Gerry Regan, who always seemed somewhat competitive with me, pressed very hard to have the official statement made by Trudeau rather than by me. I empathized with his feelings, if not with his request, since External Affairs, which might be said to cover the international aspect of every portfolio, always trod on a good many domestic political toes. However, as I well knew, the last thing the prime minister wanted was to have his own name linked with the boycott, and he promptly decided that the statement was mine to make. I, of course, associated Regan with myself in the announcement and made sure he participated in the press conference.

Unfortunately, the German link broke down in part, as Genscher was unable for various domestic reasons to deliver on his timetable, delaying his announcement until the next day. While I was able to assert that the conditions for an effective boycott were clearly present, I was not able specifically to refer to West Germany. The timing of the announcement was therefore less justified than I would have wished, though it served the minimal purpose of getting the announcement out: and of doing so before the arrival the next day of American secretary of state Cyrus Vance so that its issuance could not be attributed to American pressure.

Vance arrived in Ottawa early on Wednesday morning, 23 April, just after the abortive American attempt to forcibly rescue the besieged American diplomats at their embassy in Teheran, and in time for a full morning of meetings with me before a luncheon at the prime minister's residence. At lunch, Trudeau harangued him at length about the dangers implicit in further U.S. attempts to rescue the American diplomats confined in Teheran by the revolutionary Iranian mob. If he had realized how troubled Vance himself was by the situation, even the PM might have laid off. That same night, the secretary flew back to Washington, where he announced his resignation the next morning.

* * *

In retrospect, the Olympic boycott was only partially successful.[26] Sixty-eight countries joined it, including half of all the Middle Eastern, African, and Latin states. Another thirteen abstained because of lack of resources. Nevertheless, eighty-one did take part, and the Games went on very much as usual. On the other hand, our analyses indicated that the Soviet leadership was stung by the fact that the boycott denied them the international seal of approval that they had sought as a great and respected power.

Approximately four-fifths of the states that voted against the Soviet Union at the UN in January 1980 did not attend the Games. In particular, the absence of major Western sporting nations such as the U.S., West Germany, and Japan denied the USSR the opportunity of staging a sports spectacular proving the superiority of communism over capitalism. The embarrassing number of medals for the Soviet Union in a field lacking full competition led to a decision on the part of Soviet authorities to cease publishing a daily medal count, and Brezhnev did not attend the closing ceremony. On the other hand, the alternative games were not a great success either, with the competition there even more lacklustre.

I was disappointed with the result of my first foreign policy venture, but, being realistic, I recognized that Canada could have done nothing more to ensure the success of the boycott – that it could not, indeed, have done otherwise. The boycott may perhaps be summarized as a success with reservations, but the alternative would have been in my opinion much worse: to have let what the Soviets hoped would be a vast world endorsement of the legitimacy of their system and policy go ahead as if nothing had happened in Afghanistan.[27]

Chapter 5
The East-West Divide

The overriding international problem during the whole time that I was Secretary of State for External Affairs was the East-West divide. Chapter 7 recounts how Canada strove to ensure that the East-West conflict did not dominate the North-South agenda, but in its own right it did span the globe: Afghanistan, the Olympic boycott, Poland, the Berlin Wall, the Middle East, East Africa, Namibia and Mozambique, the Caribbean and Central America, Southeast Asia, the Ukraine, Soviet Jewry, the Conference on Security and Cooperation in Europe (CSCE), trade between eastern and western Europe. It could raise its head anywhere, at any time.

The source of the tension was, of course, the aggressive behaviour of the Soviet Union and its allies, particularly Cuba, Vietnam, North Korea, and (internally) Poland. In its more theoretical or Leninist aspect, Soviet communism was a missionary movement with a view to ultimate communization and destabilization of the world. In both the Stalin and post-Stalin eras, it may be more accurate to think of its internal dynamism as Russian imperialism pure and simple, but the effect was the same: the maximum extension of Soviet influence by the maximum destabilization of other states. In my observation, Soviet leaders and apologists professed Marxist ideology as it served their purposes; it was a useful tool, but no more.

Although American attitudes at times posed problems for Canada, I never forgot that our profound differences were with the Soviets and not with the Americans. With the Soviets, we were coming from a period of so-called détente, negotiated with Brezhnev by Nixon and Kissinger, that lasted through the mid-seventies, but with Afghanistan, it became apparent that for the Soviets détente was merely a device to ease tension in the East-West confrontation so as to obtain economic and technological benefits from the West, while continuing their military build-up in Europe. Most of all, détente for them was for Europe only, while they went ahead with expansionist and destabilizing policies in the rest of the world. My policy, along with that of the West generally, was that détente had to be reciprocal, global and indivisible, and rest on a firm foundation of deterrence.

The Marshall Plan, the Truman Doctrine and the North Atlantic Treaty Organization (NATO) were healthy early manifestations of the reaction to Soviet expansionism, as was the revival of Western Europe, leading to the Franco-German rapprochement and eventually to the European Community. The excesses should occasion no surprise, since the Bolshevik menace, as it was then thought of, was one of the historical causes of the development of Fascist governments in Italy, Germany and Spain and of Fascist movements in England and France in the unhinged aftermath of the First World War. But there was also an unhealthy side to the response: in the United States, McCarthyism and the communist fixation of the far right, and in Latin America the rise of military regimes, largely by way of negative reaction to the perceived threat to the whole of Latin America by Cuba. After World War II, the eras of John Foster Dulles and Ronald Reagan were particularly marked by psychologically unbalanced reactions in the United States. Personally, I had to cope with the first flush of triumphalist Reaganism.

Reagan was not equivalent to Reaganism; in person, he was a sunny, spontaneous, warm-hearted human being. On our first meeting, during his first visit to Ottawa on 10 March 1981, I happened to be standing with the American welcoming party as he made his way into the air force hangar at Uplands. When he came face-to-face with me, he paused for a moment, at which point I told him who I was. "Thank goodness," he replied, "I thought you might be one of my own cabinet who was so new that I hadn't met him yet."

Despite his bonhomie and his talent for repartee, he seemed largely incapable of abstract thought and therefore wholly dependent on others for his ideas. In fact, he was not really at home with ideas at all except for those that were reduced to slogans. His forte was in delivering his lines in his pleasing manner and in his simple belief in the goodness of America and all things American, and his scorn for the "evil empire" of Soviet communism. He was thus easily influenced by those who had access to him. His administration was therefore not marked by subtlety in dealing with East-West problems.

Predictably, Reagan hit it off well with Margaret Thatcher, but not with Mitterrand, Schmidt and Trudeau, who were far too intellectually sophisticated to feel close to such an intellectual nullity, who appeared to live by simple – one might say, simplistic – pieties. But even the intellectual élite could not entirely resist Reagan's human charm. He did not come across in person as an ideologue, but as a humble man, speaking to equals without condescension, and with an obvious attempt to relate to them as people. Personally, I found him a likeable human being, usually a little out of his depth, but genuinely trying, with his limited intellectual powers, to understand problems and to arrive at common-sense solutions. I reserved my venom for his acolytes, the Reaganites, who rationalized his woolly ideas into missiles for the faithful and missives against the heathen.

* * *

My period in office thus coincided with the beginning of a renewal in the Cold War. The twice-yearly meetings of NATO foreign ministers, in the form of the North Atlantic Council (NAC), were the particular Western forums for issues of the Second Cold War.[28] The annual economic summits (or G-7) were also major occasions for assessing events among the seven leading economic powers, consisting of Canada, the United States, Japan, the United Kingdom, France, the Federal Republic of Germany (FRG), and Italy, with a representative of the European Community (EC) also in attendance. They were also the gathering point for a diverse group of personalities.

It was not easy for the liberal-minded to perceive that Americans would abandon the relatively enlightened face of the Carter administration for that of Reagan. I became convinced of the impeding change of administration in the United States during the fall session of the UN in 1980, when the result still seemed in the balance. I can well remember the utter astonishment of Jean François-Poncet, the french foreign minister, when I told him of my conclusion during our bilateral meeting on 30 September.

Jimmy Carter, a thoroughly decent human being, was brought down in part because he happened to be in office during the Iranian revolution and in particular by the "student" hostage-taking of the American Embassy in Teheran.[29] The Iranians were so blindly anti-Carter that they released the hostages within a few minutes of Reagan's taking office on 20 January 1981. During his presidency, Carter managed more often than not to convey uncertainty and indecision about his intentions. From time to time, he was capable of making tough decisions well, as in the cases of the second oil crisis and the two-track NATO modernization in response to the Soviet menace in December 1979, but he usually appeared hesitant in decision-making. Part of his political difficulty, I am convinced, was his gentle Southern voice, which always sounded so flat and unemotional that he appeared to listeners to lack conviction. But the problem went deeper. Because his active intelligence showed him so many sides of any question, and because his vibrant faith made him hesitant to question the motives of others, he had the good man's difficulty in imputing evil to the wicked.

He came to his decisions with diffidence and difficulty, lending an aura of uncertainty to even his best decisions. In all, I believe it was his inability to instil public confidence in his conduct of public affairs that led to his political downfall.

* * *

My first G-7 economic summit took place in Venice on 22–23 June 1980. The U.S. was represented by President Carter, secretary of state Ed Muskie, and national security adviser Zbigniew Brzezinski – all interesting characters.

I had first met Brzezinski, who was the most anti-Soviet of the three, at a small Atlantic Conference on Sea Island, Georgia, in November 1976, just after Carter had won election but well before he had announced his cabinet. There was a lot of jockeying for position in the Carter administration among the liberal intelligentsia present, and Brzezinski, at that time a professor at Columbia, was distinguished by his harder-than-most line. In particular, he was highly sceptical of Kissinger's détente with the Soviet Union, perhaps as much from his sense of competition as from the wellsprings of policy. Brzezinski's influence on Carter in East-West issues was easily detected in Carter's tough anti-Soviet line at Venice.

Ed Muskie struck me at Venice and again at Ankara as being even more of a neophyte in foreign policy than I was. He spent a great deal of time in telling me about some hostile Arab moves in the Middle East, an account which not only sounded strange to me, but which my officials assured me was very old news – and not too reliable at that! However, guided by the always-strong coterie of U.S. advisers and by his own finely honed senatorial instincts, he always made an effective political presentation of the U.S. point of view. It was unfortunate that President Carter's defeat in November 1980 deprived Muskie of an opportunity to grow into the office, but he was very philosophical at Brussels in December about his loss, reflecting that he would now have an opportunity to make a good living for a change.

Margaret Thatcher was a sparkling presence at every meeting I attended with her, including Venice. She spoke crisply and trenchantly, whatever the subject, and was as incapable of sounding unconvinced as Carter was the reverse. After a particularly brilliant and spontaneous burst of eloquence from her at Venice, Trudeau leaned over to me and remarked, "She's very impressive, isn't she?" One could never fail to be impressed by how well she spoke. In fact, her deficiencies were not so much in foreign as in domestic policy, and domestically not so much in economic as in social matters. However, she attacked the "wets" in her own party for their tenderheartedness with the same vigour and rigour with which she assailed Brezhnev. Indeed, she entirely lacked a social conscience. Ultimately, as well, in her xenophobia against the European Community, she displayed what was probably the other side of the same "Little Englander" mentality that led her to stand up to Argentine aggression over the Falklands. She was a gifted but unusually flawed leader, whose flaws were about to do her in politically in 1982 when she was saved by the new admiration that flowed her way from her resolute defence of British interests in that short but decisive war.[30]

Lord Carrington, her foreign secretary, was one of the quickest and most incisive minds on the world scene, and he exuded an easy charm. His posture towards his prime minister was one of acquiescent tolerance. He always referred to her in a kind of devilish way as "My Mistress," which also had the effect of making it clear that he was not overawed by her. His manner was one of taking nothing seriously, but at the same time he expressed every thought with unerring precision and perceptivity.

The summit leader who consistently impressed me the most was Helmut Schmidt of the Federal Republic of Germany (FRG). Although a socialist chancellor, he was a committed advocate of a free market, a balanced budget, and a strong currency. His far-seeing understanding of foreign policy, his inherent sense of balance, and his effective presentation of his views in English particularly struck me. Trudeau was also a great fan of Schmidt's, but the German chancellor was a particular *bête noire* of the Reagan White House.

In many ways, my favourite foreign minister was Hans-Dietrich Genscher. "Dieter" was impressive, not for his expression of his views, but for his quiet wisdom. He bore the burden of being not only the foreign minister, but also the leader of the Free Democratic Party, effectively the Liberal party of the FRG. The Free Democrats held comparatively few seats, but enough to be vital to the Social Democratic government. Genscher had already managed to switch from an electoral alliance with the Christian Democrats, just as they were losing power, and he later managed a reverse switch when the Social Democrats lost power with the retirement of Schmidt. His political instincts were accordingly finely honed. He was remarkable for his common sense, for his ability to get to the root of problems, and for his constructive solutions. At later meetings, he and I worked in tandem in trying to make NATO meetings more fruitful for all of us. Although strongly anti-communist, he usually had the best reading on what the Soviets were up to, and how best to counter it.

France was represented at Venice by President Valéry Giscard d'Estaing and Foreign Minister Jean François-Poncet. Although I had a friendly relationship with François-Poncet, Giscard and Trudeau were rather distant with each other. There was no spark between them, and perhaps some competitiveness. The chemistry was much better with Mitterrand at later summits, since Mitterand and Trudeau seemed to share a common view of the world.

* * *

While the political dimension at Venice was the East-West divide in the light of Afghanistan and Iran,[31] the overall emphasis was on the closely linked economic problems of inflation and energy. Carter saw inflation as being at a crisis stage, but it was energy that became the leitmotif of the economic agenda. The summit emphasized conservation and demand restraint, especially through the use of the price mechanism, improved energy efficiency, and expanded use of other energy sources, in an attempt to break the link between economic growth and oil consumption. Canada, however, had failed to limit itself to the short-term oil import target set for 1979 and seemed to be likely to miss again in 1980. Canada's problem with imports would be taken on board only later in 1980 with the advent of the National Energy Program. In the meantime, Canadian officials made sure that the final communiqué was written in such a way as to leave a loophole for "best efforts" conformity.

* * *

At the time of the renewed Cold War, in the aftermath of the renewed missile build-up by the Soviet Union in the seventies and its aggression in Afghanistan, we in the West had no choice but to take a hard line, and particularly to couple weapons modernization with negotiations on arms in a two-track policy. This was not an issue that divided Western leadership, though it did to some extent divide citizens of the West, a substantial number of whom, fearful of the consequences of nuclear war, wanted to make a special case of nuclear weapons. On the renewed Cold War, my voice was not distinctive, but represented the common voice of the Western leadership.

What divided the leadership of the West, however, was the subtle Soviet tactic of pressuring the Poles in oppressing themselves. Aside from Trudeau, there appeared to be no Western voice to oppose blaming both the Polish and Soviet governments for this development, and I saw to it that the PM was enmeshed in a national foreign policy that was indistinguishable from the common Western policy. The point of division for others was as to the price they were willing to pay nationally for imposing sanctions on the East. The extension of credits to the Soviets to buy Western European goods and the completion of the Siberian gas pipeline, for which immense contracts had been let to Western European enterprises, were both pocketbook matters for the members of the European Community. In the long run, they had to yield on either credits or the pipeline in order to make peace with the Americans. It did not happen without a great deal of travail, but happen it did, largely by the end of 1982.

* * *

The first North Atlantic Council (NAC) meeting I attended was that in Ankara, 25-26 June 1980. This was the first NATO ministerial meeting since the Soviet invasion of Afghanistan, and not surprisingly this subject and the forthcoming follow-up Conference on Security and Cooperation in Europe (CSCE) dominated the meeting. It was also the first meeting since the two-track policy was adopted in December 1979 for Western "modernization" of intermediate-range nuclear forces (INF) with a mere battlefield range, as distinguished from theatre nuclear forces (TNF) with strategic nuclear weapons/intercontinental ballistic missiles (ICBMs). Modernization was to be combined with the second track, arms-control negotiations: the idea was very much "speak softly, but carry a big stick."

During my time in office, the two-track policy was the essence both of NATO and of Canadian policy. It involved a total commitment to rearmament to counter the increased Soviet deployment of nuclear and conventional weaponry. It also entailed a complete commitment to arms control leading to disarmament. Although it was Joe Clark who had agreed to the two-track policy on Canada's behalf, it was accepted and defended by Trudeau and used by us to justify our adherence to a nuclear alliance, our resistance to unilateral disarmament, and the testing of cruise missiles in Canada.

Under Reagan, Washington became a fierce proponent of what had originally been a Carter policy of rearmament, to the point that we and the Europeans were sometimes drawn to question American dedication to disarmament as well. This led to some tension, especially since the Reagan administration was quicker to emphasize the rearmament side.

Canada was always somewhat embarrassed when it came to talk of armaments in NATO, because we devoted a smaller proportion of our GNP to defence than any NATO country except Luxembourg. Nevertheless, we were by and large meeting the NATO target, set in 1978, of a three per cent real annual increase in military spending. Our spending, in nominal terms, had been nearly three per cent over the previous five-year period and was in excess of that amount in the short-range estimates for future years. Our proposed increase was seventeen per cent for 1982–

83 (to $7 billion) and fifteen per cent for 1983–84 (to $8 billion). Our embarrassment was that our base amount was small compared to those of others. The U.S. allowed Canada little real say on our joint defence policy. What the Americans were determined to control, they should pay for. In my view, we should merely keep up appearances, so as to confirm a common attitude towards the Soviet Union. Moreover, the U.S., even under Carter, was pressing other NATO states for further increases in defence spending, given the Soviet preponderance both in conventional forces and in INF. Carter may have given the initial impression of being soft on communism, but there was very little difference between late-Carter and early-Reagan East-West policies, except in rhetoric.

The Soviet SS-20 missiles, with their triple warheads, already provided more nuclear firing power than was planned under the entire NATO modernization program. Secretary of State Muskie warned of the growing disenchantment in the U.S. with the lack of Alliance solidarity on defence outlays. The Europeans, on the other hand, were more concerned about the lack of the political will in the U.S. for frank and timely consultation. On this issue, Canada stood with the Europeans. I made the point at Ankara that the U.S. had only nominally consulted on Afghanistan and not to good effect, the result being a bad case of crisis management.

* * *

In Ankara, I was shocked that the dialogue among the ministers at the formal sessions was almost exclusively limited to set-piece statements prepared in advance, which no doubt adequately set forth each country's position but allowed almost no room for spontaneous reaction and genuine dialogue.

Genscher, whom I found to be consistently the most imaginative and constructive of the foreign ministers, felt the same way, and in November 1980 he made a proposal for a private ministerial meeting at the next NATO session in Brussels. His objective was to bring meetings of NATO ministers into closer alignment with European Community practice, where periodic ministerial meetings were held in informal surroundings, with no officials in attendance except for one note taker. His proposal led to agreement on a super-restricted session (SRS) at NATO ministerial meetings, with only ministers and Alliance ambassadors present. The first day of the NATO meeting in Brussels in mid-December 1980 was accordingly held in SRS.

I saw Genscher's initiative as a step towards creating a more intimate, confidential and unstructured framework for ministerial meetings, and I expanded on it to propose informal meetings of foreign ministers once or twice a year in addition to the regular twice-yearly formal meetings. Initially, the French were opposed, as they were not prepared to see political co-operation diluted by more extensive consultation. The German foreign minister wisely suggested that we not push the idea further until after the French presidential election in May 1981. After the election of Mitterrand, Genscher revived the idea, and in the summer of 1982 I invited the ministers to a first private meeting at La Sapinière in the Laurentians that October. We won general agreement, and the meeting was accordingly organized. It proved to be a key setting for unlocking Alliance misunderstandings, particularly with respect to the Soviet gas pipeline dispute.

* * *

The December 1980 meeting in Brussels focussed on defence and disarmament, the CSCE meeting in Madrid and the Soviet threat to Poland. On the defence issue, there was renewed concern about the pace of the Soviet arms build-up, as the USSR continued to devote twelve to thirteen per cent of its GNP to defence spending, with an increase of four to five per cent (in real terms) each year. In the previous year, it had deployed sophisticated weapons systems and had continued with a vast shipbuilding program, with a particular emphasis on missile-firing submarines. New Soviet tanks and new aircraft were also being produced, replacing earlier-generation machines. The alarm all of this caused in NATO was somewhat tempered by the fact that a first round of U.S.-USSR talks for arms control for INF had taken place in Geneva. The Western ministers were further encouraged that the development of Pershing II and ground-launched cruise missiles was on schedule, with the first systems planned for the end of 1983. The unilateral withdrawal of 1,000 U.S. nuclear warheads as part of TNF modernization was also well underway.

The Madrid follow-up conference of the CSCE had already begun in November 1980. On that day, I flew to Madrid from London, where I had been engaged in meetings on the Canadian constitutional initiative, and I remained in Spain until 14 November. The subjects at the CSCE included the violation of human rights in Warsaw Pact states, the infringement of the Helsinki Final Act of 1975 by the Soviet invasion of Afghanistan, the expansion of military confidence-building measures, the holding of a post-Madrid meeting on the military aspects of détente, obstacles to the future development of East-West trade, and administrative impediments to the reunification of families and to family visits. Of course, the Soviet Union did not alter its conduct in response to Western criticism, but it did have to sit and listen to Western judgments of its bloc's sins against its own peoples. Perhaps nothing changed in the East as a result of this, but the USSR did not walk out.

For me, the CSCE became a fundamental element of Canadian East-West policy. It gave us an opportunity to critique the members of the Warsaw Pact, particularly on their human rights performance, and to give voice to the powerful feelings of our domestic minorities. Canada was thus an active participant in the pillorying of the Soviet Bloc and our Ambassador R. L. Rogers was a formidable proponent of the Western position. Canada was encouraged in its strong position of constant protests against Soviet treatment of its nationals and neighbours by Ukrainian and Polish immigrants in Canada and by the Canadian Jewish Congress, on behalf of Soviet Jewry. Canada never lost an opportunity to berate the Soviet Union privately as well as publicly, including the presentation of lists of Soviet dissenters like Natan Sharansky in whom we took a particular interest.

I also tried to discriminate among the states of the Eastern Bloc according to their adherence to the Final Act. Hungary was the only Iron Curtain country to allow its citizens to freely visit abroad (every three years), and it was therefore the only Eastern Bloc country that I visited during my time as SSEA, despite invitations from others.

On the final NATO subject of Poland, the process of reform that began in August 1980 through the Solidarity movement could rightly be seen as the most hopeful development in Europe since the Marshall Plan, expressing as it did a courageous effort of the overwhelming majority of Poles to achieve a more open society, an objective very much in accordance with the principles of the Helsinki Final Act. As well as an expression of an innate desire for freedom, the Solidarity movement was also an upwelling of a fierce Polish nationalism, which was immediately directed against the outside oppressor, the Soviet Union. Both of these aspects ensured that there would ultimately be a Soviet response, as, even if the Soviets could have stomached such a political revolution in Poland, they could accurately see that the same spirit would spread like wildfire among the other Warsaw Pact states. It was undoubtedly for the Soviets the greatest danger to their hegemony since the Second World War.

From the beginning, therefore, there was the danger of Soviet military intervention, which would be rendered all the easier by the presence of some thousands of Soviet troops permanently bivouacked within Poland. NATO began to grapple with this at the Brussels meeting in December 1980, but no detailed program of response was agreed on. Before I even returned to Canada, the PM stated at a press conference in Ottawa that he found ill advised any speculation as to what the West would do if there were an invasion of Poland by the USSR. This statement assumed more importance in the light of a press report that NATO Secretary-General Joseph Luns had said that there would be a military response by NATO to a Soviet invasion. This was, of course, not at all what we had agreed on. Given that the West lacked a common frontier with Poland, NATO military action was extremely unlikely from the beginning. What was seriously contemplated was a program of severe political and economic sanctions. The bottom line was to be the calling of an immediate meeting of NATO foreign ministers, who would then decide what to do, taking particular account of the degree of resistance among the Poles.

In the light of the discrepancy between the prime minister's statement and the apparent comment of Luns, it was not surprising that Flora MacDonald, the Progressive Conservative critic of External Affairs, tried to open up a dichotomy between the PM and me. That was easily enough dealt with at the time, as I said that there would be a strong and appropriate reaction to a Soviet invasion, but that we could not speculate on the form it might take. Nevertheless, this incident was a harbinger of things to come. The prime minister did not like Luns, whom he regarded as a trigger-happy Cold Warrior, and I soon came to suspect that Trudeau had no great sympathy for Solidarity, perhaps because of his antipathy to trade unions in Canada. Subsequent events would reveal at the least a considerable difference of emphasis between us over Poland.

* * *

The NATO meeting in Rome in May 1981[32] marked the first meeting of the foreign ministers with Al Haig as the U.S. secretary of state. Haig was already, as the former commander of NATO forces, well and favourably known to the Europeans, and had made an equally favourable impression on me. He was that rare American who took the trouble of listening to the rest of the Alliance and appearing to care about the opinion of other countries. He was open in manner, frank in discussion, and winning in personality. If he could not always deliver the advance consultation he professed to believe in, the Europeans assigned the blame, not to him, but to the White House. Though clearly a strong anti-communist, he talked moderation for the most part and so was not dismissed within the Alliance as simply a Cold Warrior.[33]

Haig's sensitive balancing of Alliance concerns during his opening statement created an excellent atmosphere for the rest of the meeting. Nevertheless, his strong emphasis on the necessity of devoting additional national resources to defence met with European resistance. The FRG and the U.K. in particular resisted any additional defence expenditures beyond the agreed three per cent. So did we, but I let the Europeans carry the ball. Haig complained that the U.S. had gone further to meet European concerns about arms control than Europe was prepared to go in satisfying the U.S.'s exigencies in defence. The Reagan administration itself was engaged in massive increases in defence spending.

Haig reassured the gathering that NATO was the bedrock and anchor of U.S. foreign policy and therefore attached great importance to consultations within the Alliance. It was not, however, entirely clear that this meant consultation before rather than after the fact, and in my own statement at Rome I emphasized the importance of consultations before the U.S. had made its own decisions. I also made the point that peace and security could not be assured by military means alone. The West must be ready to negotiate arms control agreements with the East. Moreover, we would lose the sympathy of the non-aligned world, which was on its own beginning to turn against the USSR, if we fell prey to the temptation to see their problems in an East-West context. Due to the lack of any immediate crisis, the issue of Poland took a back seat at Rome, everyone agreeing that the worst was yet to come. There was also little discussion of the Madrid CSCE, which was continuing without progress, but there was support for the French proposal for a conference on disarmament in Europe following Madrid.

During the Ottawa summit of July 1981, there was no division on the major political issues, but no advance either. Trudeau, speaking as chair for the group, stated in the follow-up press conference that the Soviet Union must not be allowed to achieve military superiority over the West.[34] But the door was held open for disarmament leading to peace. The unity was impressive, if temporary.

* * *

In September 1981, because it was Canada's turn, I became the honorary president of the North Atlantic Council for a year, which gave me the opportunity of playing a slightly enlarged role at the meetings. For instance, I got to make an opening address at the NAC ministerial meeting in Brussels on 10 December 1981 and host that evening's banquet. In my statement, I paid tribute to the two distinguished Canadians who had previously had the same honour: Mike Pearson, one of the original architects of the Alliance and later one of the "three wise men" whose recommendations significantly enhanced the political dimensions of NATO; and Paul Martin, who helped to break the longstanding impasse over the admission of new members to the UN in 1955 and set the organization on the road to universality, and who with his Belgian colleague initiated a penetrating analysis of the Alliance in 1967 (the Harmel Report). I added that I was personally indebted to Martin, as predecessor, neighbour, and friend, for the wise counsel he continued to make available to me.

In the light of the recent beginning of disarmament negotiations in Geneva, I referred in my presidential address to the often-popular demands of the democratic left that NATO should forego its modernization plans regardless of whether the USSR accepted corresponding reductions in its nuclear forces. I was of the view that there was a need for all of us in office to do a better job of communicating with the public, some of whom had become disoriented in the stress of the nuclear era and who needed to be reminded of the essential role the Alliance played in safeguarding our societies from intimidation. We had been successful for more than thirty years in preserving the peace, deterring Soviet expansion, and acting as a forum for political consultations and crisis management. It was a cause for justified satisfaction, but not for complacency, that the Alliance had given Europe the longest period of peace it had known in this century. We must get across to our publics the message that the purpose of our weapons was to prevent a war, not to fight one. We were not seeking military superiority, but greater security at the lowest possible level of armaments, nuclear and non-nuclear. All war, not just nuclear war, was anathema.

I got the impression that there was very general acceptance of my sentiments, and indeed the Alliance's public posture towards the European peace movement became a central theme of the meeting. The Europeans, who, after all, were in the geographical location to be most intimidated by Soviet power, were strong supporters of NATO modernization. They hoped merely that the U.S. would provide the Western nuclear missile shield – and pay for it! This was also true of our own policy.

The announcement of Reagan's proposal for a "zero option" on all land-based INF missiles[35] and the U.S. proposal to begin Strategic Arms Reduction Talks (START) in early 1982 were strongly welcomed. Even the hard-to-satisfy French were pleased, since the French nuclear deterrent would not be included. A consensus emerged that the arms reduction dialogue should be combined with an insistence on Soviet restraint in all parts of the world. Soviet conduct worldwide would thus be linked to progress in the INF and START negotiations. It was also agreed that an essential prerequisite for NATO support for deployment of U.S. forces committed to NATO out-of-area would be consultation.

No sooner had the meeting ended on 11 December than the Soviets struck at Poland through the satellite Polish government, refining their technique over their previous interventions in Hungary and Czechoslovakia to purely domestic repression. This time it was the Polish government, under

Soviet pressure, which broke off the dialogue with Solidarity and the Church, imposed martial law, and imprisoned a large number of dissidents.

* * *

On the 13 December, I awoke to the news that during the night the government of General Wojciech Jaruzelski had imposed martial law on Poland and arrested hundreds of Solidarity supporters. This was not an eventuality that we in NATO had planned for, since we had always anticipated the likelihood of direct Soviet intervention as in Hungary, Czechoslovakia, and Afghanistan. Of course, no informed person could believe that the Polish government had acted except under Soviet pressure. Indeed, Haig has asserted that "Moscow had informed the governments of every country in the Soviet bloc that martial law would be imposed in Poland *before the Russians told the Warsaw government.*"[36] Nevertheless, most members of the Alliance felt that it was important to distinguish in our reaction between an actual Soviet invasion and this "inside job." If there were no distinction, the Soviets might still be tempted to move directly, thus worsening the position of the Polish people. Only the Americans appeared to want to react as if the Soviet Union had intervened directly, and this became a point of stress between them and other members of NATO.

I felt that there had to be a strong Western reaction vis-à-vis the Polish government, and clearly its weak point, as it had borrowed so much money in the West, was its commercial credits and its imminent need for debt refinancing. There we should strike hard. We should also make the Soviets pay a price, since they had obviously caused the Polish government to act so as to avoid the greater evil of a Warsaw Pact invasion. However, I agreed with the Europeans that the USSR should pay a lesser price than if it was directly involved.

After the initial news from Poland, it soon became difficult to acquire details of what was happening, since all communications between Poland and the free world were cut. On Sunday evening, 14 December, I spoke with Haig who took a dim view of the governmental repression in Poland, but he had little more real news than what I had already heard. He offered no reaction as to how the West should respond, except that we should lay the responsibility at Moscow's door.

I made it back to Ottawa by the end of the Monday afternoon, in time to attend an evening preview of my friend Sheldon Wiseman's television special, "The Raccoons on Ice," at the National Arts Centre. Life, as always, was a mélange of the extraordinary and the more mundane.

* * *

It was 11 January 1982 before NATO foreign ministers were able to get together in Brussels, although officials had met frequently in the interim. In December 1981, President Reagan had announced a number of American sanctions against Poland and the Soviet Union. These retaliatory measures went beyond what the rest of the Alliance was prepared to accept, though Haig wrote to all the NATO foreign ministers on 9 January asking for support for the U.S. position at the upcoming meeting. My decision in advance of the Brussels gathering was that we would maintain economic assistance and fulfil existing contractual commitments but would take no new initiatives especially with respect to debt refinancing.

We agreed at Brussels to suspend any future commercial credits to Poland for goods other than food and to postpone any meetings for debt rescheduling, a decision within our existing policy. NATO also called on Poland to re-establish civil liberties and the process of reform that had begun under Solidarity's influence. Specifically, there were three demands: the lifting of martial law, the release of detainees, and the resumption of government dialogue with the Church and Solidarity. No such result was achieved, but the meeting perhaps induced the Polish authorities to lift censorship on Western reporters, and to meet with Archbishop Jozef Glemp. Moreover, the NATO agreement was a very strong inducement to a country on the verge of bankruptcy. The U.S. economic sanctions against the USSR, on the other hand, bore no apparent fruit.

As a result of American initiative, a Solidarity Day was held at the end of January, and a satellite television program was organized to carry the statements of Reagan and other Western leaders to the Polish people. Fortunately, Trudeau agreed to be one of the participating leaders.

I announced our sanctions on 23 February 1982, but these were symbolic, so as not to impose a further burden on the Polish people already suffering enough at the hands of their own government. Our sanctions were closely parallel to those of other Western states. They included suspension of academic exchanges, restrictions on the movement of Polish diplomats, as well as the common restrictions concerning commercial credits and debt rescheduling. By early May, there was some easing of martial law in Poland: eight hundred internees were released and two hundred more paroled, and some relaxation was evident of the curfew, as well as of curbs on internal travel, communications and the media.

* * *

The differences in emphasis between the prime minister and I were never more in evidence than during Question Period on 25 January 1982, the first day back for the House of Commons after the Christmas recess.

On 18 December 1981, Trudeau had put the fat in the fire with his statement that: "if martial law is a way to avoid civil war and Soviet intervention, then I cannot say it is all bad." For good measure, he had added: "Hopefully the military regime will be able to keep Solidarity from excessive demands."[37] The prime minister had been immediately rebuked for his comments by Joe Clark, and his remarks then and at his year-end television interview were picked up by the Polish regime by way of justification of their conduct.

Philosophically speaking, his refusal to condemn the invocation of martial law *a priori* was perhaps understandable, if he felt the need to consider the matter from the viewpoint of Polish General Jaruzelski's subjective conscience. The question in my mind, however, was why it was necessary to indulge in subjective moral scrutiny when the situation cried out for an objective moral and political determination. Even if it were a lesser evil, it was still an evil. Why should we in any event grant the premises of an oppressive system? And why should it be implied that excesses in political optimism by the leaders of Solidarity were a basic element of the repression? One could understand the reaction of the Opposition, of the Polish Canadian community and of the country to Trudeau's statements.

I felt it necessary to eschew any such philosophical niceties, and answered simply that I was pleased "to report again our urging, our request, and even our demand to the Polish government that it withdraw the martial law which now pertains in that country, free prisoners, and return to political dialogue."[38] The next day, the prime minister was satisfied to repeat the same three points, but he was not prepared to abandon his argument that "it was better to have martial law if that prevented Soviet invasion."[39] John Crosbie, who by that time had become the chief Conservative critic for External, paid me the backhanded compliment of having "more backbone than the prime minister,"[40] but it was not at all a matter of courage. It was not even that the PM rode his intellectual hobbyhorses to the end, whatever the cost politically – though it may have been that, too. It was mostly, I believe, that one of Trudeau's great temptations in foreign policy was a spheres-of-influence approach by which a major power could do pretty well what it wanted in its own backyard, such as the U.S. in Cuba and the USSR in Poland. This did not really justify the PM's repeated statement that Polish action was better than Soviet invasion, except that presumably he recognized that the repression occurred as a result of Soviet pressure.

* * *

The Helsinki Final Act held, in my mind, the key to what our judgment should be. In traditional international law, only states were recognized. Individual people had no status, and a state had no right to intervene with another state in its internal affairs except on behalf of its own nationals. I had a private dialogue over Poland with the PM one day in the House after Question Period in which he asked me how I could possibly justify Western meddling in the internal affairs of Poland. I replied that normal international law in this respect had been drastically altered among the signatory countries by the Helsinki Final Act, which gave the West the right to call Warsaw Pact countries to account for how they respected the human rights of their own citizens, even if the Final Act did not have the full force of a treaty. As I stated in a letter to the *Globe and Mail* on 6 March 1982, it was not the mere fact of the imposition of martial law that impinged the Final Act, but rather "the nature of the regulations promulgated under the martial law regime and their application to the Polish people in an excessive manner and over a prolonged period of time."[41] The PM had no verbal comeback to my assertion but left me with the clear impression that he continued to harbour the same feelings as before.

The Polish controversy was a most trying public period for me with Trudeau, and I was sometimes tempted to think that the PM would completely undermine the country's – and my – foreign policy. I often wondered when, and how, it would all end. I had no choice but to stand my ground, and the public seemed to understand that the prime minister's views were his alone. Despite the obvious temptations, however, I never lost patience with Trudeau. Through the whole piece, I understood where he was coming from. He was the only Western leader ever to have invoked martial law in his own country, for what both he and I agreed were good and sufficient reasons during the Quebec Crisis in 1970. In the circumstances, he could not tolerate any suggestion that the mere invocation of martial law was by itself wrong. To determine its legality and morality, one always had to examine the circumstances. And so he could not refrain from examining the circumstances in Poland. Any such examination, even if not so tortuous as the PM's, would be bound to excite misunderstanding with a public bent on judgment without ratiocination. The PM was clearly "out of sync" with the public, and suffered political consequences accordingly.

* * *

The regular NAC ministerial meeting in Luxembourg in May 1982 was largely a dry run for the extraordinary NATO summit scheduled for Bonn in June, and it also marked the appearance of Francis Pym as the successor to Peter Carrington as British foreign minister. Poland, of course, headed the list of subjects, as ministers debated how best to match carrot and stick. There was general agreement on stricter controls on credits and on technology transfers, but not enough to satisfy Washington, which as always sought the most restrictive regime possible.

My opening statement, as *president d'honneur* at Luxembourg, was that our publics must be brought to realize that the real campaign for nuclear disarmament must be waged, not in the streets, but at the bargaining table. Defence and deterrence/arms control and disarmament were the two sides of the same security coin, and could not be separated. In this context, the recent announcement of U.S. readiness to begin START negotiations that summer was welcome. I also emphasized the importance to the Alliance of consultation.

The Versailles economic summit in early June preceded the NATO summit and proved a more important event. All told, however, the formal meetings largely failed to come to grips with the broad problem of Western economic recovery, spending a disproportionate amount of time on East-West economic relations. The overriding political-economic issue was that of U.S. pipeline sanctions, which were among the measures announced by President Reagan against the Soviet Union in late December 1981 but which had not yet been brought into effect.[42] The ultimate goal of the Reagan team was to bring about the collapse of the Soviet economy, but the limited deal that Haig had in mind for Versailles was that the U.S. would drop its opposition to the pipeline in return for European agreement to restrain future credits to Moscow, a matter on which the Europeans lacked enthusiasm, to say the least, since it was not in their perceived commercial interest. Nevertheless, a rapprochement was reached at a meeting the first evening. Even on this Reagan-inspired issue, the agreement nearly broke down the next day with a contrary statement at the summit by Mitterrand.

Al Haig has subsequently commented that Trudeau "mischievously joined Mitterrand."[43] The appearance of mischief was probably heightened because I had not been able to pass on to Haig a warning as to the PM's intentions that he whispered to me to convey to Haig. I was sitting between Trudeau and him, but the discussion at the table was animated, and there never seemed to me to be an appropriate moment to break in on Haig before the PM impetuously intervened to support Mitterrand's argument for maintaining financing for the USSR. Probably, even with notice of Trudeau's position, Haig's judgment would have remained the same, as the prime minister was responding to his inner impulse to support the underdog Mitterrand and to harass the powerful Reagan.

The next event was the one-day NATO summit in Bonn. It was intended to deal with longer-term issues, and particularly with the re-establishment of consensus in the Alliance towards the Eastern Bloc in the 1980s, in contrast with the NAC ministerial meeting which had concentrated on current issues in the usual way. But mutual disillusionment between the U.S. and the others was at its highest point in years. On the American side, there was resentment at the unsatisfactory scale of the allied contribution to the collective defence effort, whereas there was widespread dissent among the European populace over Washington's handling of world affairs and among European governments over lack of consultation. Little was accomplished beyond the formal accession of Spain to the Alliance.

In the opening statement, Prime Minister Trudeau spoke of the overriding priority that nuclear arms control and disarmament negotiations should have, to the extent that they must not be linked or coupled with non-military objectives. He suggested that real progress in arms control might even provide the Soviet leadership with confidence that its security could be assured without muscle flexing.

Even though it was Alliance policy, Reagan had made no mention of linking progress on disarmament with general Soviet behaviour. In fact, in addition to reaffirming the American security guarantee to Europe in his first European visit as president, he had stated at Bonn that the U.S. would spare no efforts in order to reach equitable, substantive, and verifiable reductions to equal levels of strategic forces and to secure in Geneva a total ban on land-based INF nuclear missiles. However, in his press conference at the end of the summit, the prime minister said that he had the impression that the president was a believer in linkage, a fear that Reagan's normal rhetoric might easily inspire. Not surprisingly the press coverage portrayed the PM as anti-American.[44]

* * *

The initial reaction to the Versailles summit was that it had been a success on both East-West trade and global negotiations, but it did not take long for the summit compromise on credits to the USSR to break down.

In an interview with the Washington *Post* on 15 June, Mitterrand made it clear that France was not going to wage any kind of economic warfare with the USSR and incautiously underlined the continuing difference between France and the U.S. over the issue of credits. The White House reacted savagely, effectively taking over foreign policy from Haig and the State Department. Three days later, apparently at the direction of the president, the U.S. imposed the pipeline sanctions that had been hanging fire for months, in their full extraterritorial and retroactive force. These sanctions were announced without any consultation with or even notification of EC countries. This precipitate action followed closely on the heels of American imposition of countervailing duties on EC steel and strong criticism of the Common Agricultural Policy. The Europeans, enraged, stated that they would ignore the sanctions, and ordered their domestic corporations to defy them. Italy was the most restrained in its reaction, but France, the U.K. and the FRG were breathing fire. All of these countries had contracts to supply goods to the USSR for the gas pipeline.

The one slight gesture of reconciliation Reagan made was to order a high-level investigation to review the pipeline issue and relations with NATO partners. The French particularly felt the absence of their normal interlocutors, Al Haig and Robert Hormats, both of whom had resigned over the conflict.[45] Under the circumstances, I decided to take the initiative in a congenial meeting with Haig's successor, George Shultz, on 3 August. I suggested that either France, as the chair of the 1982 summit, or the U.S., as the chair of the 1983 summit, should convene a meeting of the foreign ministers of the Seven that month to discuss the strains in the Alliance and to restore the spirit of consultation. Such a meeting, I said, might help to limit the damage from the U.S. pipeline decision. I stressed that Canada had no national stake in the pipeline problem – except that we were strenuously opposed to extraterritoriality – and could perhaps serve as a bridge between Americans and Europeans. Shultz reacted favourably to the proposal, but admitted in the course of the discussion that he did not believe reconsideration of the pipeline decision was possible at that time. Although the meeting I had in mind would not have focussed directly on reconsideration, in the absence of its very possibility a special meeting seemed unwarranted to other members of the Seven and thus my proposal did not take. The crisis was left to be dealt with at La Sapinière in October 1982 by NATO rather than by the Summit Seven, where it had originated. Crisis management was not yet a developed art in Western practice.

Secretary Shultz, however, eventually rode to the rescue. With a hard-won mandate from the president, he used the meeting at La Sapinière to reach agreement with the other NATO foreign ministers. On the U.S. side, there was satisfaction with stronger controls over the sales of goods strategically important to the Soviet Union, including oil and gas technology through a renewed Coordinating Committee for Multilateral Export Controls (COCOM), which from 1948 to 1995 controlled the export of high technology goods to Warsaw Pact countries. Washington was also pleased with an agreement not to subsidize the Soviets in other trade and to look for alternative energy sources to avoid further European dependence on Soviet natural gas. The Europeans, on their side, were delighted to see the end of the pipeline sanctions that had threatened the "sanctity" of their contracts with the Soviets – and their economies.[46] They were also pleased that the U.S. would no longer subsidize its huge grain sales to the USSR. President Reagan consequently lifted the gas sanctions in November 1982, and in December, by intensive diplomacy, Shultz finally secured the agreement of the French, who had backslidden after the October meeting. The worst crisis within NATO since Suez thus came to an end.

Chapter 6
Arms Control and Disarmament

In the previous chapter, I outlined much of the disarmament story, but more from the viewpoint of NATO's modernization track than from that of disarmament itself. It is useful to review the record here from the opposite side of the coin, since disarmament was of equal importance to NATO states – though that was not always immediately apparent from Reagan's rhetoric. In the long run, however, the United States proved its sincere commitment to the cause of arms control.

Canada in general and Trudeau in particular were in an exemplary position with respect to nuclear weaponry. Although Canada joined with the U.S. and the U.K. as a nuclear collaborator in 1943, and the first nuclear reactor outside the United States opened at Chalk River, Ontario, in 1945, Canada was the first of the nuclear powers to eschew the development of atomic power for military purposes. As I put it in February 1982, "We are the first country that had the capability of having nuclear weapons which chose freely not to do so. We saw this form of self-denial as making a significant contribution to world peace by the example that we not only preached, but acted."[47]

But the policy was never intended to mean that Canada would not equip its aircraft or missiles with American-supplied nuclear warheads, as part of the North American Air Defence Agreement (NORAD) or of NATO. This became a matter of controversy in the early 1960s when Prime Minister John Diefenbaker refused to allow nuclear warheads to be installed on Canada's newly acquired ground-to-air missile, the Bomarc, dedicated to defending Canada and the U.S. from a Soviet bomber attack. Diefenbaker's cabinet split on the issue, and Lester Pearson gained the prime ministership in 1963 on a pledge to acquire nuclear warheads for the Bomarcs.

Trudeau, already a public figure, though not yet in government, denounced Pearson for his acceptance of nuclear warheads. When he became prime minister in 1968, Trudeau launched a review of the Canadian role in NATO, which had long since adopted a policy of the possible first use of nuclear weapons in response to Soviet aggression. This review process led to a decision to cut Canada's European-based NATO forces in half (from 10,000 to 5,000) and to retire, as soon as practicable, from a nuclear-strike role directly involving Canadian forces. The Bomarcs had already become obsolete in the face of the new threat from ICBMs against which they were useless. The Honest John battlefield nuclear weaponry was also quickly abandoned, but the Genie air-to-air missiles on CF-101s had to be retained for another decade until the aircraft was replaced by CF-18s. It was only in February 1982 that Defence Minister Gilles Lamontagne could pledge the removal, by the end of the year, of the last U.S.-controlled nuclear weapons stockpiled on Canadian soil.

The decision not to use nuclear weaponry was no doubt conscience-salving for some, but it was also slightly hypocritical in the context of our continuance in NATO, a nuclear alliance, as the fundamental element of our East-West policy. Of course, the new Trudeau government had in 1969, in reaffirming our membership in NATO, rejected any suggestion that Canada assume a non-aligned or neutral role in world affairs. If it had made any other decision, many of us would have ceased to support it.

* * *

Disarmament, and particularly nuclear disarmament, took on a life of its own in the popular consciousness.

It would be too much to say that everyone in the world was in favour of arms control and disarmament. However, both leaders and people in democratic countries were in favour of arms control and disarmament, and the more realistic recognized that to disarm unilaterally would only leave their countries prey to less well-intentioned states. As I frequently insisted while SSEA, the more fundamental concept was security, not arms control and disarmament.[48] Countries had to be reassured that their security was guaranteed before they could be persuaded to disarm. Therefore, in my estimation very few people in the West advocated unilateral disarmament as a general policy. The differences in opinion lay between those who conceived of nuclear weapons in discontinuity with other armaments and those who thought that all weapons were destabilizing and destructive. The former embraced those who wanted nuclear disarmament *per se* and the larger group whose objective was a freeze on the development and deployment of *new* nuclear weapons by the West: both were equally unilateralist.

There was, I believe, a strong element of self-absorption and shortsightedness in the disarmament movement in North America. Nuclear weapons were uniquely wrong in its eyes because, for the first time, everyone in the West was in the front line and in equal peril of destruction. Other weapons were not so dangerous because it was only the people in faraway Europe who were in danger – not that such sentiments were ever publicly expressed, but it was only in terms of such a North American-European dichotomy that the segregating of nuclear weapons from other forms of mass destruction could be rationalized.

Unilateralism was not the point of view of the NATO governments, which were for the most part European and on the literal borderline of the Eastern menace. Western Europe, even with American and Canadian military forces, could never hope to match the Warsaw Bloc in conventional strength. Public opinion in Western European countries would not support military preparedness in the dimensions, and with the costs, necessary to equalize the differential. Of course, in the Eastern Bloc, where public opinion was not tolerated, there was no restraint on military expenditures except in terms of economic affordability. What Western European leaders like Helmut Schmidt feared greatly was a lack of future U.S. commitment to the defence of Europe. Because of their range, SS-20s were a threat specifically to Western Europe, and not to the U.S. Moscow might try to break the Alliance by demonstrating that in a crisis the American nuclear guarantee to Europe would not be honoured in circumstances where the U.S. itself was not also threatened.

* * *

The Warsaw Pact states were completely uninterested in conventional force reductions. The Mutual and Balanced Force Reduction (MBFR) talks, which began in Vienna in 1973 with the purpose of establishing a more stable security situation in Central Europe at a progressively lower level of conventional military forces, had gone nowhere. NATO had not even been able to ascertain in a verifiable way the actual number of Warsaw Pact forces and arms as a basis for talks on force reductions. Nevertheless, in June 1982, NATO introduced a comprehensive draft treaty calling for a substantial reduction of ground forces on both sides.

It was only the threat of a first use of nuclear weapons by NATO in response to Soviet-inspired aggression that kept Warsaw Pact countries militarily at bay in Europe. Gromyko could well announce, as he did in June 1982 during the United Nations Special Session on Disarmament (UNSSOD II), a unilateral Soviet pledge of no-first-use of nuclear arms in Europe, but he had nothing to say about the first use of force. The NATO summit at Bonn reaffirmed that none of the Alliance's weapons would ever be used, except in response to an attack, but it wisely would not commit itself not to use nuclear arms if the Soviets attacked Western Europe. That was the military guarantee of European security, but it was accompanied by what has recently been called "the nuclear taboo,"[49] an unspoken prohibition of the actual use of nuclear weapons.

The two-track NATO policy of December 1979 embraced the goals of both rearmament and disarmament – the continued pursuit of arms control negotiations with the East, but a modernization and augmentation of NATO arms, including nuclear weapons, until negotiations were fruitful. Even under Carter, Washington urged ever-greater expenditures on conventional warfare, and promised the deployment of two new nuclear weapons, the Pershing II and ground-launched cruise missiles (GLCMs), by December 1983.

The first United Nations Special Session on Disarmament (UNSSOD I) in 1978 arrived at a verbal consensus on international disarmament strategy. The UN Committee on Disarmament, composed of forty states (including Canada), was established as the main multilateral negotiating forum on disarmament, and was given the task of drafting a comprehensive program of disarmament to try to bring to fruition the UNSSOD I goal of general and complete disarmament under effective international control. It was, however, unable to reach agreement on a document, and was asked to report further to the General Assembly in the fall of 1983.

On the eve of UNSSOD II in 1982, the Independent Committee on Disarmament and Security Issues,[50] a small number of world personages gathered together under the chairmanship of Olof Palme of Sweden, tried to jump start the negotiating process with an extensive list of immediate initiatives, including the removal of battlefield nuclear weapons from Central Europe and the strengthening of the Security Council's power to pre-empt conflicts by improving its peacekeeping capability. Despite strong membership[51] the Palme Commission could not succeed in its immediate objective of sparking agreement. The sombre international political situation in the aftermath of the Soviet invasion of Afghanistan thwarted any such attempt.

UNSSOD II ran in June and July 1982, but, despite the whole-hearted dedication of the new UN Secretary-General, Peruvian diplomat Javier Perez de Cuellar, it could not reach agreement on anything new. Its extremely modest success was limited to reaffirming the final document of UNSSOD I, to maintaining the consensus principle of operation against strong pressure for a vote from India who wanted a cessation of nuclear weapons testing and a complete freeze on their production, and to instituting a world disarmament campaign (WDC). This latter consideration offered the promise of mobilizing public opinion in all countries of the world, if such a course was actually allowed to take place in states lacking in freedom of expression. It was agreed that the WDC would be carried out in a balanced, factual and objective manner under the direction of the UN Centre for Disarmament. It was also hoped that it would include bilateral and multilateral exchanges of officials, experts, and journalists.[52]

Prime Minister Trudeau addressed the UN Special Session on 18 June. The PM's strategy was designed to deprive the nuclear arms race of the oxygen on which it fed ("suffocation"), both in the laboratories and on the testing sites. Its four elements were a comprehensive test ban, a halt to the flight-testing of all new strategic delivery vehicles, a cessation of the production of fissionable material for test purposes, and a limitation and eventual reduction of military spending for new strategic weapons systems. The combination of these elements, the Canadian government believed, would halt the technological momentum of the arms race by freezing at the initial or test stage the development of new weapons systems. In his new address, the prime minister advocated that the important strategy of suffocation be enfolded in a more general policy of stabilization. This policy would have two complementary elements: the suffocation strategy, which sought to inhibit the development of new weapons systems, and our current negotiating approach, which aimed at qualitative and quantitative reductions in nuclear arsenals designed to achieve a stable nuclear balance at lower levels of armaments. Weapons in outer space would be particularly destabilizing, so the PM proposed an early start on a treaty to prohibit the development, testing, and deployment of all weapons for use in outer space. That a policy of suffocation was necessary was made obvious by the fact that, since the first Special Session, a new INF generation had been deployed by the Soviet Union, and NATO was about to respond with Pershing IIs and GLCMs.

The lateness of Trudeau's intervention in the UN debate meant that there was no justification for my following up his address in the few days remaining before the drafting sessions began, and so I did not attend the Special Session at all. But I had already devoted a good deal of time and thought to the development of the position the PM was to put forward, beginning with a working luncheon with departmental officials and a brainstorming session with the best minds available, including Bob Ford, Si Taylor, Geoff Pearson, John Halstead, Allan Gotlieb, and Arthur Menzies, our ambassador for disarmament. Klaus Goldschlag, perhaps the most brilliant of the brilliant minds in the foreign service, could not make it for the think-tank because of his commitments as ambassador in

Germany. However, I had a lengthy dinner with him on 20 May, at which he agreed to my suggestion that, utilizing the voluminous notes from my consultation, he become the pen for the drafting of the PM's address.

The whole edifice of disarmament, the prime minister contended before the UN, rested on verification. Openness was central, but verification by national technical means, enforceable by the magic eye of highly sophisticated satellites plying their orbits around the globe, had now made traditional resistance to openness anachronistic. But even national technical means, he said, might not be adequate for verifying some modern weapons systems. Problems of verification, if not resolved, would inevitably prevent the conclusion of even well-advanced arms control negotiations and the international community should therefore address itself to verification as one of the most significant factors in disarmament negotiations in the 1980s. He added that he was encouraged by Gromyko's positive approach to verification.

Canada had been allocating increased funds to enable us to become a full participant in the international seismic data exchange, the international verification mechanism that would form part of the provisions of a comprehensive test ban treaty. We were also substantially increasing research in verification. A particularly heavy responsibility, the PM believed, rested with the two superpowers: they must give their undivided attention to negotiations to reduce their arsenals of nuclear weapons and should not deviate from that central objective by imposing political preconditions. On 7 July 1982, in contemplation of the approaching end of UNSSOD II, I announced the addition of $300 million to External's existing disarmament fund of $150 million for the then current fiscal year to assist research and teaching facilities in Canada through contributions and contracts. I hoped this would have the effect of broadening both research and public information in Canada.

In the short run, all of our ideas and words went for naught, because the international situation was not ripe for agreement. After my time in External and shortly before his departure from office in 1984, the PM tried another world initiative, which focussed much attention on the need for disarmament, but also fell short of success. Not until the appointment of Mikhail Gorbachev as First Secretary of the Communist Party in 1985 was real progress made. A nuclear arms treaty was ultimately reached in 1992; a Chemical Weapons Convention, supplementing the 1972 Biological and Toxic Weapons Convention, remains in effect.

* * *

Within a few decades of its inception, nuclear energy became a major source of electric power generation for the world, and a prized acquisition in both the developed and developing worlds. With its large supply of uranium and its development of the CANDU heavy-water process, Canada was in an excellent position to satisfy the demand for both the ore and the generating system. 5,400 tonnes of the 7,000-tonne annual production of Canadian uranium were exported in 1980, and CANDUs had the highest lifetime average capacity factor of any nuclear reactor type. CANDU use had not caused a single fatality, nor even a single injury, and Canadians felt safe in utilizing nuclear generating stations at Pickering, Darlington, and Bruce Point in Ontario, Point Lepreau in New Brunswick and Gentilly in Quebec. Our nuclear fuel waste was disposed of in the stable rock formations of the Canadian Shield. The principal instrument of government policy was the Atomic Energy Commission of Canada (AECL).

Marketing the CANDU was a major objective of Canadian export policy, but it was a difficult sell. Canada lacked the political and economic clout to make other nations want to oblige us. We were not able to consummate a sale to Japan, for example, even though an internal Japanese committee had recommended the CANDU to its government as the best system, because it was more in the political interests of Japan to enter into an arrangement with U.S. suppliers. We had to scramble for possible markets, and sometimes were reduced to dealing with regimes that were more likely than others to try to construct nuclear weapons from their peaceful nuclear programs by irradiation or enrichment cycles.

The two main international systems for keeping the peaceful uses of nuclear energy peaceful were the International Atomic Energy Agency (IAEA), created in 1956 and headquartered in Vienna, and the Treaty on the Non-Proliferation of Nuclear Weapons (NPT), which came into effect in 1970. There were 114 state parties to the NPT; but some fifty states had refused to adhere to it, including India, Pakistan, and two of the nuclear weapons states (NWS), China, and France. The NPT committed non-nuclear-weapons states (NNWS) to refrain from obtaining nuclear weapons in return for a commitment by NWS to negotiate nuclear disarmament. It was possible through the IAEA for a state on its own to agree to place some but not all of its nuclear facilities under international safeguards, thus leaving open a major loophole of a parallel, unsafeguarded program.

India moralistically insisted on the right of Third World countries to peaceful nuclear technology, but at the same time rejected the NPT, ostensibly because of the alleged double standard of the five NWS. The NWS were firmly against horizontal proliferation of nuclear-weapons technology to the NNWS, but were ambiguous about vertical proliferation (the development and augmentation of their own nuclear weapons). However, India's real reason was its determination to retain the discretion to develop nuclear weapons against Pakistan if deemed necessary. In reality, India's supposed dedication to the peaceful use of nuclear energy was exploded along with its underground detonation of a nuclear device in 1974, in Canada's view an intrinsically non-peaceful use but which India claimed was entirely peaceful. What was worse from Canada's viewpoint was that it was widely believed that India had secretly used the plutonium by-product of the irradiation of uranium fuel rods from one of the three nuclear reactors it had built under an agreement with Canada.

The agreement with India antedated the NPT and required only the then current international standards, which did not provide for monitoring of plutonium beyond the first enrichment cycle. Canada quickly decided to upgrade its standards, and from 1976 on required adherence to the NPT as a prerequisite for nuclear relations.[53] After 1976, Canadian policy made nuclear co-operation with an NNWS contingent on: first, the negotiation of a bilateral agreement requiring non-explosive use, prior consent on enrichment and reprocessing, and a fall-back political commitment that, where our nuclear partners exercised their right to withdraw from the NPT, all Canadian-supplied material would remain subject to international safeguards; and second, ratification of the NPT or an equivalent non-proliferation commitment and acceptance of NPT-type full scope safeguards on the other country's nuclear activities, as well as on-site inspection by the IAEA.[54] It would have been more profitable for Canada, from the commercial point of view, to downplay rather than to promote safeguards, but the policy of our government on this subject was morally, rather than commercially, based.

With respect to safeguards, we stood in sharp contrast to some of our competitors. France, as a non-signatory of the NPT, felt at liberty to depart from its strictures, and even the FRG, an NPT state, implemented the treaty in a free fashion. On one occasion, I raised the matter with Genscher and indicated that I found German shading of NPT standards reprehensible, particularly with respect to Argentina. At the time, he refused to acknowledge that the FRG was seeking advantage by its policy, but I always felt that it was a good idea to let other governments know that their conduct had not gone unobserved.

By the time I became SSEA, Canada had built a reactor in Pakistan (the KANUPP), was in the process of building reactors in South Korea and Argentina, and was striving to sell our technology to Mexico and Yugoslavia. We also won a contract to construct two reactors in Romania, the first of which was ultimately inaugurated by Prime Minister Chrétien in April 1996. Besides Mexico, our prospective nuclear partners were all authoritarian regimes, although our agreement with Argentina was entered into two years before the military coup took place. There was therefore some domestic heat over our program, but our safeguards were legally secure.[55]

Apart from India and Pakistan, both of which wanted the bomb to terrorize the other and with both of which we contracted before the enhancement of our safeguards, our other prospective nuclear partners had no territorial designs on their peaceful neighbours, nor to their own people who, if only for reasons of contiguity, were exempt from danger. It was the appearance, more than the reality, of dealing with Ceausescu and the Argentine military that affected public opinion. After all, Canada was not proposing to deal with such parties except on the basis of the world's most stringent safeguards. If we could sell to them with such restrictions, why should we deny ourselves the commercial benefits that could accrue to our country? If agreement proved impossible, what would we have lost? Our national interest, it seemed to me, demanded a positive answer to both questions.

Canada consistently tried to encourage the evolution of a more effective and more comprehensive non-proliferation regime than the NPT. In the meantime, we had nothing to rely on other than our own national policy, and, of course, the assistance of the NPT and the IAEA.

* * *

American testing of air-launched cruise missiles (ALCMs)[56] in Canada became a significant issue in domestic Canadian politics in the early 1980s. The U.S. request for an umbrella testing agreement was for the use of Canadian facilities and air space and was first put forward by the Carter administration in September 1980. Negotiations with Canada were continued by the Reagan administration. For some of those opposed, it was a way of resisting Ronald Reagan. For others, it was rather a linking with the greater cause of world disarmament. For those in favour, it represented a carrying out of our obligations within NATO.

What the U.S. wanted from us was an umbrella agreement for weapons testing with specific project arrangements to be negotiated for each test. Naturally, the cruise weapons would not be armed with nuclear warheads during tests, and Canada really had no objection in principle to the testing of unarmed missiles within our boundaries. This was seen as a contribution we could make to NATO's nuclear deterrence strategy. Canadian terrain was particularly valuable for testing for two reasons: unlike the United States itself, we had enough space between air corridors to provide some three thousand kilometres for flight testing; moreover, our terrain in Western Canada approximated that in the Soviet Union, including Siberia, and so could allow realistic testing.

It was not unusual for us to have agreements with the United States that allowed use of Canadian air space for military purposes. Apart from NORAD itself, there was, for example, an ongoing project with mixed military and civilian crews for airborne studies of infrared emissions of the aurora and airglow.[57] Our disposition to allow testing was encouraged further by the fact that Litton Canada had a contract with the U.S. for the missile inertial guidance systems estimated to be worth over $500 million. The question whether such testing of a new nuclear weapon was compatible with our strategy of suffocation of such systems was easily answered, since that strategy was aimed at a multilateral agreement, not at unilateral action by Canada alone, a distinction which the parliamentary opposition stubbornly refused to accept.

On 17 July 1981, I was authorized by the Cabinet Committee on Foreign and Defence Policy to conclude a five-year agreement to permit the testing in Canada of American defence systems, including unarmed ALCMs, using Canadian test and training areas and Canadian airspace. Discussion in cabinet was deferred, however, until late 1981, owing to the opposition of Lloyd Axworthy.[58] The agreement to negotiate was a secret until the story was broken in a front-page story by the *Ottawa Citizen* in March 1982. I was disturbed by the leak because it came before I had had an opportunity to inform Alberta, the site of the proposed cruise tests, of the negotiations. Opposition critics predictably jumped in to oppose the testing.[59]

There was, of course, some public opposition to cruise testing, particularly in British Columbia. I had occasion to discover this on 27 March 1982, as I began addressing the Vancouver section of the UN Association in the underground civic centre. Wild-eyed unilateralists in the audience proceeded to demonstrate their devotion to the cause of international peace by breaching the domestic peace through persistent heckling, jeering, and shouting of obscenities, and subsequently by tearing a piece of chrome from the automobile in which I was being driven away after completing my speech. There was no question period!

After the revelation of the cruise negotiations, there was parliamentary pressure for a temporary adjournment of our negotiations with the Americans until after UNSSOD II, especially with Brezhnev's announcement of a unilateral moratorium on Soviet deployment of SS-20 missiles in Europe. I seriously considered Conservative MP Doug Roche's proposal to SCEAND along these lines, but decided to reject it. Not only were negotiations with the Americans complicated enough to ensure that no agreement could be negotiated before the end of the Special Session, but I also concluded that it would send a wrong signal both to our Allies and to the Warsaw Pact states. We were, after all, very much in the aftermath of the Polish Crisis. Agreement was not reached with the U.S. until November 1982, and the official exchange of notes on a five-year agreement came in Washington only in February 1983, both after my time in office.

* * *

There was one subsequent event on the cruise testing issue in which I was involved after becoming minister of justice. While I was attending the Commonwealth Law Ministers meeting in Colombo, Sri Lanka, in February 1983, just after the final exchange of notes on the weapons testing agreement with Washington, I received a telephone call from Ed Broadbent. After the framework agreement with the U.S. for the testing of certain weapons was tabled in the House on 14 February, Broadbent had challenged the SSEA's statement that there was no agreement beyond what was tabled.[60] Cabinet had earlier accepted the actual testing of the cruise missile in principle, in March 1981, in the form of an exchange of notes, with an automatic renewal for a further five years. I had announced that fact when SSEA. The question was put to the prime minister again each of the following two days, and he denied the truth of what I had said each time.[61]

Allan MacEachen told me later that he had asked External officials beforehand whether I had ever made any statement as SSEA to the effect that we were committed to allowing cruise testing once the umbrella agreement was signed. With an appalling lack of institutional memory, the department informed him that I had not. He then said publicly that we were not so committed, and the prime minister, when challenged, backed him up: as he later told me, he could not allow his senior minister to dangle without support.

This put me in an awkward position. Confronted with the choice of telling the truth or of contradicting the prime minister and the Secretary of State for External Affairs, I took the following position: cabinet had adopted such a policy *then*, but as I saw it the prime minister, as prime minister, had the right to say that it was not the policy of his government *now*. What he could not do was to alter the fact that it had been government policy. In fact, I refused to answer Broadbent's question as such, but added, as he informed the House, that "the Prime Minister is the person who determines Government policy,"[62] thereby implying the rest.

On my return to Ottawa, I was eventually asked whether I had mislead the House in 1982. I answered the question as follows: "In my previous portfolio and in this one, I have always openly and forthrightly stated the policies of the Government exactly as I understood them. On one or two occasions when I found that I made an erroneous statement about government action or policy, as in one exchange with the Leader of the Opposition, I came into the House at the first opportunity to correct that."[63] Somehow the matter died with my statement to the House. The PM never explained further. The then SSEA never had to admit that he had been misinformed. The opposition dropped the matter, and it was not raised again.

Chapter 7
A North-South Perspective

My first eighteen months in office were a time of maximum activity on the world's poverty line, in the North-South arena. The poverty line is generally defined as the divide between North and South, with the North understood to include the United States, Canada, Western Europe, Japan, Australia, and New Zealand (the so-called "First World"), and the South to embrace Mexico, the Caribbean, Central and South America, Africa, the Middle East, Asia, and the Pacific Islands (the "Third World"). The Third World was also characterized politically as the Non-Aligned Movement (NAM) and economically as the Group of 77 (G-77). As the former, it had been organized politically by such leaders as Nehru, Nasser, and Tito as a third force between East and West. With its acceptance of Castro's Cuba and with Soviet/Cuban adventurism in Africa, however, the NAM lost any claim to ideological purity that it might have had. The G-77, with a primarily economic reference, was divided among developing countries, less developed countries (LDCs), and, the poorest of the poor, thirty-one least developed countries or LLDCs.

Although, loosely speaking, the "Second World," or Communist Bloc, was part of the North, it was generally considered to stand apart from the North-South division – from the communists' point of view because they saw problems of the South as relics of capitalist colonialism, from our point of view because they were too poor to be of any help to the Third World and too ideologically adverse for the West to want to encourage them to have a role. When the Second World did give aid to the Third World, it was usually in the form of armaments.

Countries of the North also, perhaps illogically, equated with those of the West, but the East-West terminology was reserved for issues between the NATO states and Australasia on the one hand and the Soviet Bloc on the other, with Japan and China standing aside. At the economic summits, I attended, I remarked that one of the favourite Japanese phrases was "we of the West." That made sense politically and economically, but not militarily, since the Japanese made no contribution to the common defence of the West. As for China, it was part of the Communist Bloc, but not of the Soviet Bloc, at least not after the Sino-Soviet split in 1960. It was also ambiguously part of the South. As a matter of national pride, it had rejected foreign aid, and it was classified apart from both North and South at Cancun.

Canada, on account of her ties through the Commonwealth, La Francophonie, ASEAN, the Summit Seven, and the "like-minded" smaller progressive states, was perhaps in a unique position to facilitate the North-South dialogue. In 1950, under Prime Minister St. Laurent and Mike Pearson, we had jumped into the first North-South aid program, the Colombo Plan. Since then, the general international perception that Canadian aid was motivated by humanitarian, more than by political considerations, has given Canadian assistance great credibility. In actual fact, Canadian aid was based both on our concept of social justice and on our perception of mutual benefit, through which Canada, as a major trading nation, shared in the health of the world economy. The role of Canada as bridge-builder was strongly advocated by the Commons-appointed parliamentary task force on North-South relations, chaired by Herb Breau, and generally by Canadian parliamentarians.

Animated by my Catholic belief in social justice, I had been a passionate advocate of aid to the Third World from my university days. The prime minister's inclinations were similar. At a meeting in late October 1980,[64] it was clear Trudeau was totally consumed with the North-South agenda, and particularly with the contribution Canada might make to its success. Although the North-South preoccupation of the prime minister was almost exactly contemporaneous with the Canadian constitutional crisis – which, one might have thought, would leave no prime ministerial breathing space for dreaming great visions for the world – Trudeau managed both, and many other things, simultaneously. As we discussed the upcoming summits on North-South issues, the PM was filled with youthful vigour and idealism. Accordingly, there was no area in which he and I were more completely on the same wavelength than that of North-South.

Little did Trudeau and I know of the obstacles we would encounter. It was under President Jimmy Carter's administration that the Special Session had cratered, for secondary reasons that seemed important to the Americans. With Ronald Reagan's administration, where the bipolars rode high, there was a deep visceral as well as ideological opposition, if not to the Third World itself – and this could well have been true as well, to the extent that it fell on the wrong side of the East-West divide – at least to succouring it with American money.

* * *

The first North-South issue with which I was directly preoccupied was our level of Official Development Assistance (ODA). In 1970, the Pearson Commission had endorsed the target percentage of ODA for Northern countries at 0.70% of GNP. Canada had risen as high as 0.54% in 1978, but had fallen in 1979 to 0.47%, making it ninth in the world. Only the three Scandinavian countries and the Netherlands exceeded the 0.70% target. The largest donor in sheer dollars, the United States, had a pitiful 0.19 percentage in 1979.

For better or for worse, ODA had come to be the standard by which developing countries measured their own progress. For the poorest of the developing countries that made sense, since with their primitive infrastructures they were incapable of benefiting from any other means of assistance. The better off the LDC, however, the more it would benefit from trade rather than aid.

Since the name of the game was ODA, I had to do everything in my power to raise Canada's contribution level. In this, I was greatly aided by my leading public servants. After I rejected the original CIDA draft of a cabinet document on ODA in July because our aid objectives were not presented in sufficient continuity with our foreign policy, Glen Shortliffe, then a vice-president of CIDA, produced one that was completely satisfactory to me. When the first proposal of Finance and Treasury Board for departmental spending estimates fell far short of what I needed, de Montigny Marchand, my associate undersecretary, courageously arranged a meeting with Allan MacEachen, the Minister of Finance, and persuaded him to take the major step of altering the proposal so that Canadian ODA would rise to 0.70% of GNP by 1985. This new target was the highest point Canada ever achieved in its ODA planning and was exactly what I needed for Canada's North-South strategy.

Unfortunately, the government's decision was not made in time for my opening address to the United Nations General Assembly's Special Session on North-South Issues in August 1980. Instead, I had to improvise with my CIDA officials for my first appearance during the Special Session. What I came up with I called the Futures Secretariat, with the primary mandate of informing Canadians about North-South issues and involving them to the greatest extent possible.[65] The Secretariat was a useful mechanism for exchanges with the NGOs in which so many Canadians were active, and generally for public involvement. In June 1981, I held a consultation with some forty-five NGO, church, and business leaders to introduce the Secretariat to the development community. I wanted in particular to assure them that it would not function as an intermediary between NGOs and myself. Although the meeting was successful in achieving this specific purpose, I was slightly taken aback to find that even this sophisticated group of Canadians tended to see the North-South dialogue primarily in terms of ODA.

* * *

At the meeting when cabinet approved the giant ODA increase to 0.70% of GNP, it was requested that I conduct an overall review of Canadian foreign aid. The first instalment was a review of our program for the Commonwealth Caribbean. By the middle of 1981, I was able to bring forward a larger Strategic Overview of ODA.

This Strategic Overview, which cabinet approved, established several categories of aid recipients. Category I consisted of a core group of countries eligible for conventional project assistance. Category II was a grouping of states for which selective instruments other than conventional project assistance would be utilized. Category IIA embraced countries in transitional eligibility status, which benefited only from special programs, mission-administered funds, food aid, humanitarian assistance, and technical assistance in special circumstances. The concentration of effort proposed by this new arrangement paralleled the new concept of bilateralism in foreign policy, and made possible the phasing down of the number of states eligible for conventional project assistance from fifty-four to twenty-five. To the traditional criteria for determining eligibility (need based on per capita GNP, commitment to development, performance, and absorptive capacity) the Overview added the criteria of critical factors, intended for countries like Jamaica and Zimbabwe which had suffered political, social or economic upheaval, and political and commercial importance to Canada.

At the time of the Strategic Overview, LLDCs were not recognized as a specific subgroup deserving of special status in Canadian eligibility policy, although eighty-five per cent of Canadian bilateral assistance was channelled to countries with per capita annual incomes of $625 or less, a figure which included many LDCs, as well as all LLDCs. As a result of the Overview, all of the thirty-one LLDCs, except for Afghanistan and Laos which were excluded for political reasons, were made eligible for some form of Canadian development assistance, eleven of them in Category I. The LLDCs that would benefit principally from Canadian aid were Bangladesh, Haiti, Mali, Niger, Tanzania, and Upper Volta. Such LLDCs also received much of our contribution to the concessional windows of international institutions. The balance of Canadian aid was to be dispersed to Cameroon, the Commonwealth Caribbean, India, Pakistan, Sri Lanka, Kenya, Tunisia, and Zambia.

Canadian policy towards LLDCs was slightly modified as a result of the UN Conference on Least Developed Countries in Paris in September 1981. Our major concessions to these countries at that conference were intended to be the promise of duty-free entry to LLDC imports, and the extension of the benefits of GATT Code on Procurement to the LLDCs. However, the key issue at Paris became aid volume, with the LLDCs demanding a subtarget of 0.15% of GNP for them by 1985. Such a target would have considerably surpassed Canada's LLDC contribution in 1981, and we were actually thinking of further decreases. The conference ended with a Canadian-sponsored compromise: a commitment to a 0.15% GNP subtarget, or a doubling of aid flowing from certain donor countries, which should lead to a doubling of resources to the LLDCs in the course of the eighties.

Canada did not specifically endorse the 0.15% subtarget at Paris, but on reflection I decided it was important for us to do so by way of good example. I accordingly announced our adoption of this target a few days later, during my address to the UN General Assembly (UNGA) in New York on 21 September 1981. The commitment did not carry a time limit, and I believed we would be able to accomplish it by the end of the decade.

* * *

In my address at the UN Special Session in August 1980, I spoke of Canada's consciousness of many of the realities of both North and South. Nature, which blessed us with an abundance of resources, enabled us to occupy a place as one of the world's more industrialized nations. But as a heavy exporter of natural resources and an importer of capital and technology, Canada shared many of the concerns of the developing countries about the operation of the international system in these areas.

I also spoke of the plight of the world's poorest people, almost a billion of whom lived on "the borderline of human existence." All humans in my view had a right to expect access to the most fundamental of human requirements: food, shelter, health care, sanitation, clean water, and education. Both qualitative and quantitative goods were necessary to achieve this, and that to launch a war on world poverty paid for by the richer countries, we must have widespread public awareness of the necessity of these goals. I announced that Canada would be increasing its foreign aid program for the rest of the decade, but had to speak as well of the failures of the Session, which had been intended to adopt a new International Development Strategy for the 1980s, as well as to launch a new round of Global Negotiations reflecting an integrated approach to international economic cooperation for development.

Nevertheless, the Session completely failed to reach consensus on a procedural framework for the launching of the Global Negotiations in 1981. There could not be authentic or enduring security in the world as long as there was widespread global poverty and economic injustice.

* * *

The only foreign-policy question that I believe was ever foremost in the prime minister's mind during my time in office was the North-South issue during the year of the summits in 1981. He, and I, believed profoundly in the importance of Global Negotiations, and we both devoted great effort to trying to bring them about. In preparation for the Ottawa Summit, where this was to be a key issue, the prime minister visited each of the other leaders – to canvass the world situation, it is true, but with principal emphasis on the North-South problem. I believe that this dedication to world social justice represented the prime minister's most profound interest in foreign policy – along with, I suppose, the quest for peace itself, on which he embarked on a crusade after my tenure.

The Global Negotiations were to be in five areas: raw materials, energy, trade, development, and money and finance; and marked the first attempt at an integrated approach to North-South dialogue. I represented Canada at preparatory meetings of the eleven co-organizers[66] of the North-South summit in November 1980 and March 1981, when it was agreed that the summit should be held in Cancun, Mexico, in October 1981, and that twelve developing states (Algeria, Bangladesh, Brazil, Guyana, India, Ivory Coast, Mexico, Nigeria, Philippines, Saudi Arabia, Tanzania, and Venezuela) and eight developed states (Austria, Canada, France, Federal Republic of Germany, Japan, Sweden, the United Kingdom, and the United States), plus Yugoslavia and China, should be invited. We agreed that it would be political in character, non-negotiating in form, and informal in nature, and that it would likely include four issues: food and agricultural development, trade, energy, and money and financial issues.

The Ottawa Summit in July 1981, the first hosted by Canada, was thought to be a considerable success. Certainly, it made all the right noises with respect to the North-South situation to which it devoted substantial attention, and the final communiqué was generally well received by the Third World. Summit leaders reaffirmed their commitment to co-operate with developing countries in a spirit of mutual interest and respect for independence and non-alignment. In particular, they affirmed their readiness to participate in preparations for a mutually acceptable process of Global Negotiations.[67]

The Americans, however, harboured serious reservations about the North-South dialogue. They had a strong preference for private sector rather than intergovernmental mechanisms to address developing country needs. On this basis, they opposed the initiative for a World Bank energy affiliate, supported by Canada, to foster increased energy exploration in developing countries. They also stalled the Law of the Sea negotiations because of the majority's preference for the common heritage of mankind rather than the commercial advantage of American corporations. Most ominously, they were unwilling to commit themselves to a position on Global Negotiations until after Cancun.

The Cancun summit followed in late October. It was either "a small failure or a small success;"[68] it could be said to be a success only in the sense that frank and lively exchanges of views took place without acrimony. Although it marked a positive development on the part of the U.S. toward Global Negotiations, the summit failed to achieve the public expectation of agreement on jump-starting the negotiations in the UN. Apart from the intangible atmospherics, which left everyone in a relatively good mood, it was a big disappointment for the prime minister and me that the compromise we put forward on Global Negotiations did not succeed. We had proposed that the Secretary-General convene a group of states to work out a starting basis for the Global Negotiations by the end of the year. The United States, which regarded the independence of the separate agencies as non-negotiable, was prepared to go along with the formula, but a few other participants refused to accept it. It struck me as ironic that the Third World, which had the most to gain from Global Negotiations, should have been partially instrumental in preventing movement towards them.

Although work continued behind the scenes, no further progress was made before the Versailles summit of June 1982. There was no real meeting of minds at Versailles, but there was some American flexibility of Global Negotiations, which led to a remarkable step forward. Reagan agreed to a slightly revised version of the latest G-77 text on the subject, and asked Canada to put the amendments forward in a suitably discreet way.

The G-77's meeting of foreign ministers at New York in October 1982 was a sad ending to the possibility of Global Negotiations, one for which the blame must largely lie with the G-77, who, in the end, proved uncompromising. In part, this was due to the nervousness of the OPEC states as to what they might be expected to contribute to the general good. In part, it was owing to the middle-income countries from Asia, which worried that Global Negotiations would give too much to LLDCs and too little to them. Another problem was the psychological need of the developing world to keep the North as the "fall guy." Another was the United States' failure to make agreement easy.

Despite some further efforts at the General Assembly in the fall of 1982 to find a basis for agreement, by the end of the year, Canadian officials had reluctantly come to the conclusion that it was time to look at other approaches, particularly in existing institutions on sectoral issues. The NAM summit, which took place in New Delhi in March 1983, wrote *finis* to Global Negotiations, turning instead to a program of immediate measures and a step-by-step approach to broader systemic reform.

* * *

One of the knottiest questions relating to foreign aid is the extent to which it should be influenced by the recipient country's human rights performance. This is a question that has probably increased in importance since my days as SSEA but was nevertheless a matter for concern then too. The short answer to the question of whether there is a link between a country's human rights performance and its eligibility for development aid is that Canada has always taken human rights into account in making decisions on bilateral eligibility. But the correlation is not a simple one to state.

Certainly, when the recipient country is in the hands of a madman like Idi Amin, the only response possible is to break off all aid as quickly as feasible. Canadian policy reflected this with regard to Laos and Afghanistan. But it is not usually such a clearcut issue. After all, development assistance is meant to better the lot of the poorest, and automatic denial of aid in the presence of human rights abuses would deny the very people whose rights are being violated the benefit of development, thus inflicting a double penalty.

My governing principles were always those I laid down in a Commons debate in 1981. First, Canadian policy is to assist in the promotion of genuine independence, non-alignment, and stability. Second, forms of government or economic systems are not matters to be imposed on developing countries from the outside. Third, Canada expects all governments to be vigilant in observing human rights. And fourth, Canadian foreign policy will not reward adventurism or interference.[69] As I put it more shortly, about the same time, "We try to keep our aid as politically neutral and as administratively pure as possible,"[70] and again, "Genuine independence for the Third World has to mean independence even from us."[71] I now think that such a policy is somewhat too passive.

I always carried a human rights message with me, and the approach I worked out when meeting with foreign representatives was that I was transmitting an admonition not just from the Canadian government, which might be refused by the recipient on the basis of interference with domestic affairs, but from the Canadian people. The Canadian government, I explained, had to answer to the Canadian people, who had a well-developed moral sense and would not tolerate our giving assistance or friendship to a foreign government that showed a disregard for human rights. Singapore, for example, was a problem because of our warm Commonwealth and personal ties, which were juxtaposed with that country's preventative detention law. The Canadian people, therefore, were calling both of us, our government and their government, to account.

The stormiest meeting I ever had on human rights was in a private waiting room in the Johannesburg airport with Roelof "Pik" Botha, the South African foreign minister, on 24 July 1980. Botha, a huge man, became so incensed at my defence of the rights of South African blacks that he began to storm about the room shouting that African blacks had ruined every country in Africa where they had gained power. I did not feel personally browbeaten, but took it as a performance for a hidden camera and a subsequent audience. In any event, I think I gave as good as I got, though I expect with less belligerence. I never saw Botha again, and the incident was certainly not helpful to Canada-South Africa relations, except that they were already so sheerly formal as to be of no great significance anyhow.

There was no way of knowing whether such "do better" speeches on my part had any effect. In none of the countries already mentioned did it succeed in changing the country's policy, any more than it did in China or Indonesia, whose foreign ministers I also belaboured on the human rights front. Perhaps it had some effect in preventing a worsening of the situation. The only thing I could be sure of was that it let the offending country know that there was a watching world that reacted adversely to oppression.

As mentioned earlier, the issue of withholding or lessening aid from human rights violators was a delicate one. The principal inhibiting factor in my mind was that cutting back would hurt the people already suffering from a deprival of human rights much more than it would affect their rulers. A good example of this was Haiti, the poorest country in the Americas. The specific problem there was not only the government's human rights record but also the pilfering of money and supplies from our aid program.[72] For this reason, we tried to develop (insofar as feasible) projects that were theftproof, such as educational and training programs. If money was involved, we tried to pay directly to the ultimate recipient rather than through an agent who might exact a rake-off.

* * *

I regret now that I did not give higher priority to the *public promotion* of human rights. This was an area where quiet diplomacy needed to be supplemented from time to time by public declaration. Such activity might have helped the situation in countries that allowed some public opinion, like the Philippines and Indonesia. It might also have better reflected Canadian values.

I do not think that Canada should more frequently have threatened trade or aid sanctions against countries with spotty human rights records. That is a matter of pragmatic judgment in each particular case, and, in general, my bias is that we are more effective if we do not threaten other countries. All I propose is that Canada should have made human rights a more explicit objective of our foreign policy and should probably have referred to that policy every time we had a meeting with a country where domestic rights were in question, instead of publicly concealing our divergent views and registering our dissent only privately.

* * *

One of President Reagan's favourite truisms was: "Give a man a fish and you feed him for a day; teach him how to fish and you feed him for a lifetime." Quite apart from the condescension involved in the assumption that Third World peoples needed to be educated in simple things, what is the use of knowing how to fish without a fishing rod and net? What about the need for a fishing boat? Is the person supposed to eat only fish or rather be allowed to sell or barter for other commodities? How about a transportation system for getting the fish to market? Refrigeration facilities to preserve them until marketed? Financing for the cost of business? Are there markets that are open to the product or are they closed by reason of domestic preferences? These questions give some idea of the true dimensions of the Third World problem. Canadian policy tried to be equal to the task. Reaganite policy did not.

To be fair to the Reaganites, they were not totally unresponsive to the rest of the world, as the president's change of heart at Versailles showed. Nevertheless, they were never far from their script, which always emphasized reliance on the private sector. Worse, their bipolar East-West preoccupation was always interfering with any concern about the southern part of the world beyond that orientation. They were always eager to supply economic and military support to those threatened by "communists," whom they readily identified by their opposition to vested economic interests. Senator Jesse Helms, for example, was reported to have said that "the International Sugar Agreement is a communist plot."

My approach could hardly have been more different, since I believed in insulating the Third World as much as possible from East-West contention in favour of genuine independence, non-alignment, and stability. As I saw it, economic instability was the principal breeder of the political instability on which the communists could capitalize, and so it was very much in our own interest to do what we could to relieve it. The main thrust of our policies was thus to integrate developing countries as fully as possible into the international economic system. This could best be achieved, on the one hand, by allowing natural economic forces to operate as fully as possible, and, on the other hand, by being willing to intervene selectively when warranted, as in the General System of Preferences or the Common Fund. Trade and financing, too, were matters of great importance for the economic growth of the South.

Official development assistance is of most use to LLDCs, since they are not developed enough to make use of more sophisticated instruments of growth. In earlier days, Canada sponsored many giant development projects, but we learned from experience to put more emphasis on human-scale projects. By the time I came into office, CIDA was already beginning to recognize and emphasize food and agriculture, energy, and human resources (the transfer of skills and of technology) as areas of specialization, and I did my best to reinforce the trend, with a particular stress on education and training. I always thought it better to invest in foreign peoples than in foreign governments. We in the North had to try to build the indigenous capacity for innovation, development, and democracy. Canada also learned that concentration of our efforts on a limited number of countries, or on particular sectors, could be highly advantageous. As we also counted it important to develop appropriate criteria for aid development, we made Canada's priorities the poorest countries, natural disasters, refugees, the Caribbean, and countries where we could gain a trade advantage.

The inclusion of the last group may not seem particularly meritorious, but we had to keep our own economy strong, especially as the growth of the Third World depended on ours.

Watching the 1968 World Series at Tiger Stadium in Detroit.
Left to right: Senator Paul Martin, Fred Quenneville of Windsor,
Donald McDonald, the president of the Privy Council, and MacGuigan,
the MP for Windsor-Walkerville. [Courtesy of Fred Quenneville]

Trudeau's Cabinet, 1980. Mark MacGuigan, the new
Secretary of State for External Affairs, is standing at the far left.
[Courtesy of Patricia D. MacGuigan]

Greeting her Royal Highness Queen Elizabeth II.
[Courtesy of Patricia D. MacGuigan]

MacGuigan, Sir John Ford, and Jean Chrétien toast the patriation
of the constitution, 17 April 1982. [Courtesy of Patricia D. MacGuigan]

The U.S. presidential visit to Ottawa in 1981. MacGuigan speaks
to Al Haig under the watchful eyes of Ronald Reagan and
Pierre Elliott Trudeau. Monique Bégin is to MacGuigan's left.
[NAC PA 211192]

MacGuigan (far left) with Al Haig, Ginette Reno, Trudeau,
first lady Nancy Reagan, Anne Murray, and Ronald Reagan
at a soirée in Ottawa. [NAC PA 211193]

Mark MacGuigan with
U.S. Attorney General William French Smith (right),
and Allan Gotlieb. [Courtesy of Patricia D. MacGuigan]

Discussing world affairs with U.S. Secretary of State Al Haig
on 19 January 1982. [Courtesy of Patricia D. MacGuigan]

An audience with Pope John Paul II. [Courtesy of Patricia D. MacGuigan]

Mark MacGuigan at his desk. [Courtesy of Patricia D. MacGuigan]

German Chancellor Helmut Schmidt, July 1981.
Despite the expressions on their faces, both MacGuigan and Trudeau held
Schmidt and his German counterparts in high esteem. [NAC PA 211194]

MacGuigan with Chinese Foreign Minister Huang Hua.
[Courtesy of Patricia D. MacGuigan]

Strengthening bilateral relationships, SSEA MacGuigan
signs a nuclear co-operation agreement with
Prof. Dr. Subroto of the Republic of Indonesia, 12 July 1982.
[NAC PA 211191]

Consolidating the relationship with Guinean dignitaries.
[NAC PA 210920]

**Part Three
Particular Themes**

Chapter 8
Constitutional Question ... and Resolution

The night of the Quebec referendum, 20 May 1980, I was at dinner in the Chinese Embassy in Ottawa. Before the dinner was over, a member of the Chinese ambassador's staff approached him with a well-folded piece of paper. After an animated conversation, Ambassador Wang Dong leaned over to me and said, "I have the honour of presenting you with the results of the Quebec referendum." He thereupon slowly unfolded the crumpled paper and I read the numerical and percentage results, which told me that Canada had gained a sixty to forty per cent victory. It was an extraordinarily satisfying moment – one in stark contrast to the chill period of fear I had felt when the Parti Québécois first called the referendum. Of course, I had been subsequently greatly encouraged during the course of the referendum campaign by the tactics and momentum of the pro-Canada forces, but it was very heartening to have such a decisive result.

Like other anglophone ministers from outside Quebec, I had played no part in the referendum campaign. This was not a matter of edict, but a spontaneous agreement based on simple common sense: as best I recall, the matter of our participation was never discussed in cabinet, as the issue was seen as one to be decided by Quebeckers alone. In 1980, before the later traumas, there was no question as to the strong desire of the rest of Canada that Quebec remain, and so there was no useful purpose to be served by anglophone participation.

The federal role was very effectively directed by Jean Chrétien, in collaboration with Claude Ryan on the provincial Liberal side. No doubt there were stresses and strains between federal and provincial participants, but they were not discussed in cabinet, and we anglophone ministers knew only what we read in the newspapers. The most important features of the campaign were probably the prime minister's highly successful addresses to mass audiences. In the last analysis, they probably guaranteed the federal margin of victory.

Once the referendum was over, however, the next federal steps in constitutional reform were very much in the hands of the whole cabinet. I was henceforth involved as a minister, as a member of the constitutional committee of cabinet, and, when it came to that stage, as the Secretary of State for External Affairs in dealings with the government of the United Kingdom.

* * *

On 14 May 1980, in the dying days of the referendum campaign, the prime minister had committed himself in a platform address to set in motion the process of renewing the constitution if the No side won. One did not have to know him very well to divine that this renewal would include a charter or bill of rights, which he had first suggested in 1955, and which in his mind always included guarantees of linguistic rights. In fact, the heart of the constitutional renewal the prime minister had in mind was patriation (the ending of the legal right of the U.K. to amend our constitution), a new Canadian amending formula for the constitution, and a charter of rights.

In the short run, however, a great deal of effort went into attempts to secure provincial agreement to a much larger constitutional deal. The federal government's constitutional initiative was announced by the prime minister in the House of Commons the day after the referendum, and a long summer of work at the officials' level led up to a federal-provincial constitutional conference in mid-September 1980. That meeting broke up without agreement and the prime minister and cabinet had to decide how to proceed. The decision was made to proceed unilaterally, without the agreement of the provinces, through a joint address of the Senate and House of Commons to the United Kingdom.

This initiative had already been forecast by an address that Trudeau had made in Toronto during the 1979 election campaign, when he also said that a joint address sponsored by his government would include basic guarantees of human rights. It had also been much thought about in the lead-in to the September constitutional conference and was embodied in a memorandum by Michael Kirby, the secretary to the cabinet for federal-provincial relations and accordingly a major player in the constitutional area. The Kirby memorandum was leaked by an internal federal source to the Province of Quebec, which promptly publicized it as an indication of federal duplicity in being prepared to proceed whether or not the provinces agreed. This leak substantially worsened the atmosphere of the conference and may have been one of the causes of its breakdown.

* * *

The *Colonial Laws Validity Act, 1865* provided that any colonial enactment must be read subject to any statute of the U.K. extending to that colony. Canada's constitution, the *British North America Act* (*BNA Act*) of 1867, was such a statute. Following imperial conferences between Britain and the Dominions in 1926 and 1930, the *Statute of Westminster* in 1931 would have terminated the U.K.'s mandate and that of the *Colonial Laws Validity Act*, as it did for the other Dominions, had Canadians been able to reach agreement on a substitute amending formula. But in the absence of such agreement, subsection 7(1) of the *Statute of Westminster* preserved U.K. paramountcy over the *BNA Act,* and legislative power to amend the *BNA Act* remained vested in the British Parliament. Of course, the *BNA Act* itself was interpreted to grant the Canadian Parliament and legislatures respectively legislative power over their *internal* constitutions. Legal legitimacy, as perhaps distinguished from political legitimacy, would require for patriation a final act of the British parliament renouncing its right to amend the Canadian constitution and conferring that power on Canada on the basis of some agreed-on formula.

Throughout fifty-three years of constitutional negotiations, from the first federal-provincial meeting over an amending formula in 1927 until mid-September 1980, it had been common ground that there would be no general amendment of the constitution without the agreement of the provinces – perhaps, indeed, without their unanimous agreement. As a constitutionalist, I was never of the point of view that unanimous provincial consent was required, and, on one occasion in the mid-seventies, I advocated, as a backbencher in the government caucus, that the federal parliament should act unilaterally, without the consent of all the provinces, to achieve constitutional reform. There was some disagreement with my proposal and, as best I recall, no expressed agreement from anyone. However, people were listening, and, as agreement continued to be impossible, members of the federal government became increasingly of the view that either no constitutional convention of provincial consent existed at all, or that, if it did, it was only a convention without legal effect (a political rather than a legal convention). There had indeed been unequivocal affirmations by British government spokesmen in the U.K. Parliament in 1943, 1976, and 1979 that their government and parliament were bound to accede to any amendment requested of them by the Canadian Parliament through a joint address. Early soundings of the Thatcher government's position led to the same conclusion.

In this vein Prime Minister Trudeau had a meeting with Prime Minister Thatcher in London on 25 June 1980. He explained his then broad constitutional initiative, which at that time he still hoped would lead to federal-provincial agreement. After receiving the news that ultimately there would be legislation passed in Britain, but that it was too early to predict its content, Prime Minister Thatcher gave the guarded assurance that the British government would be as helpful as possible, adding that "if you ask us to act, we will have to do so." Nicholas Ridley, the minister of state for foreign affairs, then stated that the only problem he foresaw was one of timing vis-à-vis the U.K. parliamentary timetable. Thatcher affirmed that "it will be a government measure and the whips will be on."

The foreign secretary, Lord Carrington, assured me in September 1980 that he had no serious problem about the amendment we were then beginning to formulate as to patriation and an amending formula but that he had serious apprehensions about the proposed charter of rights. It must be remembered that the Thatcher government was strongly opposed to a bill of rights for the United Kingdom itself. Carrington asked whether it would not be possible to leave the bill of rights out of the package, expressing concern about the possible effect of provincial lobbying of British MPs in causing legislative delays and even harm to British-Canadian relations. I explained to him that the charter was the heart of the proposed initiative, since it alone, with its recognition of fundamental and linguistic rights, could be said to represent a response to the vote of confidence in Canada by the majority of Quebeckers in the Quebec referendum. I also added that the federal Government would not facilitate representations by the provinces in relation to either the British government or the British parliament.

On 2 October 1980, the prime minister announced that the government would propose to Parliament a joint address for a patriated amending formula, and for a charter of rights that would have no opting-in provision for the provinces but would be binding on them from the outset. Two days later, John Roberts and I arrived in London. I was delighted to share this occasion with Roberts, the Minister of Science, Technology and the Environment, a highly knowledgeable and able minister. We had been friends for nearly twenty years, thought very much alike, and were both among the "hawks" in cabinet who insisted, when some had doubts, on plunging straight ahead with the unilateral federal initiative on the charter. On the occasion of the London visit Roberts felt that, as the senior minister, he ought to have the privilege of leading off at the meetings, but he accepted my insistence that, as the responsible minister, that was my role. The ground rules settled, we worked well together in all our encounters.

We arranged to brief the Queen before seeing the prime minister, and as she was still on her annual holiday we had to visited her at Balmoral Castle in Scotland. On the Sunday, we lunched *en famille* in a sizeable but rather informal dining room with a half dozen of the Queen's dependent relatives but none of her immediate family. Roberts, Sir Philip Moore (the Queen's chief adviser), and I were the only guests. Table conversation was pleasant but very general. The Queen's pack of some six or eight corgis was under the huge table during lunch and the Queen kept crumbling and throwing bits of food on to the carpet for them to contend over – and contend they did, tumbling back and forth at our feet. It did not strike me as particularly royal behaviour.

It was after lunch that we went into a parlour for our meeting, with only Moore in attendance. Here the Queen was royal indeed. She was very knowledgeable about Canada and was keenly interested in our project. Of course, she had no direct power to influence events, but I was sure the subject would be raised in her weekly meetings with the prime minister. We sensed by indirection that she did not see eye to eye with her first minister on everything, and indeed seemed not to have a warm relationship with her. In any event, Her Majesty could not have been more helpful to us on this occasion, indicating great sympathy for our cause.

When our meeting ended and the doors of the parlour were opened, her corgis, who were lying at the entrance in a heap reminiscent of Dagwood's pups, fell into the room barking away in delight at being received again. The formalities were well and truly over.

On the Monday afternoon, the day the Canadian parliamentary session opened, Roberts and I were closeted for the better part of an hour with Margaret Thatcher and Nicholas Ridley in her office in London. After we had made our initial presentations, Prime Minister Thatcher told us that they had no trouble with patriation and the amending formula, but that the charter was entirely unexpected and very difficult. She repeatedly asked, under different formulations, why we could not first patriate the constitution and then pass the charter on our own. She wondered how she could answer her backbenchers, since a bill of rights was contrary to her government's domestic policy. Eventually, we were able to persuade her that our prime minister was committed through an election campaign, a referendum, and a formally enunciated policy in Parliament, and that it was too late for us to back down. Not only was the prestige of the government at stake, but the future of the country. At no time during the meeting did Thatcher challenge the constitutional convention as to a joint address, and her final attitude amounted to a reluctant acceptance of the Canadian position.

Since we were not before her cap in hand but merely to explain what we were about, we never directly asked her what her position was with regard to our request. But at no time during the meeting did she challenge the constitutional convention as to a joint address, and the tenor of the meeting was that she accepted it. In fact, it was clearly because of her adherence to it that she had the difficulty she posed to us. This was confirmed by her attitude towards scheduling the required legislation, in that she completely ruled out the possibility that there might not be time for it at all. I had informed her that we would like to have our new constitution in place by 1 July of the next year, the fiftieth anniversary of the *Statute of Westminster*. She said that a failure to schedule it would be taken as a refusal.

In a subsequent meeting we had with Carrington, he again stressed the difficulty for the British of the charter, and of the timing of the whole enterprise. However, while Carrington was briefly out of the room for a vote in the House of Lords, Ridley stated that the only real problem was one of scheduling, not of substance. The next day, the High Commission received the following message:

> Prime Minister Thatcher accepts the obligation to act as requested by the Canadian Government. A serious problem exists in the Parliamentary timetable and we should not expect passage of patriation by July next unless the Bill is available in December or the beginning of January at the latest. Given that this will not be a straightforward patriation, there is likely to be Parliamentary debate. British House of Commons debates are still capable of being unpredictable.

In a telephone conversation with the Canadian government House Leader, Yvon Pinard, U.K. House Whip St. John Stevas was even more pessimistic as to timing. Timing, however, while important, was never of primary concern to the Canadian government. It was Stevas' warning of the unpredictability of British parliamentarians that eventually came to bedevil our relationship with the U.K.

Margaret Thatcher made her first public statement on the Canadian problem in the House of Commons on 9 December 1980. She affirmed that the British government would deal with the expected Canadian request as expeditiously as possible and in accordance with precedent. It was all we could have asked for as a statement of government policy. However, at Thatcher's request, Prime Minister Trudeau received Francis Pym on 19 December as Thatcher's personal representative. As expected, Pym opened the conversation by emphasizing that the Thatcher government had reaffirmed its intention not to look through the Canadian proposal but rather to place before parliament any proposal as submitted. He emphasized, however, that the charter was very controversial and that, even though the U.K. government would pay no attention to the opposition of Canadian provinces, many MP's and lords would. Similarly, the U.K. government recognized that the court proceedings in Canada were of no direct relevance, but these could greatly affect the attitude of backbenchers. Passage would be extremely difficult and a great deal of work would have to be done. If the charter were dropped, the measure would go through easily.

Trudeau replied that dropping the charter would not diminish opposition in Canada. Pym said that the U.K. government was extremely anxious to deal with the Canadian measure as proposed and would regard the failure to do so as an absolute tragedy. He added that a positive decision from the judicial reference in Manitoba would make an enormous difference. The prime minister said that if the government lost in Manitoba it would have to review its whole strategy. Pym stressed repeatedly the difference between the British government's assurances and the reaction in the two houses of parliament, where there was a strong feeling that they should not be asked to amend the constitution while patriating it. He stated that the charter was not their business, and that the U.K. government hesitated to put something forward that it knew would not pass. He recognized that Trudeau had little room to manoeuvre and suggested that we await the report of the U.K. Select Committee (called the Kershaw Committee after its chair, Sir Anthony Kershaw) and the judgment of the Manitoba Court of Appeal and then meet again.[73]

The work and report of the Select Committee on Foreign Affairs of 30 January 1981 was an unmitigated disaster for the federal government. In November 1980, the committee had undertaken its study of the role of parliament in relation to the *BNA Act* on its own motion, without the necessity of parliamentary authorization, in response to intense provincial lobbying of the British MPs. It held only two substantive sessions, and it represented the views of only eleven out of some 630 members.[74] The report took the position that the Westminster parliament need not give automatic endorsement to any request for amendment it received from the Canadian parliament but should give effect only to a proper request. On the basis of testimony before the committee by legal experts and representatives of provincial governments, the committee concluded that the proposed Canadian constitutional resolution directly affected the federal structure of Canada and was therefore an improper request since it was made without provincial government consent. It was the charter, and particularly the guarantee of language rights with corresponding restraints on provincial legislatures, which led the committee to conclude that the proposal directly affected the federal structure of Canada. The next Tuesday, the Manitoba Court of Appeal came down with its opinion substantially supporting the federal position – a judgment that reached entirely opposite conclusions than the Kershaw Committee.[75] What I found most offensive was the Kershaw view that Westminster must serve as the guardian of the federal character of the Canadian constitution. The Canadian Parliament must answer to the Canadian people, whereas the British Parliament could not do so. The British Parliament therefore lacked any moral authority or legitimacy over the Canadian constitution.

In mid-January, 1981, Justice Minister Chrétien announced the extensive amendments to the charter that the government was prepared to accept, and the Special Joint Committee of the Senate and House that had been reviewing the resolution reported to Parliament in mid-February. Debate in the House and the Senate began a few days later. The Official Opposition filibustered the report stage (including a seven-day procedural filibuster) to the point that, on 31 March, after the release of the Newfoundland reference,[76] the prime minister felt impelled to offer a deal that would involve awaiting the result of the appeals to the Supreme Court of Canada before pressing the British to pass the resolution. A deal was actually reached on 8 April by which votes on all proposed amendments to the resolution would be taken on 23 April in the House, the Senate vote to be held the following day, after which the resolution would be referred to the Supreme Court for hearing on 28 April. The final vote would await the result of the Supreme Court hearing. After the deal was reached, Ridley informed Deputy High Commissioner Christian Hardy that the tide in the British House was at last beginning to turn in our favour.

* * *

I had an awakening perception of the dimensions of the U.K. problem early on. On 28 October 1980, I sent a memorandum to the prime minister that my department was now a good deal less certain than it had been that the U.K. government was prepared to co-operate in expediting our bill through their parliament. The most significant of the triggering events that I mentioned was a London *Guardian* story that quoted an unnamed senior minister as saying that "if the present discussions with Mr. Pierre Trudeau's Liberal Government failed to persuade the Canadians to withdraw their request for a Bill of Rights there would be a major hold up to legislation planned for the new Parliamentary session." Although the British High Commission reassured us that this report did not represent government policy, the report, when combined with other indicators, suggested to me that their government had shifted ground, at least in their degree of willingness to expedite our request.

I speculated in the memorandum that most of the apparent stiffening in the British position arose from concern for their parliamentary timetable and perhaps also for the propriety of proceeding with our bill while it was *sub judice.* On the plus side, after earlier hesitations, they had now decided that they would not discuss constitutional items with provincial representatives. As for the non-favourable MPs and lords, I divined four reasons for their hostility: a distaste for passing a charter for Canada when they were opposed to the same thing in the United Kingdom; a resentment at being called upon to go beyond the minimum to include a controversial charter; a concern at being drawn into a Canadian controversy which Canadians themselves had not been able to resolve and which was before the courts; and sympathy for certain provinces and native groups. I concluded that, although the U.K. government had reasons for viewing our bill as a source of embarrassment and difficulty, I did not anticipate any direct request for a substantive change, despite continuing rumbles about the problems it caused. The greatest effect would probably be on the timing of action.

* * *

The first question I had been asked by the press after being sworn in as minister was whether I would be keeping Jean Wadds as Canadian high commissioner in London. Wadds, a former Conservative MP, had been named to the post by the short-lived Clark government and was an immediate success. I answered purely on instinct and on my reluctance to play the patronage game that I had no plans to replace her, but I soon learned that Trudeau did. He wanted to appoint Don Jamieson, a Newfoundlander and former Secretary of State for External Affairs, to London. Trudeau had no compunction about using his powers of patronage to the fullest extent. Personally, I was not an all-out opponent of patronage, provided that the nominees were worthy of their roles. In the long run, I could not prevent the prime minister from sending Don Jamieson to London, but I did stall successfully for nearly three years. It could not have been an entirely easy role for Wadds to rationalize, but she was totally loyal to the Trudeau government's policy and our most effective single lobbyist in London.

Once the constitutional crisis began, I was greatly aided by Wadds's obvious merits for the job, including her natural talent for ingratiating herself with the British upper crust and her political value as an embodiment of Conservative backing for a Liberal initiative. As to our strategic plan, I saw her as "key," partly because her office gave her an entrée and her personality a cachet that no other official had. I recommended that she should develop a full and enriched program of entertaining and contacts oriented to the constitutional issue. We should have frequent visits of ministers and high officials to London, and, because we had the support of the New Democratic Party, we should encourage federal NDP members of Parliament to assume a special role in contacts with Labour MPs and lords.

The U.K. press reports led to some sharp questioning in the House from Progressive Conservatives in late October. Although I had to acknowledge that we had had free-flowing discussions with the British during which many possibilities were canvassed, I was able to rely on the many formal expressions of co-operation we had received from the British government to reassure the House that the British had made a commitment to us which we expected them to honour.

In retrospect, I might have been more suspicious of the British high commissioner to Canada, Sir John Ford. We had heard rumours in Ottawa about his antagonistic talk to Canadians with whom he had met regarding our initiative, but when approached in October 1980, Ford vehemently denied playing any double game and stated that his warnings of difficulties had been offered only to senior federal officials. He gave a solemn assurance that his code of conduct was merely to reflect his government's policies.

Ford became increasingly troublesome in the new year, lobbying senior federal officials, as well as Opposition and provincial politicians, to oppose the constitutional amendment. On 5 February 1981, Ed Broadbent, the leader of the NDP, informed me that he was very upset by the way in which Ford had lobbied one of his MPs, Ian Waddell, against the Canadian constitutional initiative at a recent social occasion. Broadbent proposed to raise the matter with me in Question Period, and to inform the House that the high commissioner had directly attempted to influence Canadian representatives on this internal Canadian issue. As this was the first I had heard of the matter, I was not able to say anything very useful that day, except that the conduct alleged would be doing a great disservice to the government of the U.K. and was completely unacceptable to the Government of Canada. The same day, Ford gave a press conference in which he tried to deny everything but effectively admitted that he had tried to make Canadians understand the depth of negative feeling in the British Parliament as to the Canadian initiative.[77] I later discovered that Ford had lobbied New Brunswick Premier Richard Hatfield, who subsequently confirmed this in a telephone conversation with me. Unfortunately, Hatfield refused me permission to use his name publicly to that effect.

Nevertheless, I had enough to go on to commission Allan Gotlieb to fly to London on 9 February 1981 to discuss the problem with British officials. We perhaps could have demanded that Ford be withdrawn immediately, but we eschewed anything that dramatic lest it provide the Official Opposition with more fodder for raising doubts about the intentions of

Her Majesty's Government – even if I shared such suspicions myself. Instead, the British offered to speed up the assumption of office by Ford's successor, Lord John Moran, and I was pleased to accept that offer. The British made the announcement the next day, and Ford was recalled to London for consultations.

Officially, both we and the British denied any connection between the change of high commissioners and Ford's lobbying. I felt it would not do to emphasize Ford's unseemly actions, given our already great difficulties with the British. It would threaten the perception in Canada of U.K. government support, and it might even serve to undermine our position in the U.K.

* * *

In the first half of February 1981 there was a massive leak or leaks of Canadian diplomatic cables from London to Ottawa, including one from Jean Wadds in which she speculated that her telephone was being tapped, presumably by the British. I have already referred to the leak of the Kirby memorandum the previous fall, with the view of making it appear that the federal government was not in good faith at the Federal-Provincial Constitutional Conference in mid-September 1980. Although the government refused to confirm that any of the material made available to the press was genuine, we knew that it was, and it was seen as such by the press and the Opposition. The February leaks were very embarrassing to the officials named in the telegrams, to our government, and to the British government.

When the investigation of the leaks was handed over to the RCMP, they succeeded in pin-pointing the culprit or "mole," who turned out to be a well-placed foreign service officer whose primary loyalty was to the separatist government of Quebec rather than to Canada, and who had been acting as a spy for Quebec, probably for years. His services were, of course, immediately dispensed with, but, in order to avoid a political furor and a backlash both against Quebec and from Quebec, no public announcement was ever made, and he was allowed to retire for personal reasons in the course of the year. I found this manner of proceeding somewhat against the grain, but it was probably forced by the position of the RCMP, some of whose own wiretaps might have been of dubious legality, and who, I was told, absolutely refused to prosecute. The decision was ultimately made by the Prime Minister's Office. Even now, it is hard to be sure what the fallout would have been from a confrontation with Quebec over the spying, though my guess is it would have wounded the Parti Québécois in Quebec.

* * *

Canada had its defenders from without. Gough Whitlam, the former prime minister of Australia, visited Canada in early February, had meetings with both the prime minister and myself, and offered the public advice that Canadians should not tolerate any British intervention in Canada's constitutional affairs. Of greater importance was the support given by Sir Shridath "Sonny" Ramphal, the secretary-general of the Commonwealth, who had a sister in Toronto and was quite pro-Canadian in feeling.[78] I talked with him briefly in Ottawa on 29 October 1980 and had a meeting with him at Marlborough House in London on November 10. He did not have to be persuaded, but merely to have the issue drawn to his attention. Since he was a fierce proponent of the independence and equality of Commonwealth members, he took it very much amiss that there would be any question of the United Kingdom's not acceding to our constitutional resolution. In a subsequent meeting with Lord Carrington, he appeared to have threatened dire consequences in the Commonwealth in the event of a British failure to act.

The British resented our playing the Commonwealth card, especially when Trudeau coupled it with a public statement that rejection could imperil Britain's membership in the Commonwealth. By the time Trudeau met Ramphal in Ottawa on 31 March 1981, we were in the position of trying to restrain the secretary-general's strong feelings so that they would not be counterproductive with the British. Indeed, until the Opposition filibuster became effective and the Newfoundland Reference was decided on 31 March, progress appeared to be being made with the British. There was even a suggestion that Prime Minister Thatcher might want to act quickly.[79]

* * *

The Canadian government naively expected the Supreme Court decision to be favourable and speedy. It was initially thought that the decision would be handed down in late May or early June 1981, still leaving a possibility of British passage by 1 July, the fiftieth anniversary of the *Statute of Westminster*, and the long-preferred date for proclamation. Much planning went into this possibility, which was to be heralded by a royal visit. By 18 June, however, it was clear that the decision would not be announced before the Court rose for the summer on 25 June, although there was some lingering hope that it might be recalled for that purpose during that season. In a meeting in London on 26 June, Prime Minister Thatcher informed Trudeau that, in such a case, British passage before their summer recess in late July was highly unlikely.

In the event, the Supreme Court decision was not delivered before 28 September 1981. The expectation was that it would be a federal victory and that the so-called "Gang of Eight" provinces would continue the fight, probably with a high-profile incursion of the eight premiers to London. Carrington gave me the unwelcome news that Thatcher would be unlikely to refuse to receive the premiers if they came as a group.

When the members of the Supreme Court delivered their decision at a televised hearing in Ottawa, Trudeau was on his way to Melbourne for the Commonwealth Heads of Government meeting, and I was at the United Nations in New York, but we had both made arrangements for speedy transmission of the results. The Court's decision was an unfortunate one for us, because it came down on both sides, thereby leaving the political issue unresolved. By a 7–2 margin, it held that in strict law Ottawa could proceed unilaterally:

> [T]he one constant since the enactment of the *British North American Act 1867* has been the legal authority of the United Kingdom Parliament to amend it. The law knows nothing of any requirement of provincial consent, either to a resolution of the federal Houses or as a condition of United Kingdom legislative power. [80]

Nevertheless, a majority of the judges (six of nine) held that a substantial degree of provincial consent – to be determined by the politicians and not the courts – was required by convention for the amendment of the constitution.[81] The minority, which included Bora Laskin, the chief justice of Canada, took the position that "it cannot be asserted, in our opinion, that any view on this subject has become so clear and so broadly accepted as to constitute a constitutional convention."[82]

Although the government's official position after the judgment was that, having received a green light as to the law, we would press ahead, the effect of the decision was to induce negotiation, especially in the light of the British reaction. Despite the apparent counsel of her advisors, Prime Minister Thatcher was very supportive when she discussed the matter with Trudeau in Melbourne, but it soon became manifest that British opinion required at the least a serious attempt to negotiate a resolution of the crisis.

Eventually, even negotiation in good faith was not enough. At Cancun in October 1981, Carrington let me know that the British government had reluctantly come to the conclusion that it could not assure the passage of the joint address in the current circumstances; backbench opinion was just too intransigently opposed for even the whips to make a difference. Although I did not take this counsel of gloom as being necessarily the final British word on the matter, I realized that it had not been said lightly, and I passed it on to the prime minister at once as a serious assessment. Carrington's view was later confirmed by a story in *The Guardian* on 30 October to the effect that there was no Commons majority for the measure and that the British government was reconciled to possible defeat. The situation in the British parliament was undoubtedly a significant factor in the PM's willingness to compromise at the Federal-Provincial Conference he called for 2 November.

The compromise of the night of 4 November 1981 was the result of two factors. First, on their scale of priorities, the provinces placed a satisfactory amending formula first, whereas the federal priority was the inclusion of the charter in the constitution. Each side therefore had something to safeguard and something to bargain with. One could envision in advance the federal acceptance of the provincial amending formula in return for the provincial acceptance of the charter, perhaps with a limited opting-out feature. Second, the inept tactics of Quebec Premier René Lévesque broke the unity of the Gang of Eight. Lévesque had joined the other premiers on 16 April in a patriation plan that abandoned Quebec's traditional search for a veto over constitutional amendments, in exchange for financial compensation for opting out of new federal programs. Then, on 4 November, Saskatchewan Premier Allan Blakeney advanced a proposal for a new amending formula that would give Quebec neither a veto nor compensation. Trudeau cleverly put forward a counter-proposal for a national referendum on the charter and baited Lévesque into accepting it. This breaking of ranks by Lévesque dumbfounded the other premiers. The unity of the Eight having been splintered, the way was open for a nighttime deal to be negotiated by Jean Chrétien, Roy McMurtry, and Roy Romanow in the conference kitchen. As Trudeau pointed out in a subsequent article, it was Premier René Lévesque who "plunged the knife into the heart of the very accord he had signed less than seven months earlier."[83]

The committee of the federal cabinet dealing with the charter was called into session at 9:45 p.m. on the night of 4 November. Only the legal rights guaranteed by the charter were to be the subject of the legislative override that would allow the provinces to withdraw specific legislation for the five-year periods from judicial review. If I had understood that this was also to be the lot of the fundamental freedoms, I could not have then agreed to the proposal. In a subsequent private conversation with Premier Hatfield of New Brunswick he expressed the view that Ottawa would have gained exemption from the override for the fundamental freedoms if it had pressed sufficiently hard. Now, years later, I am reconciled to the result, given the overwhelming pro-charter sympathy of the Canadian public, which has almost entirely foreclosed the possibility of the provinces by-passing the charter.[84]

The agreement between the federal government and all of the provinces except Quebec led to the adoption of the joint address by the Canadian Parliament in early December and its transmission to the United Kingdom by Chrétien on 7 December 1981. The *Canada Bill* received first reading in the British House before it rose for the Christmas holidays on 23 December. We expected that would be the end of the drama surrounding the matter, but both Quebec and many Canadian Indian bands, who were concerned with what the charter did not include, lobbied hard in London against its passage. Quebec also brought a legal challenge in Canada, which was ultimately resolved against it.[85]

Alberta Indians went so far as to bring a legal challenge in U.K. courts. After a panel of the English Court of Appeal granted leave to appeal, the British government decided to postpone second reading until after the hearing of the case. Fortunately, the legal proceedings did not take long,[86] and by mid-February the House was able to grant second reading on a 334–44 vote. The other stages followed quickly and the Queen gave royal assent to the *Canada Bill* on 29 March 1982.

The stage was therefore set for the official proclamation of the *Constitution Act, 1982* by the Queen before a vast outdoor assembly in front of the parliament buildings in Ottawa on 17 April 1982. By strength of his steel-willed determination Prime Minister Trudeau had triumphed over the most intense opposition in patriating the constitution with a new amending formula and in entrenching the *Canadian Charter of Rights and Freedoms*. It was a victory for him to savour, one in which most Canadians could join.

Among those who shared Trudeau's triumph most were the activists in the Liberal party and especially the members of the cabinet, who with comparatively minor disagreements had stuck together through thick and thin. The only potential of a split occurred not on substance but on procedure, and originated with Allan MacEachen, the Minister of Finance, who was regarded as the best House Leader in memory. At a meeting of the Cabinet Committee on Priorities and Planning in early December 1980, MacEachen threatened his resignation if plans to impose tight time constraints on parliamentary debate on the resolution were carried through. Although he was the only minister who expressed such qualms, the prime minister did not proceed with the plan for time allocation and the unity of cabinet was thus preserved.

The immediate consequence of MacEachen's threat was that the government was unable to get the constitutional resolution through quickly, which would have avoided the all-too-evident danger of allowing the opposition time enough to organize. The ultimate effect of MacEachen's position was to allow for the judicial references in Canada and the mobilization of hostile opinion in the United Kingdom, with the consequent failure of the federal government to have its way without compromise. Although I was very much on the other side at the time, I have to acknowledge now that MacEachen's democratic instincts were perhaps right in the long run. It was probably the most important decision to be made by Parliament in its history and therefore one on which the more usual processes, including delays and filibusters, should be followed. Moreover, it may well be better to have a constitution towards which all regions of the country can feel at peace than a superior one forced by a majority on a protesting minority. No doubt MacEachen saw a Commons reconciled to the resolution, or at least to the process by which it was arrived at, as a happy harbinger of consensus across the country. Ultimately, he proved to be a good prophet.

The most notable exceptions to the general euphoria over the resolution of the constitutional question were the supporters of the separatist Parti Québécois and some other nationalists in Quebec. Even though the charter was as popular with the public in Quebec as elsewhere and almost all of the federal members from the province voted in favour of the federal resolution, the PQ took the purely separatist position that only the provincial government represented Quebec. The reaction in the Quebec National Assembly would probably not have assumed major significance had it not been clothed with credibility by a subsequent Canadian prime minister, who gave currency to the myth that Quebec had been betrayed in the constitutional negotiations by the rest of Canada. This myth was a staple fiction of the PQ, who exploited it through the Meech Lake and Charlottetown deliberations and the referendum of 1995.

Once enacted, the charter assumed a momentum of its own in Canadian history. It looms large in public consciousness, with the populace having enthusiastically embraced it. Moreover, it is itself causing the development of a new sense of national community. In other words, it is not, as perhaps it might have been, a purely individualistic phenomenon, but the leading edge of a new belief in the strength of shared value and opportunities. In this, it very much reflects the central thesis of Prime Minister Trudeau's parliamentary address on the *Charter* on 23 March 1981: "Lest the forces of self-interest tear us apart, we must now define the common thread that binds us together."[87] The *Charter*, as a common thread of liberty, was Pierre Elliott Trudeau finest achievement.

Chapter 9
Managing the American Relationship

Managing the American relationship is the greatest challenge for any Canadian government. The principal bilateral issues between the Americans and ourselves during my term of office were maritime boundaries and fisheries, transboundary air and water pollution on our side, and the National Energy Program on their side. We also had to deal with a crisis in prime ministerial credibility. Managing these issues led us to what Allan Gotlieb has called "the new diplomacy."[88]

* * *

When I became Secretary of State for External Affairs, the most important bilateral issue in our relations with any country was the boundary/fishery dispute in the Gulf of Maine with the United States. On 29 March 1979, Canada and the U.S. had signed linked treaties providing for a co-operative fisheries management regime in the Gulf and for submission of the underlying boundary dispute to the International Court of Justice (ICJ), or alternatively to an ad hoc court of arbitration. President Carter had submitted the treaties to the Senate the next month, and, effectively, nothing had happened. At issue was sovereignty and jurisdiction over 22,700 square miles of continental shelf, as well as fisheries management of the area.

The problem had arisen because, in January 1977, Canada had extended its fisheries jurisdiction beyond the traditional twelve-mile limit to two hundred miles, and the United States had taken the same step two months later. The respective fisheries zones, of course, crossed. The East Coast Fishery Resources Agreement of 1979 provided on a permanent basis for co-operative management and for access and entitlement to specific fish stocks. It was a complicated well-worked-out treaty that had taken eighteen months of intricate negotiations because of constant consultation with the fishing communities of both countries. All in all, it represented a major advance in handling international disputes, especially in recognizing the need for permanent co-management of a depleting and constantly moving resource, independent of the location of the international boundary. Unfortunately, most U.S. senators took the view that the fisheries issue was a regional matter on which they should follow the lead of the New England senators who were directly concerned. Despite the assiduous consultation with American fishers, only those in Maine supported the treaty, and those in Massachusetts and Rhode Island were adamantly opposed. Nova Scotians and New Brunswickers were in support of the treaty, even though they had to make concessions with respect to redfish, cod and haddock, as well as to scallops.

I got a first-hand feel for the situation when I had a tête-à-tête dinner with Rhode Island Senator Claiborne Pell on 21 October 1980. In this one-on-one setting, he was totally frank. He warned me that, with his opposition, the Fishery Resources Agreement would never pass the Senate because, on this kind of matter, the other senators defer to the senator affected. His own opposition was guaranteed simply because his fishing community was opposed. That was not going to change, and so we were at a complete stalemate over the treaty. Canada's only hope was to proceed with international arbitration under the boundary treaty.

Although I bore Senator Pell's advice in mind, I continued to lobby publicly and strongly for the treaty, since I regarded it as an indignity for Canada to have to submit to two sets of negotiations. In truth, it was a welcome relief from a hopeless situation. Secretary Haig announced on the eve of his first trip to Ottawa in March 1981 that the U.S. would delink the two treaties and proceed only with the East Coast Boundary Adjudication Treaty, which provided for arbitration by a five-judge chamber of the International Court of Justice.[89] At this time, this was the only solution that could be accepted by both sides.

The final two events in the Gulf saga, the hearing and the decision, occurred after I was no longer Secretary of State for External Affairs. As such, I had a continuing role in the arbitration, and I found myself before the ICJ in the Hague on the afternoon of 2 April 1984 making the opening plea in the Canadian case. In my statement, I concentrated on the U.S. claim to dominance geographically, legally, and politically with respect to the clear object of the dispute, Georges Bank. Canada claimed less than half of the Bank, but the U.S. claimed it all. If the U.S. claim were upheld, it would exclude Canada from fishing and hydrocarbon resources which it had claimed and utilized since 1964. I stated squarely that "it was precisely the extravagance of the United States' claim that made prudence and reasonableness seem unnecessary to those United States interests that lobbied against ratification of the 1979 agreement on east coast fishery resources."

For the United States, I reasoned, the non-division of Georges Bank had become an equitable principle in its own right, clothed in the theories of the natural boundary and single-state management. Moreover, the notion of dominance was implicit even in the American view of geography, which gave the coast of Maine a dominant character because it was allegedly a "primary" coast, to which the coast of Nova Scotia, as a secondary coast, must yield. One consequence was that there would be no need for co-operation in the management of overlapping fish stocks, which I referred to as "a new form of isolationism, and no form of law." Canada's position, on the other hand, resulted "from the application of law to geography," with its equitable character confirmed by non-geographically relevant circumstances.

Oral proceedings before the ICJ were completed in May 1984, and the decision was rendered in mid-October, by which time I was on the bench and a new government was in office in Ottawa. The result was a 4–1 decision, including Judge Stephen M. Schwebel's concurrence in which he took exception with the majority's position of including the Bay of Fundy as part of the Gulf of Maine. The presiding judge was the dissenter, rejecting the parties' agreement that a single line should be drawn for both boundary and resource purposes. The Chamber rejected both countries' arguments, taking the view that the waters in the Gulf of Maine, like the continental shelf, formed a single continuous ecosystem and could not be differentiated by supposed natural boundaries of differing ecological units.

The upshot of the principles applied was a substantial victory for Canada. Not only was the Chamber's boundary line closer to Canada's, but at the northern end of the inner gulf it awarded Canada more than it had claimed. Much more important, Canada got the ultra-rich northeast segment of Georges Bank where it was estimated that fifty to sixty per cent of the Bank's scallops, an essentially sedentary species, were found. It also covered the area where seventy-five per cent of the hydrocarbon permits issued by Canada since 1964 were located. The judgment came into effect as of midnight on 26 October, two weeks after its release. On the whole, Canada could feel very satisfied with the result.

* * *

The west coast fisheries problem was largely simultaneous with that on the east coast. The west coast crisis, focusing on albacore tuna, was ignited by Canada, which asserted its jurisdiction under the *Coastal Fisheries Protection Act*, a jurisdiction which was consistent with the consensus at the Law of the Sea Conference[90] that a coastal state is entitled to exercise "sovereign rights" over fisheries resources within a two-hundred-mile zone.

Only the United States and Japan took a contrary position, and Canada consequently arrested nineteen American tuna vessels fishing without Canadian licences off the British Columbia coast in 1979. The vessels were brought to Canadian ports and released on the payment of heavy fines. In these circumstances section 205 of the U.S. *Fisheries Conservation and Management Act* automatically embargoed exports from Canada of tuna and tuna products, thereby causing economic loss to Canadian fishers. The U.S. law was regarded by Canada as contrary to the General Agreement on Tariffs and Trade (GATT) and was referred by Canada to a GATT dispute panel for adjudication.

Both countries were anxious to resolve the dispute, and in 1980 an interim agreement was entered into which provided for port access for Canadians in return for fisheries access for Americans. It was also agreed that every effort should be made to have a longer-term treaty in force by June 1981. In fact, we succeeded in having the *Albacore Tuna Vessels and Port Privileges Treaty* signed on 26 May 1981, ratified by the U.S. Senate on 20 July 1981, and in force on 29 July.

Much to the dismay of the United States, Canada let it be known throughout the negotiations on the treaty that it intended to proceed with the adjudication. The GATT panel made its report on 22 December 1981 and the report was subsequently adopted by the GATT council. The report understandably did not find section 205 of the U.S. legislation contrary to established rules, but it did state that the American embargo on imports of tuna and tuna products from Canada was not consistent with Article XI of the GATT.

Given that it always seemed likely that Canada would emerge victorious from the GATT proceedings, it may perhaps be asked whether we got as good a deal as we should have in the treaty, since what we won would have come our way anyhow, assuming that the U.S. accepted the GATT result. External Affairs' role, however, was to obtain what British Columbia fishers and the Department of Fisheries and Oceans were certain they wanted, namely an immediate agreement as signed without the one- or two-year delay that any other course of action might incur. This seemed especially desirable since the highly migratory albacore tuna normally enter Canadian fisheries waters only once every three or four years, and Canadian fishers may have calculated that they did not have much to lose during the three-year currency of the treaty. Canadian fishers were also relatively pleased with the landing ports designated by the treaty, although they clearly would have preferred the more southerly San Diego to the northern California port of Crescent City.

The west coast agreement caused a good deal of soul-searching on our part because of its simultaneity with the east coast problems. I was determined that we would not again be put in the position of having an agreement negotiated with a U.S. administration subject to the threat of renegotiation in the U.S. Senate. Never again in my view should we conduct foreign policy on such a basis. Ideally, we needed some kind of assurance from the U.S. Senate that a given treaty would be ratified by it.

* * *

In an exchange of notes in mid-November 1978, the governments of the United States and Canada agreed to commence discussions on transboundary air pollution. Discussion actually began in December of that year and continued until agreement was finally reached in March 1991. It was an indication of changed times that the principal Canadian complaints against the U.S. had become environmental rather than directly economic.

The principal air pollution problem was acid precipitation, which quickly came to be called acid rain. It came from the burning of coal and the smelting of ores, in which processes sulphur and nitrogen oxides were converted in a series of complex chemical reactions into acids and which returned to earth as components of rain, snow, hail, and dew. Preliminary indications suggested that such acid precipitation might have severe ecological impact. Lakes could become so acidic that they could not support fish life. Agricultural crops could be reduced in yield from the effects on foliage and the leaching of minerals from the soil. Productivity of forests and of forest products, such as maple syrup, could be lessened. There was also the danger of corrosion of buildings, as well as possible health risks downstream.

Canada herself was far from innocent. The INCO smelter at Sudbury was the largest single source of sulphur dioxide in North America, and coal-fired production of electric power by Ontario Hydro in plants such as that at Nanticoke on Lake Erie was a constant matter of constant controversy. Nevertheless, the U.S. exported two million tons of acid rain a year to Canada against our export of half a million tons to them. The Canadian-caused air pollution in the New England states was only eighteen per cent of their problem, and thirteen per cent in the next affected states. New smelters in Canada had better than ninety-five per cent containment, and sulphur dioxide was being reduced in Canada by about fifteen per cent every year.

I expressed concern on 19 March 1980 about President Carter's proposal to reduce reliance on imported oil by converting some U.S. utilities to coal. My complaint was that the proposal did not take into account the effects on Canada or on the Summit Seven pledge at Tokyo regarding the use of coal without damage to the environment. We had conveyed the same message to Washington before the U.S. announcement, and I subsequently raised the issue, first in a meeting with U.S. Ambassador Kenneth Curtis, and then with Secretary Vance during his April visit. Some progress was made with the Carter administration, though not on its coal-conversion program, where Canadian interests ran head on into coal and utilities lobbies. We wanted the U.S. to build sophisticated pollution control techniques into its conversion program, but the utilities lobbies were opposed to the increased cost, which would diminish their profits.

By 5 August 1980, however, the U.S. was prepared to sign a memorandum of intent (MOI) on transboundary air pollution, with the aim of negotiating a bilateral agreement as soon as possible, beginning no later than June 1981. The memorandum established five work groups to prepare for the negotiations and called upon both governments in the interim to vigorously enforce existing laws and further to develop domestic air pollution control policies.

The next event was an International Joint Commission (IJC) report on water quality in October 1980, to the effect that all parts of the Great Lakes' watershed were receiving precipitation containing five to forty times more acid than would occur in the absence of atmospheric emissions, and that many inland lake ecosystems might be irreversibly harmed within ten to fifteen years. Both countries were said to be responsible and were urged to reduce emissions of the oxides of sulphur and nitrogen. On 24 June 1981, however, Interior Secretary James Watt told Judy Erola, our minister of state for mines, that it was not clear to the U.S. that there was an acid rain problem at all and that our countries should await further scientific research before taking action. Canada, he said, was guilty of undue pressure on an "excessively emotional issue."

Others were perhaps less blunt, but a meeting in early July produced a disturbingly unyielding American response. There seemed to be no likelihood of progress with the Reagan administration; our only hope seemed to be with Congress and American public opinion. This was a dangerous road because it was likely to incur administration resentment, and indeed it was not long before we began to receive administration reaction to our congressional lobbying. The American side insisted that the evidence was not yet sufficient to indicate the best solutions. It was also made clear by U.S. officials that Canadian questioning of American motives was not appreciated and that our efforts at emissions control had failed to impress

In February 1982, Canada presented a draft treaty, which promised a dramatic fifty per cent reduction in Canadian emissions of sulphur dioxide by 1990, contingent upon parallel action by the United States. But the U.S. soon made it apparent that it could not accept this offer, arguing that it was premature because of scientific uncertainties. As it turned out, the impasse was to continue for a long time.[91]

* * *

Since 1889, the Garrison Water Diversion Project in the Missouri River Basin had been a dream in North Dakota. It would be a means of irrigating dry farmlands, of augmenting municipal and industrial water supplies, and of controlling flooding. An original plan to cover a quarter of a million acres was authorized by Congress in 1965, and Canada had been raising concerns about possible adverse effects on Manitoba since 1969.

The problem for Canada was caused by the close geographical proximity in North Dakota of two great drainage systems, which had been entirely separated since the last Ice Age: the Missouri Basin, draining through the Mississippi into the Gulf of Mexico; and the Red and Souris rivers, arising in North Dakota and Saskatchewan. It was feared that Missouri basin waters would be transferred across the natural continental divide between the basins, with consequent deterioration of water quality in Manitoba, and the introduction of new diseases, new parasites and new fish species into Lakes Winnipeg and Manitoba. Such a transfer of biota might possibly cause an ecological disaster in Manitoba, threatening the existence of native Manitoba freshwater fish like whitefish and pickerel, and thereby affecting the commercial fishing and tourist industries. Biota transfer could also cause greatly increased water treatment costs for communities that took their water from Manitoba rivers.

Canada had allies amongst the American environmentalists, particularly the Audubon Society, which was troubled by the devastating effect it foresaw the Garrison Diversion Unit (GDU) having on prairie marshes and their associated wildlife. We were also aided by the fact that there was less pressure in Washington to do something for a state with a single member of Congress than there would have been for a more populous region.

The United States assured Canada in a note in 1974 that no construction would be carried out on parts of the project that could affect Canada unless it was clear that the U.S. treaty obligation not to pollute transboundary waters to the injury of health or property in Canada would be met.

Subsequently, the two national governments referred the issue to the IJC, which released its report in 1977. It concluded that the construction and operation of the Garrison Diversion Unit as envisaged would cause significant injury to health and property in Canada as a result of adverse impacts on water quality, and on some of the more important biological resources in Manitoba. The commission therefore recommended that those portions of the diversion that could affect waters flowing into Canada not be built at that time. However, it further advised that the Lonetree Reservoir, the hub of the principal supply works for the whole project, could be constructed without an unacceptable risk to Canada so long as all outlet works from the reservoir were located so as to discharge only into the Missouri River Basin. The U.S. Department of the Interior accordingly proposed a much downscaled 96,300-acre project, which pleased neither North Dakota nor Canada: for North Dakotans it was too little; for Canada too much.

In April 1980, Washington officials adopted a phased concept to accommodate Canadian concerns. Although this represented great progress, Canadian concerns remained as to whether there was significant American commitment to ensure that no biota were transferred into the Hudson Bay system. It was always for us an open question whether phased development did not merely mean a gradualist approach to complete development in the long run.

Because of the likelihood that arose in June 1980 of a congressional appropriation of $9.7 million for the GDU, enabling construction to begin on the Lonetree Reservoir dams and dikes, I released to the U.S. the text of a diplomatic note opposing any appropriations until Canadian concerns had been dealt with and stating that full agreement on the eventual outcome should precede such spending decisions. My colleague, Lloyd Axworthy, the effective Minister of Employment and Immigration and, more important in this context, the only government minister from Manitoba, made similar representations on a visit to Washington on 28 June to members of the administration and of Congress. This represented a significant hardening of our position.

On 18 November 1980, the Department of the Interior announced that the portion of the appropriation relating to works that would affect Canada would be set aside in a reserve fund pending the conclusion of consultations with Canada. There was considerable alarm in Ottawa in early March 1981 over reports that the Reagan administration proposed the appropriation of an additional $4 million for Garrison. A unanimous House of Commons resolution on 5 March expressed "strong concern," which I conveyed to Washington. The new funds did not, however, represent a new initiative, but were merely a confirmation of the amount that had previously been requested by the Carter administration for the 1982 fiscal year.

We had a small contretemps with Manitoba over GDU. Although co-operation between Ottawa and the province had been close and satisfactory over the years, the newly elected NDP premier, Howard Pawley, had unwarily made an election promise to establish an independent Manitoba office in Washington. This was a definite no-no as far as I was concerned. Washington was an exclusively governmental centre without commercial, economic, or cultural interest, and a Manitoba office with the objective of governmental lobbying would directly challenge Ottawa's ability to speak with an effective, coherent voice in our general responsibility for foreign policy. I informed a provincial delegation that External would do everything in its power to block Manitoba's access to the U.S. administration. Manitoba backed down, accepting my offer of a provincial officer in the embassy and the facilitation of Manitoba visits to Washington, and at Manitoba's request we created a federal-provincial coordinating committee on Garrison.

Reagan, during his March 1982 visit to Ottawa, offered his assurance that the United States would not pollute Canadian waters. However, we concluded after our initial consultation meeting that his administration would be much more in favour of the GDU than its predecessor. Through considerable lobbying on our part and Manitoba's, the Democratic-controlled House rejected a North Dakota-inspired proposal for new construction. U.S. officials conveyed the message at an October meeting that domestic political considerations might soon result in a major revision of the Garrison Project as originally proposed (which would eliminate or postpone interbasin water transfers), and that North Dakota was now turning to a new irrigation project with South Dakota. Our concerns persisted.

In June, the impact of Canadian lobbying was demonstrated by a decisive House vote to delete the Garrison funds, the first time this had happened in the GDU's seventeen-year history. The $4 million funding, however, was restored by the House-Senate conference committee. The eventual bill included the stipulation that none of the funds could be used for construction of project features affecting water flow into Canada. It was still the Canadian belief that this authorized plan would sooner or later cause severe damage to Manitoba waters, and the House of Commons adopted a motion of dismay and disappointment that the project was still proceeding.

Canadian concerns about the GDU were not alleviated until the passage of the U.S. *Reformulation Act* in 1986, thanks to lobbying by Canada and by American environmental groups, as well as to financing considerations. The GDU was not killed entirely, but its emphasis was shifted from irrigation to the supplying of municipal, rural, and industrial water to North Dakota. What irrigation remained was confined to areas in the Missouri River Basin, and Canada wisely continues to keep a watchful eye on the situation.

* * *

Nothing illustrates better than our transboundary pollution problems the disparate, disorganized, and scattered state of U.S. politics at that time: individualism ran rampant and the lowest common denominator held sway. At its best, the U.S. system of government works when an enlightened and strong-minded administration provides effective leadership over the regional and sectoral interests that otherwise prevail in Congress. In post-Watergate Washington, the development of a more democratically organized Congress, where seniority was no longer a first principle, led to more individualism and a weaker party structure than ever before, and the Reagan administration, though strong-minded, was not enlightened. It consistently did its level best to ensure that environment controls were weaker and more industry-friendly.

It was my conviction at this time that Canada must manage her relationship with the United States coherently and productively, with a clear sense of our own priorities. The first consequence of this for the U.S. was the development of the "new diplomacy," an in-their-face representation of our interests by which we would press our case on any issue unremittingly and in all directions.

Traditional diplomacy limited states to conducting official business with foreign ministries or with other government departments. It also forbade intervention in domestic affairs. In the words of Allan Gotlieb, "Traditional diplomacy ... was a recipe for ineffectiveness, a prescription for marginality, or, even worse, irrelevance" in the Washington of the 1980s.[92] With the new diplomacy, we were no longer dealing just with the U.S. administration on a state-to-state basis but actually plunging into the hurly-burly of American politics. In post-Watergate Washington, it was no longer possible to draw clear lines between the executive and the legislature, or between foreign and domestic policy. What was critical was access to the decision makers. Canada became a political actor on the American scene, trying to influence and, if necessary, forge alliances with congressmen and senators, and with various domestic interest groups. As Canada, we could have little influence in American political forums, but as allies of various domestic groups and their representatives, of people who actually held voting power in the United States, we might hope to have an effect.

Of course, the new diplomacy also required a good deal of legwork on the part of the whole embassy, keeping in touch with senators, congressmen, and perhaps most important of all in the American *realpolitik*, their staffs; as well as the administration, the press, interest groups, and other lobbyists. I had encouraged our new ambassador to the United States, Allan Gotlieb, to pick his own "team" for Washington, which included the brilliant Jeremy Kinsman. We also engaged our own lobbyists, which meant a sizeable increase in budget for the embassy, an initiative I gladly sponsored. I also tried to do my share from the beginning: addressing numerous councils, committees, and conferences in the U.S., as well as conjoining meetings with news media when feasible, and lunching with senators. The new diplomacy would probably be possible only in the open-ended political system of the U.S. and, even there, it quickly drew reproof from the Reagan administration, which did not want to see Canada as a political player.

Gotlieb and I were completely *ad idem* on the new diplomacy. It was, in fact, a joint policy, though most of the details were his. Indeed, he and his wife Sondra were just the catalysts the new diplomacy needed. Gotlieb proceeded to make himself a celebrity in the capital on the basis of his sheer intellectual power, and his wife, Sondra, ably matched him by becoming a celebrity in her own right through her exceptional wit. People wanted to be seen in their company, and this gave the ambassador contacts, influence, and leverage. Their access to the power centres of the Potomac ensured that Canada was always *au courant* with the prevailing winds, even of the innermost secrets of the White House.

When I announced the policy of bilateralism, I suggested that the relationships to which we were giving priority had to be subject to central policy management, but our U.S. relationship is so vast and multifarious that it will always resist this form of management. During my time in office, the substance of our American strategy was provided by the "Third Option," and was principally reflected in the National Energy Program.

* * *

In the fall of 1972, Mitchell Sharp, then SSEA, published a paper on the future of Canada-U.S. relations,[93] a subject that, despite its overriding importance to Canada, had been inadequately treated in *Foreign Policy for Canadians* (1970). The options Sharp saw for the future were the following: first, Canada could seek to maintain more or less its current relationship with the United States with a minimum of policy adjustments; second, Canada could move deliberately toward closer integration with the United States; third, Canada could pursue a comprehensive long-term strategy to develop and strengthen the Canadian economy and other aspects of its national life by turning towards a contractual link with Europe and Japan, and in the process reduce Canadian vulnerability. The government called it the "Third Option." "Trade diversification" would have been a more felicitous phrase. Canada's distinctness was seen as having only one meaning: distinctness from the United States. The Trudeau government therefore moved over the next decade in an increasingly nationalistic direction, one that I strongly supported; though perhaps with less fanaticism than some of my colleagues. Petro-Canada, the Foreign Investment Review Agency (FIRA), the Canada Development Corporation (CDC) and ultimately the National Energy Program (NEP) were all fruits of this approach.

***

In 1977, Canada and the U.S. signed an agreement that was to lead to the construction of the world's longest pipeline, some five thousand miles in length. Parliament established the Northern Pipeline Authority (NPA) to supervise the construction of the Canadian portion of the line. Late in the decade, the Americans became so avid for natural gas that they proposed a "prebuild" to obtain Alberta gas quickly. Initially, the government was convinced that the prebuild should go ahead only if there was an ironclad guarantee of financing for the whole project, but before long it recognized the overriding advantage to Canada of the prebuild even by itself and passed the required order in council in 1980.[94]

The United States was always greatly interested in Canadian energy policies, if only because they imported so much more from us than we did from them.[95] Events in Iran and the second OPEC oil crisis led to a sudden international concern with energy in 1980, and the Liberal party's platform in the energy-inspired election campaign of that year were cognizant of this reality.

The National Energy Program (NEP), a joint policy of Marc Lalonde, the Minister of Energy, and Allan MacEachen, the Minister of Finance, emerged simultaneously with MacEachen's first budget of 28 October 1980. The NEP represented an attempt by the government to exercise more federal power over the provinces in the energy field with corresponding fiscal advantages, building on a predicted rapid increase in petroleum prices and hence in revenue flows for producers and producer provinces. Though it was a highly meritorious program, it produced some unfortunate political side effects. First, being introduced in the same month as the federal constitutional initiative, it inevitably embittered the already heated Canadian political atmosphere, ensuring a hard line by the three western oil-producing provinces against the federal constitutional initiative. Second, the forecast price increases did not occur as expected. What did happen instead, although not as a result of the NEP, was a high-interest rate economy with interest in the neighbourhood of twenty per cent, along with a depressed oil and gas industry. This created general discontent with federal government policies. Third, with the electoral victory of Ronald Reagan, we were about to be confronted with an aggressively nationalistic and determinedly America-first administration that came to see the NEP as specifically directed against the United States.

The stated objectives of the NEP were: first, security of supply and independence from the world oil market; second, widespread participation by Canadians in industry expansion; and third, fair pricing and revenue-sharing for all Canadians no matter where they lived. One observer tersely summarized the objectives as "more money, more Canadians and more oil."[96] It was said by a critic that the hidden agenda was more federal power over the producer provinces as to the value and control of oil and gas resources, and the creation of a new industry outside the producer provinces with funds from the revenues of the industry and the producer provinces.[97] In my opinion, the second hidden consequence was no part of the intention, but the first could fairly be said to be. From the early 1960s, the federal government had controlled the pricing and supply of oil and gas outside the producer provinces as far east as the Ottawa Valley. Most of Ontario had thus been held as a captive market for the producer provinces for two decades. Moreover, from the mid-1950s, the federal government had been much involved in the financing of national pipelines, to the benefit of the producer provinces. It seemed only reasonable that the favour should be returned through general sharing of the expected revenues of the producer provinces in a time of prospective windfall.

Among the proposals to achieve the NEP objectives was a made-in-Canada oil pricing system that was blended to account for the different costs of domestic and imported oil; the price might rise to eighty-five per cent of the lower of world or U.S. prices.[98] This pricing system was to be financed through a petroleum compensation charge on refiners. The natural gas pricing system increased gas prices less than oil prices and added a new federal tax on gas produced. This decision to keep wellhead prices down for both oil and gas, thus benefiting consumers rather than producers, was probably the key element of the policy. I had been a consistent supporter of lower consumer prices. At the time of the first oil crisis in 1973, the government introduced the outline of a new National Oil Policy to develop Canadian self-sufficiency in oil by the end of the seventies. Elements of the policy included a rapid increase in oil production in Canada, including the development of the Alberta oil sands, the creation of a national petroleum company (Petro-Canada), the construction of a Sarnia-to-Montreal pipeline, the establishment of guidelines for energy conservation, and the insulation of Canadian energy users from full world oil prices so that consumers who continued to depend on imported oil would not pay higher prices than those who had access to cheaper domestic supplies. It was this last feature that was my particular concern because of the harsh effect of the potential doubling of fuel prices in Atlantic Canada.

Under the NEP there was to be a new petroleum and gas revenue tax (PGRT) on production revenues without a deduction for royalties and expenses. Depletion allowances were to be phased out in favour of a new petroleum incentives program (PIP) for oil and gas exploration and development by Canadian-owned and controlled companies. There were to be additional incentive payments for exploration on lands under federal jurisdiction, which would probably have the effect of moving exploration activity from provincial to federal lands. A new Canadian ownership levy would finance the takeover of foreign-owned oil and gas companies by Petro-Canada, a Crown corporation. The government also reserved a twenty-five per cent share of all oil and gas developed in the Canada lands without any offer of direct compensation. This became known as the "back-in" and was a target of particular American venom. There were also provisions requiring the use of Canadian goods and services by oil and gas companies that operated on Canada lands or in major non-conventional projects.

Before the NEP, prices for oil and gas had been established by agreement between the federal government and the producer provinces. The response of Alberta, which produced eighty-five per cent of Canada's oil and gas, to the NEP's attempt to fix prices unilaterally was a series of production cutbacks. These actions eventually forced an Ottawa-Alberta agreement on 1 September 1981 and a redrafting of details of the original legislation. Under this agreement, the ceiling on oil prices was to be seventy-five per cent of the world price for old oil (i.e., from existing projects) and a hundred per cent of that price for new oil. The agreement would increase returns to oil and gas companies by $10 billion over five years over the original NEP.[99]

It was, of course, the additional federal presence in the industry that upset the producer provinces. For the United States, however, it was Canadianization that was the sticking point. Canadianization was intended to create at least fifty per cent Canadian ownership of oil and gas production by 1990, particularly with respect to Canadian content of larger companies, and to increase the share of the oil and gas sector owned by the federal government. Little more than a week after the introduction of the NEP, the U.S. first made known its concerns about the program, principally with respect to trade policy and investment policy.

Objections heightened under the Reagan administration and included an attack on the operation of the Foreign Investment Review Agency (FIRA), which for a number of years had scrutinized all foreign investment in Canada. FIRA was important to Canada because of the extent to which Canadian industry was foreign-controlled: about sixty-five per cent in oil and gas (versus eighteen per cent foreign ownership in the U.S.), about forty per cent in the mining industry (as opposed to five per cent in U.S.), about eighteen per cent for manufacturing (versus three per cent in U.S.).

There was nothing new about FIRA's operations in 1981, but it was less tolerable to free-market Reaganites than it had been to previous administrations.

Washington was stampeded into action not only by the adverse reaction of American oil and gas giants to the NEP and the ideological opposition of the Reagan administration to the NEP and FIRA, but also by the outraged American reaction to takeover attempts of domestic American businesses by Canadian companies in the earlier part of 1981.[100] There was little in these latter events to alarm any genuine free trader, but it was typical of Reaganites in particular and to some extent of Americans in general to want a "level" playing field tilted in their favour. After several lower-level exchanges, Al Haig sent a formal note to the Canadian ambassador in March 1981, itemizing the administration's concern about the NEP with the threat that, should the balance of concessions be disturbed, the U.S. would be obliged to consider how a new balance might be achieved. The note was withdrawn on 9 March, presumably because it seemed too harsh in tone on the eve of Reagan's first official visit to Canada, but the substance of the message was nevertheless unmistakeable.

We took U.S. complaints seriously and, as minister for the carrying department, I pushed strongly for concessions that Lalonde announced on 14 May because I felt that the Americans had identified weak points in our program that ought to be rectified. Bill C-48, the proposed legislation to implement the NEP, was accordingly amended to remove any ambiguity over whether Canadian companies would have preference over foreign companies in the purchase of goods and services; it was made clear that the intention was only to ensure that Canadian companies had a right to have their bids taken into account, not given priority. In fact, the problem that the legislation had sought to address occurred because American companies were given to making contracts with U.S. suppliers without competitive bids. Another 14 May concession was that *ex gratia* payments would be paid to companies on whom a twenty-five per cent federal equity interest was being forced as part of the back-in provision.

Washington was not satisfied. The changes were welcomed but the *ex gratia* payments were said to be inadequate as compensation in that they did not take into account the true commercial value of the assets. Nevertheless, we felt that American agitation was easing. Still, we had not counted on continuing Canadian business takeovers in the U.S. and on the inflammatory effect this had in Congress. The Reagan administration, and particularly its allies in Congress, began considering retaliation. Congressional threats were made to link the air pollution question with the NEP, and there were threats as to the continued viability of the Auto Pact, which the Canadian government regarded as essential to Canada's industrial well-being. There were also threats of various trade sanctions. In October, Treasury Secretary Don Regan demanded more concessions, particularly as to the back-in and as to purchasing requirements for mega-project bids, as well as to the possibility of further Canadian legislative activity of the same kind. We were unyielding on the procurement and back-in issues. Grandfathering of currently operating companies and payment of proportionate asset value, as the Americans demanded, were not possible since they would strike at the heart of the program. In our view, the problem with respect to procurement was imaginary; there had been no grievances with respect to the Alaska gas pipeline, where the problem and the solution were largely identical.

We felt strongly about the back-in, which turned out to be the most strongly felt American *bête noire* in the NEP. It applied to Canada lands north of the sixtieth parallel and all offshore development, where the land or seabed and the subsurface oil or gas was owned by the federal government. All that corporations had been granted under exploration permits was the right to explore and to apply for a lease. Under a lease, they had obtained the right to produce oil, but no title to the subsurface oil itself.

We also felt confident of our position internationally on both the NEP and FIRA. The 1976 OECD Declaration on International Investment and Multinational Enterprise provided for "national treatment," so that all foreign investors would be assured of equitable treatment relative to national investors and other foreign investors. Canada was under no legal obligation to accord national treatment to foreign investors.[101] The bottom line was simply that a state must extend a minimal standard of protection to foreign investors, and we were confident that we had done so.[102] Washington continued to press for unrealizable changes, especially when the Energy Security Bill that implemented the PIP was introduced in 1982, but we were resolved to yield no more.

The fundamental weakness of the NEP, as events developed, was that it was based upon a perception of a huge windfall profit to oil and gas producers and producer provinces as a result of the second OPEC crisis. This perception was the reasonable one at the time the NEP was proposed. But the OPEC countries drew back from their own handiwork when the general economic and financial crisis into which their actions had plunged the whole world became apparent. The rise in oil prices stopped and partially reversed, and the effect on the oil and gas sector became a negative one. At the same time, the general economic and financial crisis had an enormous impact upon Canadian fortunes – and on those of the government.

The National Energy Program went a bit too far in its original expression, as our subsequent modifications indicated. However, I do not believe that this excess in the details was responsible for its problems. It was a strong assertion of the national interest, both domestically and internationally, and this led to the resistance to it. The Reagan administration in particular was simply not prepared to accept such an assertion of Canadian interest that was so contrary to its views of how the rest of the world should behave. It made that attitude manifest by its blind refusal to come to terms with the NEP even after it would have become obvious to any reasonable observer that no further amendments would be made. There was no notion of graceful – or even grudging – acceptance of stalemate. No doubt, the stubborn American response was also prompted by the continual undermining of the federal position vis-à-vis the United States by Alberta and by Canadian business. In the long run, the Reaganites lucked out in finding a subsequent Canadian government that was more interested in pleasing them than in standing up for Canadian interests.

In the meantime, a new crisis was just beginning, focussing on the person of the prime minister.

* * *

There were any number of reasons for a poor relationship between Ronald Reagan and Pierre Elliott Trudeau. As an intellectual, Trudeau had his own ideas, many of them profound and far-reaching. Canadians found themselves frequently persuaded by them, at least during every second election. He was an intellectual, political, and social star, even on the international scene.

Reagan, on the other hand, was not an intellectual, and his ideas tended to amount to vague echoes of the wider concepts offered by the ambitious people behind him. He was incapable of absorbing ideas in a pedagogical way, needed to be jollied along, and above all to be reassured that we sympathized with him in his central preoccupation with Soviet communism.

In my view, given the global and bilateral issues with which we had to strong stand with Reagan, we could not afford to challenge the United States frontally on fundamental East-West questions *unless our own interests demanded it.* We could, and I often did, take the U.S. to task for its lack of adequate consultation with its allies, but, when all was said and done, Canada's East-West interests were substantially identical with those of our southern neighbour. Unfortunately, Trudeau came to entertain what I saw as the quixotic view that the USSR was more in need of understanding than of reproof, and that it could be negotiated with on a reasonable basis. In this attitude, I believe he was several Soviet chairmen too soon.[103] The prime minister was incautious enough to give expression to his feelings on the occasion of his receiving an honorary degree at Notre Dame University in May 1982. His subtle but implicit equating of the two superpowers on what could be taken to be the same moral plane was drastic enough to provoke a Reagan reaction, especially when delivered in the American heartland. The situation proved absolutely galling to Reaganites, but the final blow was yet to come.

In June 1982, Lubor Zink, a person generally reviled as a figure of the far right in Ottawa, published an article on Trudeau in the *National Review*. This was quickly brought to Reagan's attention. Though it was a one-sided diatribe entirely lacking credibility in Canada, it could, presented as fact, deceive an unsophisticated audience. In it, Zink presented Trudeau as a "combination of Jesuit sophistry and Marxist certitudes," a man who lied his way to power through public deceptions by distracting people with a "yearning for escape from the drabness of sub-arctic life" by his social antics. According to Zink, Trudeau's sins included the crippling of Canada's contribution to NATO's front-line defence in Germany, his freezing of the defence budget, his 1971 Friendship Treaty with the USSR, his recognition of China, his embrace of Castro, his promotion of détente, and, above all, his "sweeping transformation of Canada from a liberal parliamentary democracy into a centrally planned state," aided by his exploitation of Canada's anti-Americanism. Inspired by Harold Laski, Machiavelli and Mao Zedong, he had made Canada "a happy hunting ground for Soviet-bloc and Cuban agents who have found in Canada a handy base of operations against the United States."[104] Although a few of Zink's facts were correct, the overall context led to a total distortion of Trudeau's life and of the Canadian people.

But President Reagan, no doubt remembering the NEP, was taken in by it, and had come to believe that Trudeau was anti-American in general, and anti-Reagan in particular. This obviously presented a problem for future relations between the two men. In June, Allan Gotlieb sent off a top secret letter[105] to Michael Pitfield, the clerk of the Privy Council, relating the situation and urging a campaign to rehabilitate Trudeau in the president's eyes. In a letter to me, Gotlieb suggested that the prime minister seize an early opportunity to write laudatory things to Reagan about anything.

That the White House had heard that Trudeau had referred to Reagan as an imbecile further complicated matters. Gotlieb was able to assure Washington that this alleged statement could not be true, as the prime minister had too much respect for the office of the presidency to use such derogatory language. In my view, that assurance was safely given. In sixteen years of parliamentary and four years of cabinet association, I never heard Trudeau make any personal comment on another international leader.

There were never any explicit threats as to what the president might do in retaliation. I never discussed the problem directly with Trudeau, so I have no first-hand knowledge of how seriously he took this development. But we in External took it seriously, and the prime minister was moved, under Pitfield's influence, to co-operate with the rescue operation, at least to the extent of making favourable noises from time to time regarding Reagan's policies, and especially with public statements in 1983 in favour of cruise missle testing.

The situation was a cyclical one, with periodic ups and downs, and was never wholly resolved before Trudeau retired. But progress was made, although suspicion of Trudeau lingered among Reaganites right to the end of the prime minister's mandate. This suspicion certainly did not help Trudeau's late-1983 international peace initiative in Washington circles, though with Gotlieb's guidance he did successfully handle his peace-initiative meeting with Reagan in December 1983. I think that on balance the problem did not lead directly to any deleterious consequences in Canadian-American relations, although it had the potential to do so.

Although in this case the leaders' personal animosity did not get out of hand, human relations do matter a good deal in foreign policy, particularly with respect to the willingness to accommodate. Because Trudeau and Giscard were competitors rather than friends, Canada in Giscard's era could always expect a certain lack of support from France over Quebec issues. With Mitterrand exactly the reverse was true. This was not a matter of party affiliation, since Giscard's middle-of-the-road party might be supposed to be closer to the Canadian Liberal party than Mitterrand's Socialists. The prime minister and Margaret Thatcher respected each other, but as no personal bonding took place, Canada–U.K. national relations were correct but not close. Thatcher promised to do what she had to do with our constitutional resolution, but she was not in the least supportive of our initiative. With Reagan the leaders' relations were the most nominal, and our bilateral problems were probably the worst they had ever been. The Reaganite agenda was, of course, so much at odds with ours that we could not have expected a smooth ride in any event. But with a good rapport between the leaders, the Reaganites might have backed off after they achieved much of what they wanted in relation to our NEP. They did not because they had neither policy nor personal reasons to do so.

As far as I could tell, Trudeau was entirely indifferent to the personal element of foreign policy – just as he was to the personal aspect of domestic politics. With the active co-operation of our ambassadors and officials, I did my best to make up for Trudeau's lack of rapport with Reagan, but we could do only so much. Other than half-heartedly following the conciliatory program Gotlieb and Pitfield orchestrated for him towards Reagan after 1982, I am unaware of any efforts on his part ever to ingratiate himself with anyone. Normally all that is required to win people over is to display empathy towards them. Trudeau, I believe, was too set on his own way to have such relationships. Canadian foreign policy – and indeed Canadian politics – was the worse for it.

Chapter 10
The Caribbean, Central America, and Latin America

The Commonwealth is a voluntary association of independent states, comprising nearly a quarter of the world's population and united for consultation and co-operation. It is the former British Empire, grown to maturity and independence. Active membership in the Commonwealth has been and continues to be a fundamental orientation in Canadian foreign policy. My own principal activity with the Commonwealth was in connection with the Commonwealth Caribbean.

If Trudeau came slowly to an appreciation of the advantages of the Commonwealth, by my time in office, he was certainly an ardent advocate of it and had developed close personal relationships with many of its national leaders, like Sonny Ramphal of Guyana, Lee Kuan Yew of Singapore and Julius Nyerere of Tanzania. Indeed, it would not be too much to say that Canada had become the effective leader of the Commonwealth. Thatcher was as unpopular, as Trudeau was popular, with Commonwealth leaders.

My instinct was that Canada ought to assume a particular responsibility with respect to the Commonwealth Caribbean, including Guyana. We were the closest Commonwealth country with the ability and willingness to help the area, we had had a long history of trade and tourism, we had many immigrants from "the Islands," and, perhaps most of all, the problem was a limited one as world problems went, and a major increase in our aid could make a crucial difference. Indeed, the Commonwealth Caribbean, with its five million inhabitants, was already the largest per capita beneficiary of Canadian aid largesse.

To this end, I announced in March 1980 that the government would be reviewing its policy toward the Caribbean, where its interests were strong and growing. Then, at a cabinet committee in July, I proposed an increase in real ODA for the Commonwealth Caribbean, and I was authorized to prepare a recommendation to this effect for cabinet consideration before the end of the year. The full cabinet approved the Caribbean policy review in the fall of 1980.

What I came up with was a plan to double our total ODA to the Commonwealth Caribbean over five years from $43 million in 1981/82 to about $90 million in 1986/87. In terms of direct bilateral aid (as opposed to that through other agencies) our assistance would rise to $70 million from $34.5 million.[106] The most needy Commonwealth states, specifically the Leeward and Windward Islands, Jamaica, and Guyana, were classed as "core countries" and received the largest share of our giving. Barbados and Trinidad received much less, being classed as countries where selective instruments were used. Belize was a country in transitional eligibility status and so obtained the least.

In January 1981, I made an official visit to the Caribbean. In Barbados, the most prosperous and stable state in the Eastern Caribbean, I had meetings with Prime Minister Tom Adams and Foreign Minister Henry Forde. Adams was a political junkie with an encyclopaedic knowledge even of Canadian politics. I also signed a water development loan agreement and turned the valve to declare open a completed CIDA project, the giant Lodge Hill Water Tank. I well remember that event, as I had to stand without shelter at noon on one of the highest points in Barbados under a burning sun. By the time the ceremony ended, I was in desperate need of the ceremonial glass of water I was offered from the tank! In St. Kitts, I handed over the beautiful new Golden Rock Air Terminal Building, which had shortly before been completed with CIDA funding. I then moved on to Jamaica for a Canada-Caricom Joint Trade and Economic Committee meeting, at which I was able to announce on 15 January 1981 the dramatic increase we proposed in aid to the Commonwealth Caribbean. This I followed with bilateral meetings with newly elected Jamaican leaders, at which time I decided on the spot that Jamaica merited a doubling of Canadian bilateral aid.

* * *

Grenada was a major problem for Canadian ODA in the Caribbean. The Marxist government, which came into power by a coup, had closed the only free newspaper on the island, was detaining a hundred people without trial, and refused to commit itself to the holding of free elections. Moreover, Prime Minister Bishop aligned Grenada with Cuba's foreign policy in the NAM and was allowing the Cubans to build an airport on the island. Grenada also voted in the minority in the General Assembly in support of the Soviet invasion of Afghanistan. The U.S. and the U.K. had both distanced themselves from the Bishop regime, and the Commonwealth secretary-general was very negative on Grenada, regarding it as completely alienated from its Caribbean neighbours and as part of an expanding leftist political presence in the region. In May 1980, I raised the question whether Grenada was a Soviet satellite like Cuba, and, if so, whether it should continue to receive Canadian aid.

In response to my query, our energetic high commissioner to Barbados, Allan Roger, conducted an extensive series of *tours d'horizon* with regional leaders in the Eastern Caribbean, as well as with the British and American heads of post. The consensus was that Grenada had not been irrevocably lost to the Eastern Caribbean family, despite the distasteful Cuban presence on the island, and that Canada would be making a serious mistake to withdraw aid. Moreover, it would be regarded as something of an empty gesture, since by an accident of staggered planning, all of our programs there had in any event run out.

The one concern to which I did agree was the military vulnerability of the smaller mini-states, particularly St. Vincent, Antigua and St. Kitts, to any handful of adventurers. They did not have the means even to exercise any normal civil control over their inshore waters. Canada therefore agreed to assist these mini-states in the security sector, without arousing resentment or apprehension on anyone's part. Nevertheless, I was prepared to go no further than to supply unarmed harbour patrol boats.

I accepted this consensus of the democratic and friendly governments in the Eastern Caribbean, especially in the hope of countering leftist movements fed by the discontent among unemployed youth in the area. I therefore approved an aid program for Grenada that, while providing no funding in relation to projects involving Cuban or Eastern Bloc participation or any partisan interests of the government, would emphasize economic development aimed at benefiting the more disadvantaged sectors of the population. I looked with particular favour on a cocoa rehabilitation project that was in the planning stage.

* * *

The Caribbean and Central America region was the playground par excellence for the bipolar extremists of both superpowers. On the one hand, there was poverty, unfair distribution of wealth, social injustice and, naturally, instability. On the other hand, East-West rivalry piggybacked on the existing instability caused in part by Cuban/Soviet-encouraged expansionist opportunism, in part by U.S. economic interests which were usually involved with those who were exploiting the poor. Politically unaware churchmen, journalists, and intellectuals also adopted a bipolar view, focussing not on East-West considerations but on social injustice. The "godly" judgmentalists were the particular victims of left-wing bipolarism, seemingly because they found it hard to believe that those who were struggling against real oppression could be as evilly motivated as an impartial analysis of their actions would imply. Because they lived closer to and understood better the motivations of the rich capitalists, they apparently found it easier to perceive their evil. My position was a plague on the houses of both kinds of oppressors. As I put it on 20 March 1981, "I do not have any more confidence in the leftist forces in El Salvador than I do in the extreme right wing there. I deplore them both."[107] Both forms of bipolarism left me cold, since both failed to take account of the whole of regional reality.

A liberal perspective tried to see the world as it was, without ideological preconceptions. I favoured those who were striving for democratic decision-making, free elections, and the reducing of income inequalities. I disfavoured those who sought, for whatever reason, to undermine those values.

The Soviet Union was involved only at a distance, supplying food and armaments, usually through its proxy, Castro's Cuba, which was independently dedicated to seeding socialist revolution wherever possible. In the first flush of Castroism in the 1960s, there were ill-planned and uniformly unsuccessful expeditions to Haiti, the Dominican Republic, Panama and Venezuela that alarmed Cuba's hemispheric neighbours.[108] Reacting against Cuban interference were countries that, by the way of countercause, fell into the grip of right-wing elements, such as Argentina, Brazil, and Chile, and landowner and business groups in many countries. In most countries in the region, those smaller numbers who stood between right and left were conspicuously lacking in social, economic, and political power. It was a parlous time for liberalism, which always seeks the middle ground between extremes.

I liked neither Cuba's domestic repression nor its policy of large-scale military intervention in East Africa and Angola, and I was particularly persuaded of the wisdom of the cabinet decision in 1978 that Canada should cut off its aid program to Cuba so as not to indirectly subsidize Cuban adventurism abroad. In 1980, Cuba remained a residual problem for Canadian ODA, in that since 1978 it had continued to receive aid through Canadian University Service Overseas (CUSO) in the agricultural and health fields. In the fall of 1980, I therefore had cabinet committee recommend the revocation of all aid to Cuba.

When the matter came to full cabinet, the prime minister asked me privately before the meeting if I would consider withdrawing it, but I explained to him that I felt I did not have that kind of leeway either under the earlier cabinet decision or the newer one. Although I refrained from saying so, I thought he was seeking special consideration for his friend Castro, based on personal preference rather than on principle. I suspect he did not accept my stated reason, but he allowed the committee recommendation to pass cabinet without adverse comment.

* * *

The crisis in El Salvador, a small country of under five million people and with one of the worst income inequalities in all of Latin America, began just before I assumed office. In October 1979, a revolutionary five-man junta bent on reform ended the military dictatorship of Carlos Humberto Romero. This coup brought to an end fifty years of military government, but the junta itself was immediately subject to pressures from both left and right.

This event followed on an even more momentous change, the overthrow of the repressive Nicaraguan dictator Anastasio Somoza on 19 July 1979.[109] A coalition of groups was involved, but the Marxist military forces within the Sandinista coalition acted in such a way as to induce all of its moderate members to leave office. In the short run, however, the Sandinistas disowned elections and pluralism and began directly supporting revolution in neighbouring El Salvador. Initially, the Nicaraguan revolution had been highly favoured and generously supported by the United States, but Sandinista support for overthrowing the Salvadoran government led President Carter to suspend American aid before he left office.

Because the conflict in El Salvador was continuing, the Canadian public became more interested in that country than in Nicaragua. In January 1980, the three civilian members of the new Salvadoran junta resigned, but the Christian Democratic Party under José Napoleón Duarte joined it in an attempt to stabilize the situation. No doubt owing to Duarte's influence, the junta promised free elections in 1982, was able to institute reforms of the banking and landholding systems in the spring of 1980, and also began an agrarian reform program. However, Archbishop Oscar Arnulfo Romero, a well-known supporter of social reform, was assassinated in his chapel in March 1980. The secretary-general of the Canadian Conference of Catholic Bishops (CCCB) immediately blamed the junta for precipitating the archbishop's death. Archbishop Joseph MacNeil of Edmonton, president of the CCCB, accused the junta of not being representative of the people, and denounced a $50 million American military aid package it had received.[110]

By early July, Monsignor Rivera y Damas (the apostolic administrator, later appointed Romero's successor as archbishop) estimated that violence was claiming the lives of over two hundred peasants and workers a week. Violence between left and right accelerated throughout 1980, with an estimated nine thousand deaths during the year and twelve thousand more in 1981. Moreover, six opposition leaders were murdered on 27 November 1980 and three American nuns in early December. The government denied involvement.

Following the murder of the American nuns, the U.S. suspended economic and military aid to El Salvador and sent a special presidential commission to investigate junta involvement. The commission found that, although no evidence existed to implicate senior government officials, some members of the military had been involved in an attempted cover-up. The U.S. renewed non-military aid and pressured the junta into a reorganization in which the Christian Democrat Duarte was made president. However, at the same time, control of the army passed from a left-leaning junta member, who was dropped, to a conservative member. Overall, the change therefore probably made the moderates' position within the junta more difficult.

In the meantime, various guerrilla groups had united to form the Farabundo Marti National Liberation Front (FMLN), which subsequently formed a diplomatic commission with the Democratic Revolutionary Front (FDR) to gain international support.[111] I met two representatives of this commission on 26 January 1981, when it was engaged in a massive, Cuban-supported campaign to gain international support. I reiterated Canada's opposition to any external interference. Their professed fear was direct U.S. intervention, which I was able to assure them I would oppose, but I made it clear that I was equally opposed to interference from the Marxist side. I also deplored the gross violations of human rights from both right and left. I had frequently made representations to the junta against right-wing oppression, and this was a welcome opportunity to do the same with the left.

The diplomatic commission of the FMLN and FDR was at pains to emphasize that it was seeking to establish a pluralistic state. In the light of the Bolshevik Revolution itself, the Eastern European experience after the war, and that in Nicaragua in 1979, I had grave doubts that, given the opportunity, it would actually carry out such a democratic policy. There was no doubt in my mind, however, that Guillermo Ungo and his National Revolutionary Movement, represented in the FDR, were genuine democrats. In my opinion the Reaganites, who had just come to power in the United States, were totally mistaken in identifying all opposition to the junta with totalitarian movements.[112]

In January 1981, I discussed U.S. military assistance to El Salvador with Secretary Haig and made clear Canada's opposition to any supply of offensive arms. The Reagan view was that resupply of the armed forces of El Salvador was required to counter the leftist offensive made possible by the supply of arms from Marxist countries. I accepted that this was a reasonable position in itself but knew that the U.S. retained no control over the arms once they arrived in El Salvador and that they could as easily be used by rogue military against the general population as by the armed forces acting officially in response to foreign-supported aggression. In other words, it was a situation in which the uncontrolled availability of arms was itself a danger.

In the circumstances, however, where the U.S. believed it was acting only by way of response to aggression, I felt that it would be counterproductive for Canada to mount a strident public protest against the U.S. action. We continued to disagree with Washington, both privately and publicly, but without raising the decibel level. This was the context in which I stated in the House of Commons, on 9 March 1981, that "we are prepared to contest the U.S. policy of military aid, but not to protest it; we are prepared to pronounce on it but not to denounce it; we are prepared to criticize it but not to condemn it.... [W]e believe in doing so in terms which are appropriate to the cause and not wildly inflated because of some paranoia of the left." [113] In this position, I was at odds, not only with the left, but, I think for the only time during my mandate, with a sizeable portion of the Canadian public, who wanted a loudly voiced denunciation of American policy regardless of the consequences – presumably for the moral satisfaction it would give them. Quiet diplomacy was not seen to be enough, even if it carried the right message. In their view, this was an occasion for moral outrage.

It would have been easy enough to give in to the clamour. I felt sure that the prime minister would not have objected to a more outwardly anti-American policy. Indeed, my own initial impulse had been strongly to oppose American policy in El Salvador, because of its two-faced nature: while officially supporting the moderates, the Americans greatly applauded and assisted the right-wing extremists. But I immediately came to see that such a policy would be a betrayal of Canada's liberalism: the only hope for El Salvador was through the one clearly democratic figure in the country, Napoleón Duarte. I felt we must support Duarte, distinguishing him as clearly as possible from any unworthy supporters in the military.

As a secondary consideration, I did not see it as being in Canada's long-range interests to appear overly anti-American, nor did the officials who advised me. It was in fact parallel to the situation during the Vietnam

War, when there was a similar public outpouring of moral condemnation against the United States. But like my predecessors at that time, I held fast against the tide. Not only did I think quiet diplomacy was the better policy vis-à-vis the Americans, but I did not see how we could attack Washington for what was essentially a pro-junta policy when that policy was morally required by my own philosophical liberalism. We already opposed the U.S. arming the Salvadoran government. What more could we disapprove of without betraying our own beliefs?

The tone of my approach particularly annoyed the left and the naive in Canada. I identify both with the NDP policy of the time, for whom it was an article of faith that the right and the Salvadoran government – for them it was all the same – were at fault, and that Americans made it all possible by their support. Of course, no level of protest against Washington could have satisfied these critics, so long as we were not also prepared to denounce the Salvadoran junta unequivocally.

My policy resembled that of the United States only in its acceptance of the predominance of hardline Marxist elements among the guerrillas and of the Sandinista role in supplying them, and in our constant attempt to shore up Duarte's government. Where we parted company entirely with the Reaganites was in their tolerance for the military elements on the right. It was revealed by the Truth Commission in 1993 that Salvadoran military forces massacred hundreds of innocent civilians in El Mozote in 1982, and that U.S. officials covered up the truth for years afterwards.[114] Recently declassified American documents "reveal that former presidents Ronald Reagan and George Bush and their senior officials worked with, and provided money to, political and military leaders they knew through intelligence reports to be involved with El Salvador's spectacularly brutal death squads."[115] However, none of the subsequent evidence has impeached the bona fides of Duarte, reliance on whom was the bedrock of my policy as the only hope for eventual resolution of the problem.

On 21 December 1981, I met Ruben Zamora, Secretary of the FMLN/FDR Political-Diplomatic Commission, and Oscar Dada, the FMLN/FDR representative in Canada. Zamora explicitly recognized the good faith and integrity of many Christian democrats, including Duarte and Jorge Bustamente, the electoral commissioner. The rebel representatives themselves admitted that their funds for buying weapons on the international black market had come from kidnapping and bank robberies, as well as from money raised internationally by sympathizers.

The leader of the NDP, Ed Broadbent, argued in an address to a rally on Parliament Hill a week later that it was the rebels' right to get their arms from Nicaragua, since they had no other way to overthrow their government. This unbridled right of revolution apparently justified for him the rebels in whatever they did – despite twenty-eight assaults on foreign embassies, the assassination of the Swiss chargé d'affaires, the thirty-day kidnapping of the French ambassador, the three occupations of the Costa Rican embassy, the bank robberies, the many kidnappings of foreigners, and the hundreds of ordinary citizens murdered in their communities. Broadbent also expressed the view in a House of Commons debate on 16 June 1981 that an election in El Salvador would be a travesty of democracy in current circumstances.

In a letter to two representatives of the CCCB on 4 May 1981, I stated:

> In my view, the areas of disagreement between the positions of the Conference of Catholic Bishops and the Canadian Government on the basic issues may be more apparent than real. We both oppose military aid and foreign intervention in El Salvador. We both support a political solution to the difficulties and deplore the continuing violations of human rights in that country.
>
> We appear to disagree on the source of violence in El Salvador. Your position appears to be that the right is responsible almost exclusively for the continuation of the violence. The Government of Canada's position is that while the right is indeed responsible for much of the violence, the left and undisciplined members of government security forces are also at fault. For this reason, we continue to make vigorous representations to the Government of El Salvador on human rights issues and played a leading role at the 37th Session of the United Nations Commission on Human Rights in supporting a resolution calling for the appointment of a Special Representative to investigate violations of human rights.

On subsequent reflection, however, I believe the problem was even more fundamental than the source of violence in El Salvador. It was rather the very characterization of the government itself.

In my view, there were three orientations in the country: the rebels on the left, the military assassins on the right, and Duarte in between. It is now known to be true that the right-wing murderers came from the Salvadoran military, nominally under the junta's direction, but it was widely known at the time that the junta had only imperfect control of its forces, and that there were many local power centres at play in the countryside. Ernesto Rivas, the Salvadoran ambassador to the U.S., admitted to me that government forces had been responsible for violence but argued that this had not been authorized by the military high command and was the result of what he described as "cultural violence" at lower levels of authority where violence had been endemic for many years.

Archbishop Rivera y Damas, in a March 1981 sermon, strongly condemned left-wing and especially right-wing violence, but made it clear that the Church in El Salvador looked very favourably on the willingness of the junta to search for a political solution. The Vatican's policy was to support the local national episcopate. It was never obvious to me that the CCCB followed the same policy.[116]

The left, both in El Salvador and in Canada, demanded that before an election was held, there should be negotiations on a political settlement with a view to creating a new political order and integration of the FMLN and government armies. In their meeting with me on 21 December 1981, the rebels rejected as insufficient the recommendation of the Dupras Subcommittee that elections should be preceded by an internationally supervised ceasefire and be conducted under international supervision. Their prerequisite to elections was "a comprehensive political settlement." On the model of Nicaragua such a comprehensive settlement would in my view have assured control of the government by the rebels before the election was held – if it ever was. Some slight credibility had been given to the rebel position by a joint declaration by France and Mexico in August 1981 that the FMLN/FDR should be recognized as "a representative political force" and should therefore participate in any political settlement in El Salvador. This declaration was supported by the Soviet Bloc and by Cuba, Nicaragua, and Grenada. However, no other country in the Americas endorsed it.

From the beginning the election, eventually set for 28 March 1982, was the key to the eventual resolution of the Salvadoran problem. The only question Canada was confronted with was whether to send official observers to witness the election. We would have been most willing to participate in an international observer force, as we had for elections in Zimbabwe and Uganda, but no such process was envisaged. To try to make a judgment on the election in the whole country with a few observers of our own, without even a resident ambassador, seemed too forbidding an undertaking, despite the American desire that we do so. I also lacked confidence that the election would be run fairly and that the right-wing elements in the country would accept the result. Despite our best efforts to provide an advance dialogue between the various groupings as to the election, no such meeting was ever held, and there were no leftist parties on the ballot. I therefore announced, in reply to a question in the House on 18 February 1982, that we would not send observers. I did, however, request our ambassador to be present for the occasion.

Despite my concerns, the election proved to be a resounding success. More than eighty per cent of the electorate voted, a startling endorsement of the democratic process. The left made strenuous efforts to stop the democratic process, even to the extent of large-scale intimidation of electors not to vote at all. The guerrillas threatened to attack those who voted and did attack many of the election stations. At least fifty people were shot down on election day.[117] The Catholic episcopate in El Salvador, on the other hand, urged citizens to participate. It was also important that right-wing parties appeared on the ballot and henceforth no longer had to operate covertly under the mantle of the government. The principal right-wing grouping was the Arena party under the leadership of extremist Roberto d'Aubuisson.

Even so, the election results were inconclusive. There was talk of a coalition of five right-wing parties with a view to excluding the Christian Democrats from government. I was sufficiently alarmed by the possibility of d'Aubuisson's becoming president of the country as a result of behind-the-scenes pressures that I telephoned Al Haig at the first of the week to ask him to use all his weight to ensure that he did not, and to inform him that continued Canadian support of the El Salvador government depended on the Christian Democrats' retaining the government. I am sure he knew as well as I that none of the potential good of the election would occur if d'Aubuisson became president and that it would not even be seen to be a democratic outcome. In the result, d'Aubuisson became president only of the Assembly. The new head of state was a neutral and respected figure from the World Bank, Alvaro Magaña, and the Christian Democrats remained the chief force in the government.

This was very far from the end of the story, but the election of 1982 marked the beginning of the process by which, a decade later, reconciliation and fuller democracy came to El Salvador. Major d'Aubuisson used his political power to paralyze land reform in the short run, and the civil war continued. Duarte succeeded Magaña as president. Soldiers killed and mutilated six Jesuit priests and two associates as late as 1989. Only the end of the Cold War, and the consequent ending of communist aid to the guerrillas, made peace a possibility.

* * *

Cuba and Central America were political necessities forced on Canadian foreign policy. In general, however, Canadian policy towards Latin America was based on our economic self-interest as expressed in the notion of bilateralism.

I always gave a very high priority to trade matters, and tried to coordinate my efforts in this regard with Ed Lumley, our enterprising minister of state for foreign trade. Mexico was an early target of both of us, since, at that time, as an oil-producing country, it was an economic high-flyer with apparently boundless potential and with an interest in acquiring nuclear technology. Canada stood ready to oblige with its CANDU reactor. We also hoped to sell the Mexicans wheat, corn, and dairy products. In recognition of Mexico's special status as a country of concentration in our foreign policy, we had one of our best foreign service officers, the late Claude Charland, in place as our ambassador.

During my first visit to Mexico in April 1980,[118] the Foreign Minister Jorge Castañeda and I established a genuine rapport, which carried through many subsequent associations. He had a keen mind and was possessed of a deep suspicion of the United States which, as I quickly learned, seemed to be a characteristic of most Mexicans. The anti-Americanism that existed to some extent in Canada was nothing compared with the prevalence and virulence of anti-Americanism in Mexico. Nevertheless, Castañeda and I found much in common in our general approach to world problems.

Bilateral trade began to increase dramatically. Following the Mexican president and foreign minister's state visit to Canada in May 1980, Canada began to import fifty thousand barrels a day of Mexican oil. We also began to participate as fully as possible in Mexico's industrial development program. Following another trade-oriented visit to Mexico with my colleagues Lumley and Whelan in early 1981, the Canadian corporation Bombardier won a $100 million contract for railway cars for the Mexico City subway. By January 1982, Prime Minister Trudeau was able to announce that there had been a fourfold increase in Canada-Mexico trade since the May 1980 visit. If it had not been for the subsequent collapse of the Mexican economy, no doubt succeeding figures would have been even more impressive.

* * *

The Caribbean Basin Initiative was an American idea to encourage increased social and economic development in the region. The United States, Canada, Mexico and Venezuela came together by American invitation and by common will at Nassau in July 1981 to launch the initiative. By that time, I had already announced a doubling of previous levels of Canadian assistance to the Commonwealth Caribbean and a corresponding tripling of assistance to Central America. I had also announced increased aid to the Dominican Republic and Haiti.

What drew Canada, Mexico and Venezuela together at Nassau was involving the United States *constructively* in the Caribbean for perhaps the first-time – or perhaps it would be more accurate to say to help the United States to become involved. As I saw it, it was a conspiracy against the American Congress by the American Administration, and I was happy to be that kind of co-conspirator. The United States planned to give exports from the region, with the exception of textiles and apparel, duty-free treatment for twelve years, along with tax incentives for investment, and a supplemental aid program for specific projects.

The initiative was not really an overall plan for economic development in the Caribbean. Each donor country was left free to co-operate with whatever countries it chose and in whatever manner it chose. The Nassau Four agreed that there was to be no military-security component, that economic assistance should be without military considerations or political pre-conditions, and that no country in the region would be excluded.

Did the program succeed in hoodwinking the American Congress into believing that a great multinational effort was in place to which the U.S. must contribute or lose face? In part it did. The aid component of the program was adopted after a complex legislative battle. However, as George Shultz admitted, "The trade and investment aspects of the program came harder: special interests are always wary and watchful of potentially competitive imports."[119] Important parts of the program became law by mid-1983, but duty-free entry was never provided for the basic Caribbean crop, sugar, because it was in direct competition with American sugar beet interests. The limits of Reaganite altruism were typically narrow.

* * *

During my tenure, I was always conscious of the enormous trade advantages to be gained from a heightened relationship with South America, and, in 1982, I was able to make official visits to Venezuela and Brazil.[120] Venezuela was a large export market for Canadian-made auto parts, and under our new policy of bilateralism was one of our most important trading partners in Latin America.[121] Brazil was the other country of concentration in South America for Canadian foreign policy. Our goal was to emphasize Canada's value as a partner in economic development and as a valuable interlocutor on political and economic issues of international importance, so that we would be front and centre in Brazil's mind as it embarked on economic liberalization and diversification of trade.

* * *

In my view, one could not focus on bilateralism in Latin America for long without realizing the fundamental necessity of Canadian membership in the Organization of American States (OAS). Canada had always stood aside from the OAS, accepting only observer status, since it had always appeared to be the playground of the U.S., with which we already had many occasions for disagreement. I found that the larger Latin states like

Argentina and Brazil were supremely uninterested in whether or not we joined the OAS, but the smaller states like Venezuela and Colombia were passionate advocates of our entry.

Officials of the Department of External Affairs were just as strongly opposed as I became in favour. I think they just did not want any occasions for collisions with the U.S. and they had not yet come to a realization of the importance of the region for Canada. I resolved to change all of this. As I said on 27 May 1982, "I have tried to insist on linguistic capacity, particularly in Spanish-speaking countries."[122] I had established the policy anyhow of seeing all outgoing and incoming ambassadors so as to keep tabs on what was going on. I began asking of each proposed ambassadorial appointment for the region whether the putative appointee spoke Spanish, or Portuguese for Brazil. Most of all, I decided that, in order for us to be really treated as a seriously interested neighbour, we had to join the OAS. Indeed, it was very difficult to explain to any Latin country why we had not done so years ago.

Since this would be a major departure in our policy, I raised the matter first with the prime minister in the House one day in the spring of 1982. I told him I had become convinced we should belong to the OAS and asked for his views. He assured me that he had always felt that Canada should be a member of the OAS and that I could proceed in that direction with his blessing. With this backing from the top, I informed MP Maurice Dupras, the head of the House Sub-committee on Canada's Relations with Latin America and the Caribbean,[123] of the lay of the land and assured him that, if his sub-committee was to recommend membership, the government would welcome such a recommendation. I planned to move on the matter as soon as I received the sub-committee's report in the fall.

Alas, from that point of view, intervening events saw to it that I was no longer the responsible minister by the time the favourable report appeared. In fact, on what turned out to be my last day in office, I revealed at a press conference that I had in mind Canada's joining the OAS. However, my successor Allan MacEachen did not pick up my initiative. He seemed to be listening to the departmental naysayers, since during his mandate a cabinet document was put forward recommending against membership in the OAS. With considerable support from Francis Fox, I was able to defeat the document in committee – MacEachen was not present to defend it – so that it never went forward to cabinet. But this was a negative victory, and within bureaucratic procedures I had no way of substituting a recommendation to the contrary. It was therefore left to a later government to take the bold step of joining the OAS in 1990, by which time my own party had forgotten that it was originally our policy.

Chapter 11
Southern Africa

Canada's problems with South Africa related to its policy of apartheid and to its treatment of Namibia.

Successive Canadian governments had forcefully condemned apartheid and the systematic violation of human rights it entailed. It should also be said that Canada did not recognize the governments of the so-called "independent homelands" for blacks that the South African government had established. The Diefenbaker government had forced South Africa out of the Commonwealth, and Canada had instituted a voluntary arms embargo in 1963, before supporting the institution of a mandatory arms embargo as a member of the Security Council in 1978.

But Canada never endorsed the idea of an embargo on peaceful goods, as we did not believe it would achieve the objective of encouraging reform in South Africa. We were also concerned about the potential impact of such an embargo on black states in the region. Nevertheless, we did withdraw Canadian trade commissioners in 1978 and close our consulates in Johannesburg and Cape Town. We also withdrew Export Development Corporation facilities for exports to South Africa (further extended in 1981), and insurance for investments in South Africa. In the same year, we issued a Code of Conduct on Employment Practices for Canadian companies with South African subsidiaries, with the aim of improving working conditions for non-white employees. In January 1980, the Clark government terminated our trade agreement with South Africa which accorded it preferential tariff access to the Canadian market.

Action had also been taken in the area of sporting contacts. Given the importance attached to sports by many white South Africans, the Canadian government actively discouraged sporting contacts between officially representative Canadian and South African athletes. Beginning in 1972, the government refused to provide funds to Canadian sporting bodies for competitions in Canada to which South African representatives were invited, or for Canadian athletes to compete in South Africa. Canada had also imposed a visa requirement for all South Africans in 1978 and had since then refused to issue visas to South African sportsmen or officials who intended to participate in competitions or meetings on a nationally representative basis. In February 1982, I introduced further measures to restrain competition between Canadian and South African athletes in third countries.

It was also *de rigueur* each fall at the UN General Assembly to deliver strongly worded denunciations of South African apartheid.[124] Nevertheless, we continued to maintain diplomatic relations with South Africa with the hope that we might still have a means of communicating Canadian opinion regarding the need for change in the policy of apartheid to the white minority. That way, we were able to assist the black population through mission-administered funds and to contribute to UN programs of education, training, and relief for South African refugees. Canada also supported South Africa's right to participate in the activities of the United Nations and other international organizations because of our general belief in universality of participation and in order to continue to expose South Africa to world public opinion. Our continuing relationship enabled me, for example, to have our concern about a new wave of detentions against prominent clerics, trade unionists, students, and academics brought to the attention of the South African foreign ministry in December 1981, and specifically our concerns about detention without trial.

* * *

Before the election of the Reagan administration, there was no gulf between Canadian and American policy towards South Africa. But Reagan said that the United States should try to be "helpful" to South Africa as long as "a sincere and honest effort" to make headway on its racial problems was underway. The South African government naturally welcomed his remarks.[125]

In my eyes, he was right in seeing South Africa as a bulwark against the communist threat in Angola, but wrong in believing that this fact should itself determine the Western relationship with South Africa. Nevertheless, Reagan had already forecast during his election campaign the priority that the Angola situation would have in his mind by his expressed support for U.S. aid to Jonas Savimbi, the leader of the anti-communist National Union for the Total Independence of Angola (UNITA). Reagan's feelings against the predominant Popular Movement for the Liberation of Angola (MPLA) were undoubtedly heightened by the presence in Angola on the MPLA's side of fifteen to twenty thousand Cuban troops, as well as three to four thousand Cuban civilians such as teachers and physicians. The

MPLA defended the presence of the Cubans on the ground that they were needed as long as South Africa continued to attack bases in Angola used by guerrillas of the South West African People's Organization (SWAPO), which were fighting for the independence of neighbouring Namibia. From the Canadian point of view, the independence of Namibia, not the Cubans in Angola, was the key issue in the area.

In 1920, under the League of Nations mandate system, administration of the former German colony of South-West Africa was handed over to South Africa. After the replacement of the League of Nations by the United Nations, the UN offered South Africa the trusteeship of this territory, but the South African government refused to enter into such an agreement on the ground that it had already assumed sovereignty over it. The UN did not accept this status quo, and in 1967 the General Assembly created an eleven-member council to be the legal administering authority for the territory it voted to rename Namibia the next year. Canada abstained on the resolution and from the first did not accept the authority of the UN Council for Namibia, a position in which the International Court of Justice (ICJ) effectively confirmed us in 1971. All UN members were required to recognize the illegality of South Africa's role in Namibia and to avoid dealings implying recognition of, or lending support to, its administration. Canada accepted the IJC opinion and a month later issued a formal declaration to this effect in a diplomatic note to South Africa.

Canada's involvement in the Namibian negotiations came as a result of membership in the UN Security Council. In April 1977, the Western members of the Security Council formed what became known as the Contact Group. At the same time, and with the same objective, Angola, Botswana, Mozambique, Tanzania, and Zambia joined together as the Front Line States. Discussion among the Contact Group, the Front Line States, SWAPO, and South Africa led to proposals to bring about early and peaceful independence for Namibia, and, in September 1978, the Security Council adopted Resolution 435, a plan for Namibian independence through UN-supervised elections. By the end of 1980, all of the substantive difficulties preventing the implementation of the resolution and the associated UN plan appeared to have been settled. South Africa, nevertheless, refused to proceed on the subjective grounds of the UN's alleged partiality towards SWAPO and its consequent incapacity to supervise elections impartially. It also soon became apparent that the Reagan administration was determined to link independence for Namibia with Cuban withdrawal from Angola. Thus, American as well as South African intransigence became a factor that the other members of the Contact Group had to deal with, as free and fair elections for Namibians were thus held hostage by events in Angola.

This was brought forcefully to my attention at my meeting with Secretary Haig in Rome on 3 May 1981. I was at a twofold disadvantage in this contretemps. First, at an advance officials' meeting of the Contact Group in London a few days before, the Canadian representative had, without my knowledge or authorization, pretty much agreed to the linkage the Americans wanted. This was not a prohibitive problem, since I repudiated my official's agreement at the beginning of my meeting with Haig. More important was the fact that at the Contact Group meeting which immediately followed my unpleasant but inconclusive meeting with Haig, no other foreign minister was prepared to back me up in taking on the Americans and excluding any reference to Angola. I felt I had the sympathy of the German and French ministers, but they were not prepared for a confrontation. The British, of course, because of their extensive commercial interests in South Africa, were always soft on South African issues. Lacking any support, I had to give way partially, and we ended up by adopting language which referred to the Cuban presence in Angola in such a way that the Americans could give it one meaning and the rest of us another. Canada's position continued to be that, although the withdrawal of Cuban troops from Angola was a highly desirable goal in itself, such a withdrawal should in no way stand as a condition of a Namibian settlement. In our view, South Africa could not create conditions where it had no rights.

The Cuban factor was always more of an American than a South African consideration, and South Africa was happy to seize on the Cuban issue as an excuse for further delay towards Namibia. Earlier, when it had seemed possible that South Africa was contemplating the possibility of freeing Namibia, it was almost certainly because it seemed at that time that its sympathizers in the Namibian Democratic Turnhalle Alliance could win an election there. As those prospects decreased with the continuance of the guerrilla struggle with Angola, so did South African willingness to negotiate.

At the next meeting of the Contact Group in September 1981, on the margins of the General Assembly, some apparent progress emerged. South Africa had tentatively agreed with Washington on an implementation date before the end of the following year. A new initiative was therefore launched, involving senior officials of the group, who would travel to Africa with new proposals based on Resolution 435. This mission would be the first phase of a new timetable and would consist of the presentation of a package of constitutional principles based on the general democratic practices of states, the principles of the UN Charter and the Universal Declaration of Human Rights. Phase II would deal with the negotiation of the remaining issues identified in exchanges with the South African government.[126] The talks with all parties (SWAPO, the Front Line States, the Organization for Africa Unity, and South Africa) generally went well, but led to no South African commitments. The Contact Group as such had no contacts with Angola. That was left entirely to U.S. initiative.

The negotiations dragged on into 1982. By May, the South African government was raising the question of international assistance for a newly independent Namibia, both to replace South Africa's current subsidies and to encourage a post-independence government to pursue a moderate course. In particular, South Africa wanted the Western five to use their economic and political leverage to protect property rights in Namibia. I was opposed to this as it would involve us directly in the domestic Namibian issue of compensation for white landowners and leave us open to charges of duplicity from the other side. Besides, the constitutional principles on which all parties were close to agreement had been devised with a view to meeting concerns about property and civil rights. Our offer of support was therefore a highly qualified one.

On 21 May 1982, I met Ambassador Becker with the purpose of conveying to Pretoria that, while Canada remained unilaterally opposed to apartheid – a stance which had led to limitations on its relations with South Africa – it wished to maintain a mutually beneficial dialogue on matters such as the independence of Namibia. I also wanted to provide positive reinforcement of South Africa's announced policy of gradual integration of Indians and coloureds into the central organs of government, as well as of conferring some political rights on blacks at the local level, steps that I hoped would be the beginning of greater liberalization. Our discussion of Namibia was superficial and short, as the ambassador was not well briefed on the subject. He did refer to the importance of Cuban withdrawal, at which point I reiterated the Canadian position of no linkage between Namibian independence and Cuban presence. I also drew to his attention that South African support for Savimbi's UNITA was an important reason for the continuing Cuban role.

I had a very revealing moment with Al Haig at the Bonn summit, where we happened to be sitting side-by-side at the opening ceremonies. I had just heard from Genscher that the South Africans had let it drop recently to the FRG that they were open to a Namibian settlement even without a Cuban withdrawal. That was the first time we had had such an unequivocal statement, and I confronted Haig with it in a whispered conversation. His devastating reply was, "I don't think I could sell my boss on that." In other words, Cuban withdrawal was a pre-condition for Namibian independence on which Reagan would not yield even if Pretoria did. That admission let me know that there was no possibility of a Namibia settlement in the short run.

George Shultz was to be no more effective than Haig in influencing Reagan in this respect. Indeed, it was only at the end of Reagan's mandate in 1988 that agreement proved possible. On 6 December 1988, an accord was reached among South Africa, Angola, and Cuba, with a signing ceremony on 22 December 1988, ending colonial rule in Africa.

Chapter 12
The Pacific Rim

The Pacific Rim was for Canada not so much a geographical entity as a trade concept. It embraced Japan, Korea, China, Taiwan, Hong Kong, the five countries of the Association of South East Asian Nations (ASEAN – Indonesia, Malaysia, the Philippines, Singapore, and Thailand), Papua-New Guinea, Australia, New Zealand, Samoa, and Fiji, as well as potentially the United States, Mexico and Latin countries on the Pacific Coast. In trade, it embodied almost limitless opportunity.

We already had considerable trade with many Pacific states.[127] With ASEAN, our trade was almost in balance: $414.6 million in exports, $412.4 million in imports (1979). But the potential for increase in trade was enormous for several reasons: the large populations in many Pacific Rim countries (China was the world's most populous state, Indonesia the fifth largest), the incipient state of development (particularly in China), and the fact that our exports were mostly commodities (wheat, coal, copper, oil, seeds, potash) or unprocessed or semi-processed goods (pulp and paper, fish products) which we could strive to sell in a more finished state, perhaps even as end products. In order to stir more Canadian interest in these Pacific markets, the first Pacific Rim Opportunities Conference (PROC I) was held in 1980 in Vancouver. The conference was only for Canadians – business and labour leaders, provincial representatives, Canadian diplomats, and academics – and was intended to focus their attention on trade and economic relations with the Pacific world.[128]

I was firmly convinced from the outset that it was not sensible to try to build more fruitful trade relationships with countries in isolation from other relationships. That was my philosophy in general, but I thought it was of particular importance in the Orient, where human relations were more delicately handled than in many other parts of the world. At the conference, I therefore stressed a total approach, including cultural and academic relationships, so that we might become genuinely engaged with the people of the Pacific world and function as whole human beings, not just as commercial zealots. Accordingly, the creation of a Pacific foundation that would enhance Canada's presence in the Pacific community emerged as one of the recommendations of PROC I.[129]

PROC II was held in Toronto in February 1982. This time, I emphasized that trade must be the number one priority of both federal and provincial governments, since Canada was a country that earned roughly one third of its GNP through trade. By strengthening Canada's ability to act as a nation, we would be able to bring greater benefit to Canadians, and we would do so in part by providing full federal support to provincial initiatives.

* * *

A decision to enhance the Canada-Japan relationship was taken by the prime ministers of both countries in 1974 and confirmed during Trudeau's visit to Japan two years later. In the aftermath of this visit, important steps had been taken to give substance to that relationship; most notably, by the creation of a framework for economic co-operation and a cultural agreement concluded in 1976. Canada and Japan established a Joint Economic Committee, which met annually at the senior official level to review the broad range of economic relations. Our most important objective in the Japanese relationship was a multilateral one, to support a more active international role by Japan, which was generally a laggard in that respect among Western nations.

I visited Tokyo for consultations in November 1981, where I met with Foreign Minister Sunao Sonoda. One of my most vivid memories of Sonoda was the distorted interpretation that occurred at one of these meetings. The foreign minister, who was not highly regarded by his officials, apparently indulged in some idiosyncratic foreign policy of which official government circles did not approve. Accordingly, what he said was not interpreted by the Japanese government's interpreter, who substituted what the minister should have said for what he actually did say. My officials hastened to inform me of the deception *sotto voce* in the course of the meeting.

Such a subordination of the ministerial role would have been inconceivable in most other countries. But it expressed rather well the Japanese reality, in which, as I understood it, bureaucrats centred in the Ministry of Finance and the Ministry of International Trade and Industry (MITI) actually ran the country – not subject to the political will of parliamentarians and ministers. Moreover, the Japanese bureaucracy operated by a cumbersome consensus system, so that in order for policy evolution to occur a whole group of people – perhaps even leaders of industry – had to be persuaded of the wisdom of any change. Bargaining with the Japanese was thus a time-consuming, and often frustrating, exercise because their negotiators were not empowered to do anything more than listen.

The Japanese government also tended to make its major decisions on the basis of Japan-U.S. relations and problems, automatically assuming that these decisions would be satisfactory in relation to Canada; for example, with regard to automobiles. The main bilateral problem we had with Japan was over their flooding our market with Japanese-made automobiles at a time when our industry was still vulnerable. Ed Lumley and I were determined to bring about both an automobile import restraint program on their part and also further Japanese investment in the automotive parts industry in Canada, which in the fiscal year 1980 increased by twenty per cent to US$920 million. It took a ruthless determination on our part to threaten a surtax and to delay routine customs examinations at points of entry to bring the Japanese – slowly – to agree to restraint in automotive exports to Canada. This was a political initiative taken without much support from our public servants. It was not easy for free traders like Lumley and myself to act as occasional protectionists, but it was sometimes necessary in the national interest.[130]

During a February 1982 meeting, the ambassador acknowledged that Japanese decision makers did not always perceive a separate set of issues and that it would take some time to effect any significant change in the Japanese approach. He also noted that Lumley's aggressive automotive stand had come as a surprise to Tokyo only because they had not been listening until we started screaming, and problems like this were time-consuming, given the Japanese decision-making process. In any event, our extreme measures eventually got Japanese attention, and a satisfactory restraint agreement was reached.

* * *

Trudeau's 1970 recognition of Beijing as the sole legal government of China was a landmark of Canadian foreign policy and also an integral step for the People's Republic of China (PRC) in obtaining its seat in the United Nations, and diplomatic recognition by virtually every other state, including eventually the United States.

In establishing ties with China, Canada recognized the importance of China as the world's most populous country and as a potential great power. We accordingly sought to draw China out of its international isolation and to move it towards active membership in the world community. For our own national benefit, we also sought to expand trade and other contacts. This task was rendered easier by the major modernization program that Deng Xiaoping launched when he finally gained full power in 1978.

Two things were always guaranteed to make the PRC government see red: any interference with its hegemony in Tibet and any threat to its claim to Taiwan as an integral part of China. The second was a constant but small source of friction, given the number of Canadian entrepreneurs who wanted to trade with Taiwan. For example, the Chinese chargé d'affaires in Canada made an official protest in August 1980 against the establishment of a "Liaison Centre of the Chamber of Commerce of the Republic of China" in Toronto. We regretted the use of the name "Republic of China," but because a legal resident of Canada had established the office, we had no means of enforcing a change of name.

I made an official visit to the Peoples' Republic of China in August 1981, and Vice-Chairman Deng Xiaoping, Premier Zhao Ziyang, and Foreign Minister Huang Hua received me. On this visit, I was able to inform the Chinese that China was now eligible to receive CIDA development assistance, a matter which had had to be carefully negotiated with Chinese officials so as not to offend their sensibilities as to receiving aid. The program I proposed was a modest one.

Deng was particularly well disposed to me because of the personal good turn I had been able to do him the previous year. His son, Deng Pufang, had been forced to jump out of an upstairs window by hostile cadres during the Cultural Revolution, breaking his back in the incident. He was thereby rendered supine and came to Canada for a secret back operation. The operation was highly successful, and the younger Deng was henceforth able to sit up. Although I had done only what any Canadian foreign minister would have done in similar circumstances, at Deng's instigation I was given what External officials referred to as "a prime ministerial tour" of China, which included Beijing, the monumental Great Wall, the recently unearthed statues at Xi'an, the spectacular gorges of the Yangtse, and the wartime capital of Chongqing (Chungking).

My forty minutes with Deng were spent mostly on internal factors, such as Chinese social and economic developments and the role of capitalism in the socialist system. Deng insisted in our conversation that he would accept only the techniques of capitalism and not its substance. I expressed polite skepticism as to whether that was possible.[131] I suggested that the techniques of capitalism could work for them, as they had for us, only in a matrix of freedom. Indeed, on 20 August I had given an address on international law and human rights to the Chinese Law Society in which I had delivered the following paragraph:

It is sometimes thought that what is most remarkable about Canada and other countries of the West is our advanced technology and material well-being. However, the source of our progress is not technology, but rather the rule of law, which protects citizens from arbitrary action by the state and guarantees the fundamental values of a free society: freedom of conscience and religion, freedom of speech and of the press, freedom of assembly and of association. It is this freedom in the framework of the rule of law which renders possible our social dynamism, economic progress, and even technological innovation. For us, the rule of law has proved to be the matrix both of collective progress and of personal fulfilment.

I felt that this was the message we most urgently needed to convey to the Chinese leadership.[132]

Huang had been the first Chinese ambassador to Canada in 1971, had headed the PRC's UN delegation, and had become foreign minister in 1976. At the time of my visit, he was in his late sixties. Huang and I focused in our meetings principally on international issues, particularly Soviet aggression in Afghanistan and Cambodia. He was regarded as being circumspect even by PRC standards, but I cultivated an excellent relationship with him.

During my time in Beijing, I also met Premier Zhao, who provided a briefing on his contacts with Southeast Asia, Party Vice-Chairman Li Ziannian, who enlightened me on developments within the party, and Vice-Premier Bo Yibo, with whom I discussed economic relations. The most substantial of my talks outside of Beijing was in Chengdu, the capital of Sichuan Province, which was a hotbed of economic reform. I called on the deputy governor in charge of economic affairs and also visited a people's commune and a tool factory.

While I was in China, there was some press misunderstanding of my reply to a journalist's question, which was interpreted to mean that we would now supply weapons to China. The truth of the matter was that, as a result of a review the previous winter, China had been placed in a category similar to that of most countries with respect to strategic goods such as defensive equipment, transport aircraft, and high technology items, but we sold *offensive* weapons only in a NATO/NORAD context. In fact, we had no intention of discussing even strategic goods with the Chinese, and the matter never came up.

I did my best to sustain the impetus from my visit to China through the rest of my time in office. The question that lingered in our minds, however, was who would replace the aged Deng.

* * *

ASEAN was established in 1967 as a regional economic, social, and cultural grouping, but it was only with the Bali summit meeting of ASEAN heads of government in 1976 that political co-operation made real progress.

The economies of the ASEAN countries were amongst the fastest growing in the world, and the association instituted a formal dialogue mechanism with its major economic partners: Canada, the United States, Japan, the European Community, Australia, and New Zealand. The first Dialogue with Canada was held in 1977, but none was held in the next two years. However, recognizing the priority status that ASEAN merited in our foreign policy, I made a point of attending the ASEAN Foreign Ministers' Meetings in 1980 (Kuala Lumpur), 1981 (Manila) and 1982 (Singapore). These meetings were considerable events, not only as to business but also as to the camaraderie that developed among participants. The meetings always began with a Five-Plus-All session, which was always focussed on multilateral issues and always included a social evening. The individual encounters with other foreign ministers were known as Five-Plus-One meetings.[133] Vietnam and Cambodia were the multilateral preoccupation of all the ASEAN states at the annual sessions.

The political cohesion of ASEAN had been given further impetus by the Vietnamese invasion of Cambodia in January 1979 and by their installation of a pro-Hanoi regime under Heng Samrin. Despite some differing perceptions of the relative threats posed by Hanoi, as well as Beijing, the ASEAN states nevertheless recognized the need for solidarity in their approach to the continuing Vietnamese occupation of Cambodia.

With two hundred thousand troops in Cambodia and a puppet regime installed under Heng Samrin, Vietnam gave promise of remaining in control indefinitely. It did not, however, command the loyalty of the Khmer (Cambodian) people. But then neither did the predecessor regime of Pol Pot and his Khmer Rouge, domestic communists who in an excess of Maoist revolutionary fervour had slaughtered perhaps as many as two million of the Cambodian middle class and some ethnic minorities, and who, ousted from power, constituted the Democratic Kampuchea (DK) resistance.[134] The DK was by then nominally led by Khieu Samphan, but Pol Pot continued as the military and real leader. There was also a non-communist opposition led by the aging Son Sann, though it was no match militarily for the Khmer Rouge.

Canada's policy, following the lead of ASEAN, was to continue to recognize the Pol Pot government as the legitimate holder of Cambodia's seat in the General Assembly, a matter which came up for a vote every fall. This was not out of any affection for the murderous Pol Pot, against whose policies the Clark government had spoken out at the General

Assembly in 1979. Indeed, we had no diplomatic relations with the DK. However, we felt we could not recognize the alternative People's Republic of Kampuchea, which was sustained in power only by Vietnamese troops and organized by Vietnamese "experts."

This was the general Western position, although Australia had announced its intention to derecognize the DK in the midst of an election campaign, at a time when a large sector of their public was opposed to continued recognition of a government guilty of such gross violations of human rights. Vietnam's pretext for its continued occupation of Cambodia was that China was threatening collusion with the DK. This was an attempt to fuel traditional concerns about Chinese interference in the region. At the same time, by increasing pressure on Thailand through stepping up military activity along the Thai-Cambodian border, it tried to make the Cambodian problem appear as a border problem with Thailand. It also tried to gain international respectability by international lobbying, particularly with the European Community.

The United Nations staged a successful International Conference on Kampuchea (Cambodia) in July 1981, which established the basis for a peaceful resolution of the problem. In my address at that conference, I rejected both the illegal Vietnamese occupation of Cambodia and the restoration of the genocidal Pol Pot government. Instead, I endorsed the proposals that were adopted for a ceasefire, the creation of a United Nations peacekeeping force, the supervised withdrawal of foreign troops, and the holding of UN-supervised free elections. China was isolated in its opposition to a UN peacekeeping force, which it saw would interfere with the untrammelled freedom of action of its client state, the DK. In any event, Vietnam and the USSR remained intransigent.

Canada's relations with Vietnam had been minimal since it invaded Cambodia in 1979. Prior to then, we had provided wheat flour and medical supplies to Vietnam, and a Canadian company had been actively involved in oil exploration. The only active component of Canada/Vietnam relations in my day was the Family Reunification Program, under which some 2,300 Vietnamese and Sino-Vietnamese came to Canada, in addition to the 82,000 Indochinese refugees resettled in Canada since 1975.

Cambodia was on the brink of starvation during the early eighties and was kept going only by large-scale relief from the democratic world through the two ports and the few border-crossing points open. Unfortunately, both sides in the conflict used food denial as a weapon of war and food distribution as a political tool. As a result, large-scale deprivation was the norm in most of the country. Through UNICEF, the International Red Cross, the United Nations high commissioner for refugees, and various non-governmental organizations, Canada provided $29 million in humanitarian assistance for Cambodia in 1979–81. The assistance went to Cambodians within Cambodia, along the Thai border, and within Thailand, and to Thais displaced by the refugee influx into Cambodia.

In the months following the International Conference on Kampuchea, a serious attempt was made to put together a coalition government embracing both the non-communist and communist Cambodian opponents of Vietnam. This was ultimately successful, at least in name, and Prince Sihanouk was named president and Son Sann the prime minister of a new Coalition Government of Democratic Kampuchea. Son Sann visited Ottawa on 21 December 1981, at a time when the coalition government was not yet fully established. When the coalition government was finally established, we gave our strong moral support, and Prime Minister Trudeau wrote Son Sann expressing the hope that the formation of the coalition government would bring closer the day when the country would be free from foreign occupation.[135]

Chapter 13
The Middle East

Canada's interest in the Middle East was not limited to the Arab-Israeli conflict. The Arab world was the fifth largest market for our exports and our highest export growth area in the previous decade. In 1979, we had merchandise exports to the value of $620 million as well as service contracts to the extent of $400 million with Saudi Arabia alone. Our imports from the Arab world were even larger: $1.5 billion in value in 1979, including forty per cent of our total oil imports. Our trade with Israel was much smaller: exports of $109.5 million in 1979, imports of $563 million. Nevertheless, the Arab-Israeli conflict was the dominant foreign policy issue in the area and assumed a large role in international diplomacy generally, because of Arab linkage of almost everything else with it.

The Jewish-Arab conflict had been an international issue at least since 1897, when Theodore Herzl founded the Zionist movement for a Jewish national home in what was then Palestine. It was given impetus in 1917 by the Balfour Declaration and crystallized in 1948 with the proclamation of the state of Israel and its recognition by the United Nations. Its contemporary form stems from 1967 when Israel, in the highly successful Six Day War, took possession of the Gaza Strip and the Sinai from Egypt, the West Bank from Jordan, and the Golan Heights from Syria. This occasioned the passage of Security Council Resolution 242, which established Israel's security with recognized borders in exchange for its withdrawal from the territories it had occupied, a step Israel has not fully taken even to this day. Nevertheless, our acceptance of Resolution 242 has been the bedrock of Canadian policy toward the problem ever since.

The Israeli Labour Party had been in power from the founding of Israel until the 1977 election. The new Labour leader Shimon Peres was, if anything, more enlightened, but had less political rapport with the Israeli people, probably because he lacked a military background. In that year, the Labour Party was defeated by the hard-line Likud Party under its politically fundamentalist leader Menachem Begin, with his determination to claim for Israel permanently the whole of what was called *Eretz Yisrael*, the Biblical land of Israel. Begin's regressiveness was even more striking in contrast with the far-seeing statesmanship of Anwar Sadat, who had succeeded Gamal Abdel Nasser as the president of Egypt, by far the most populous Arab state.

Sadat, with his symbolic visit to Israel in 1977,[136] brought about the first signs of peace between Israel and its neighbours and led to the eventual restoration of the Sinai to Egypt. Both the United States and liberal Israelis, like Attorney General Aharon Barak (the chief Israeli negotiator), pressed Begin into agreement. The Israeli leader, however, could not be pushed at all in negotiations over that part of the Camp David Accord dealing with an interim five-year period of partial self-rule for the Palestinians in the West Bank/Gaza, which was clearly intended to be followed by fuller autonomy, but to which he subsequently gave such a narrow reading (autonomy only in limited respects) as to be tantamount to bad faith.

To my mind, Begin was consistently an irascible and irrational barrier to progress toward peace. He was also particularly disliked by Prime Minister Trudeau, who greatly resented his apparent meddling in the Canadian election campaign of 1979, when Trudeau was for a nine-month interregnum replaced as prime minister by Joe Clark. Begin's immediate objective at that time was Canada's recognition of Jerusalem as the capital of Israel in place of Tel Aviv, a step Trudeau had consistently refused to take since coming into office in 1968. Indeed, in a private tête-à-tête during the Israeli leader's 1978 visit to Canada, Begin asked Trudeau to recognize Jerusalem as the capital. When the prime minister refused, Begin threatened that he would have no alternative but to take his case to the Canadian people. In carrying out his threat, he did succeed in making Jerusalem an issue in Canadian politics, although officially it was denied that the subject of Jerusalem had arisen.[137] Clark, the new leader of the Progressive Conservative Party, was persuaded by him and made a campaign commitment to move the Canadian embassy to Jerusalem, thereby recognizing it as the Israeli capital – although it could be argued that the whole of Jerusalem was illegally occupied by Israel.[138]

Both Arab and Muslim non-Arab states protested strongly, Saudi Arabia being one of the loudest voices against the move. Arab states threatened to exclude Canadian companies from future business, and even to breach existing contracts. Bell Canada was in a particularly vulnerable position because of a contract with the Saudis. The Arab monetary fund decided to boycott all Canadian banks and financial institutions. The situation worsened when Ron Atkey, otherwise a successful minister of immigration, stated that the Arabs' bark was worse than their bite, since this was taken by many Arabs as a canine allusion. Canadian business and the provinces were almost unanimously opposed to the Clark move. The comment I heard again and again from members of the public during this period was "It's all so unnecessary." The public perception of Clark's competence began to be undermined. It seemed that Canada needed the Arab world more than it needed us.

Arab-Israeli issues were normally very much entangled with domestic politics, with Canadian Arabs on one side and Canadian Jews on the other. The strange thing about the embassy issue is that moving it to Jerusalem did not seem to be a particular objective of politically conscious Jews in Canada. It was a Begin initiative, rather than a domestic cause. Trudeau continued to have a good relationship with the Canadian Jewish community, but he understandably had it in for Begin.

Specific Arab sanctions were held in abeyance in the hope of further clarification of the situation. Clark was forced to do something to still the clamour both inside and outside the country and on 23 June 1979 announced that he was appointing Robert Stanfield, his predecessor as Conservative leader and a man highly respected for his probity and objectivity, as a special representative to consider Canada's contribution to the Middle East peace process, including the location of the embassy. This was seen by Arab states as a conciliatory gesture since Clark made it clear that every question was left open for Stanfield's consideration. Stanfield made an interim report at the end of October 1979 recommending against the change in embassy location until Israeli-Arab agreement had been reached in the Middle East negotiations. The Jerusalem crisis therefore came to an end.

I regarded myself as pro-Israel in that I had no time for talk of Israel's dissolution, or for its international isolation, or for general condemnations of Zionism or of Israeli policy. Indeed, the department regarded me as pro-Israel. The conventional wisdom was that the so-called "departmental Arabists" controlled External Affairs, except for Gotlieb and myself. Nevertheless, I found the department, under the capable direction of Michael Shenstone, the assistant undersecretary for the Middle East and Africa, indispensable in interpreting events and in deciding how to react.

Despite my pro-Israel starting point, as events will show, I was far from uncritical of Israel's behaviour, whether to its Arab subjects in Gaza and the West Bank or in Lebanon, and of its knee-jerk response to everything related to the Palestine Liberation Organization (PLO). I had had first-hand experience with the depths of Arab feeling on the question in 1975, when I was attending the annual session of the International Labour Organization (ILO) as parliamentary secretary to the Minister of Labour.

In the course of the meeting, the PLO was admitted to the ILO with observer status, an event that led to a thunderous demonstration of approval from Arab and Arab-sympathizing delegates. It seemed as if the whole huge assembly hall – not including the Canadian delegation, I hasten to add – was on its feet jumping about and wildly cheering as the PLO representatives walked down the aisle. It was a happening etched in my memory.

Nevertheless, I was never seduced by the illusion that Canada was – or could be – a major player in the conflict. The United States had had a special relationship with Israel from its inception in 1948, originally no doubt because of President Truman's stalwart defence of Israel's right to exist, and subsequently by reason of its billion-dollar annual subsidies to Israel for both military and economic aid, the steady American emigration to Israel out of idealism for the new Jewish community, and the political strength of the Jewish lobby in the U.S. It was always clear to me that it was only American pressure that could move Israel at all from its belligerent ways and that even American pressure was often not equal to the task. But it was all that we in the West had going for us.

* * *

At the time that I became foreign minister, Canada was not only firmly committed to the Camp David peace process but was still optimistic as to progress. Alas, we had not sufficiently counted on Begin's intransigence with regard to any degree of real Palestinian autonomy in the West Bank/ Gaza, and by May of 1980 the process had clearly reached a complete impasse. We continued to speak of our dedication to Camp David, but we no longer had any substantial belief in the likelihood of success.

Initially, I pulled my punches towards Israel in making private rather than public démarches to Tel Aviv. I did this not primarily out of friendship for Israel, but more out of fear that any public criticism might incite public opinion in Israel in Begin's direction, at a time when everyone believed he was certain to lose the 1981 election if nothing happened to change the direction of Israeli public opinion. In keeping with this policy, I made quiet early representations to Tel Aviv on Israeli incursions into South Lebanon and on the lack of progress on Camp David, both of which I argued would have the effect of further isolating Egypt within the Arab world. It was, after all, the only Arab state that had trusted Israel and had little to show in return.

Moreover, on 23 March 1980, on a close 8–6 vote, the Likud cabinet had approved a new Israeli settlement in the former Jewish quarter in Hebron, the largest Arab town on the West Bank, with a further agreement to allow other new settlements in the occupied territories. This was, to my mind, an attempt to prejudge the ultimate outcome of the peace negotiations just as they were about to begin again. On my instructions, our ambassador to Israel, Joe Stanford, conveyed my strong feelings to the Israelis a few days later.

In June, I had meetings with the Israeli ambassador, the Egyptian ambassador, and the other Arab ambassadors. I informed them that I did not plan to implement as such the final Stanfield Report, which had been presented to the Clark government on 20 February, just before the election. The report called for a more activist Canadian policy in the Middle East, one that was less supportive of Israel at the UN and more critical of Israel in general. It was, nevertheless, a moderate and sensible document, one that I followed in effect. I also told the Israeli ambassador that Begin's policy of encouraging more West Bank settlements was "folly" and that the only thing working in Israel's favour was that Palestinian policy was even more foolish than that of Israel. I delivered the same message to the Arabs. The only Israeli defence of the new Begin settlements policy was that the new communities would be limited to ten.

I had my first meeting with the Canada/Israel Committee (CIC) on 12 June 1980, with whom I generally enjoyed excellent relations during my time in office. The principle figures were Harold Buckwald of Winnipeg, the head of the CIC, who was usually supplemented at meetings by Irwin Cotler, the president of the Canadian Jewish Congress and a distinguished international civil libertarian and personal friend. Both were embarrassed from time to time by Begin's antics. On this occasion, I met only Buckwald and CIC Executive Director Mark Resnick, whom I told that Canada would not be adopting a high profile position on the Middle East because there was little contribution we could make to the peace process. Any initiatives we would take would not be radical.[139]

In late July, the Likud-dominated Knesset passed a bill affirming that Jerusalem was an integrated whole and the capital of Israel, thereby effectively annexing East Jerusalem. On 1 August, I stated that Canada did not recognize the legality of Israel's annexation of East Jerusalem and reaffirmed Canada's traditional policy that the status of Jerusalem could be resolved only as part of a general settlement of the Arab-Israeli dispute.

In the meantime, I also had occasion to protest to the Israeli government about the use of counterfeit Canadian passports by Israeli intelligence agents, an issue which arose again with greater force several months later, after an Israeli bearing a fraudulent Canadian passport attempted to assassinate a PLO official in Cyprus. I had my strong disapproval conveyed to the Israeli ambassador on 15 January 1981. The Israeli accused pleaded guilty to the attack and received a two-year sentence.

Over the Easter weekend in 1981, the Israeli Defence forces (IDF), and the Christian militia in southern Lebanon allied with them, took aggressive action in response to attacks on neighbouring Israeli territory by PLO forces. I was particularly disturbed by the large number of reported cases of death and injury of innocent civilians. I issued a press release calling on all parties to refrain from further hostilities, followed by a démarche in Tel Aviv calling for restraint. Israel went on to bomb the Beirut area, and Christian Phalange units proceeded to attack Palestinians in Beirut and Zahle, east of Beirut on the edge of the Syrian-held Bekaa Valley, provoking serious Syrian shelling.

In June 1981, Israel bombed Iraq's French-supplied OSIRAK research reactor, and I publicly denounced the action. The attack was especially provocative in that Iraq was an NPT signatory, whereas Israel was not. Given the quality of Israeli intelligence, I believed that it was probably true that Iraq was secretly engaged in the late stages of a nuclear weapons program, but even in that context I could not approve of such a unilateral preemptive strike. Israel's action was unanimously denounced by the Security Council, as well as strongly condemned by Canada. Nevertheless, Canada and other Western states were not in favour of the suspension or expulsion of Israel from the International Atomic Energy Agency. Our policy was one of universality of membership in the agency, and, moreover, there was no provision in the IAEA charter for membership sanctions.[140]

The issue of Canadian participation in the Sinai in a multilateral peace force, which came to be called the Multinational Force and Observers (MFO), arose about the same time. The MFO was a consequence of the Camp David peace process, of which Canada was generally a strong proponent. But because of the opposition of Arab states other than Egypt, the MFO could not become a UN peacekeeping operation, in which Canada would have been prepared to participate. Instead, it was now to be a U.S.-led peacekeeping force, and we were privately urged by both the U.S. and Israel to participate. The Canadian contingent to be involved would have been small, since it was the symbolic quality of our support that Israel in particular prized.

If I had ever thought that Canada's participation would have made the difference in the actual deployment of the force and in Israel's official return of the Sinai to Egypt in 1982, I should of course have been willing to go along. Indeed, it took me some time to make up my mind, but I was not ultimately disposed to offer any moral support to Begin or to do any favours to an unduly aggressive Israeli government, especially since, against all the odds, Begin had succeeded in defeating Peres again in the June 1981 election, and his new coalition was accepted by the Knesset.

Undersecretary Gotlieb disagreed with my decision not to participate in the MFO and asked my permission to carry the matter to the prime minister. I collaborated with him by sending to Trudeau Gotlieb's memorandum that we should agree then in principle to the MFO, with actual participation to come later; thus appending my own hand-written comments that we should initially decline participation, leaving the door open as to the future. The prime minister was even less disposed than I to accommodate Begin. As a result, we did not take part in the MFO, and all parties adhered to the polite fiction that we had not been invited – which was true in a formal sense – so that no one was embarrassed by our refusal to join.

* * *

By the autumn of 1981, Israel had agreed with Egypt to renew negotiations on Palestinian autonomy, but had also expressed its intention to assert its sovereignty over the occupied territories at the conclusion of the interim autonomy period. International attention had switched from a European Community spring initiative on the Middle East, which endorsed self-determination for the Palestinians, to a more far-reaching Saudi eight-point peace plan which proposed complete Israeli withdrawal from the occupied territories, including dismantling of Israeli settlements, and the establishment of a Palestinian state with Jerusalem as its capital.

Canada had never gone as far as the EC in recognizing the PLO and calling for a Palestinian state, though realistically our position was not far from that. We favoured a defined territory for Palestinians, which we usually referred to as a homeland, within a clearly defined territory, which we identified as the West Bank/Gaza. We took the view that Palestinians must be represented in the determination of their own future but that it was up to them at an appropriate time and in an appropriate way to choose their representatives. We accepted that the PLO was *a* representative group, but not necessarily *the* representative group, of the Palestinians.[141] Moreover, I thought it was too soon to endorse without qualification the idea of a separate Palestinian state. Gaza in particular was largely a wasteland and might well be a permanent international "basket case." It might, it seemed, make more sense for the West Bank/Gaza to be united with Jordan. But I never rejected the possibility of an independent Palestinian state. So, as I approached Israeli Foreign Minister Yitzhak Shamir on the margins of the UN General Assembly in September 1981, accompanied by our new UN ambassador, Gérard Pelletier, I could assure him that Canada not only accepted Israel's right to exist, to be secure and to have recognized borders, but also had an open mind as to the shape of the future.

My overall point of view, however, was that Israeli actions had made it more difficult for Canada to continue its strong moral and voting support. I had four counts in my indictment. First, Israeli policy towards the West Bank/Gaza Palestinians was incomprehensible in its unreadiness to negotiate their future. Second, the attack on the Iraqi nuclear facility was extraordinarily dangerous. Third, Israeli's bombing of Beirut and its actions in south Lebanon were regrettable. Fourth, Israel's settlements policy completely undermined the Camp David peace process. In sum, Israel had disastrously lost the propaganda battle in the previous year.

Shamir was rather avuncular in manner and at that time seemed considerably more moderate than Begin. He refused to take offence, and his response was defensive and explanatory, not aggressive. But as events were to show, his moderation, if it existed, had little effect on Begin's government.

* * *

Anwar Sadat's assassination on 6 October 1981 was a blow to the prospects for peace in the Middle East. Begin attended the funeral and had a meeting with Mubarak in which both pledged that the search for peace would continue. But Sadat's death ought to have been taken by the Israelis as a sign of how incredibly difficult the path was for moderate Arabs, and the basis for a resolve to do what they could do to bolster the position of such sympathetic interlocutors. Instead, Begin was entirely preoccupied with his own country's immediate interests. In December, the Knesset legislated that the law, jurisdiction, and administration of Israel be extended to the Golan Heights taken from Syria in the Six Day War. The Israeli ambassador to the United Nations insisted that this did not constitute annexation, but it was hard to see the difference, especially since the justification Shamir offered me in a message on 14 December was on the basis of security considerations and *the necessity for clearly defined boundaries.*

I replied that we saw the Golan action as an attempt to extend Israel's sovereignty. Such a move was completely incompatible not only with Resolution 242, but also with the General Assembly's 24 October 1970 declaration on the Principles of International Law Concerning Friendly Relations and Cooperation among States, which provided that no territorial acquisition resulting from the threat or use of force should be recognized as legal. The Canadian position was made public, and, in consultation with the prime minister, I also decided to vote in favour of a General Assembly resolution condemning the Israeli initiative on the Golan.

Shamir had assured Herb Gray that Israel would fulfil its Camp David commitment to withdraw from the Sinai. On that it was as good as its word, but at the same time it launched its greatest folly. On 6 June, Israel invaded Lebanon, in what was stated to be a response to over a hundred terrorist attacks on Israel and to what was said to be the last straw – the shooting of the Israeli ambassador in London. The action was argued to be in full accord with international law as a valid exercise of the inherent right to self-defence, in order to destroy the large quantities of PLO tanks, missiles, artillery and ammunition in Lebanon. It was emphasized that Israel had no territorial aspirations in Lebanon but also that the simple restoration of the *status quo ante* was out of the question.

The prime minister issued a public statement addressed to Begin on 9 June, stressing our dismay at the Israeli escalation of the conflict, calling for a ceasefire and an immediate Israeli withdrawal. Begin replied privately a week later, accusing Canada of a lack of understanding, and stating that in "Judea and Samaria there stalks a neo-Nazi organization called the PLO." I replied by supporting a UN General Assembly resolution condemning Israel for its non-compliance with the Security Council resolution to withdraw its forces.

* * *

While the Israeli siege of Beirut was going on, Canada was engaged in its own small conflict with Israel. The Canadian ambassador to Lebanon, Theodore Arcand, was the only Western ambassador who remained at his post in Beirut during the turbulent summer of 1982, and as a result suffered Israeli indignities not visited on any other ambassador. He stayed, not only to assist those who needed visas and other help, but also to help keep up the spirits of the populace. It was bad enough that his residence was shelled from time to time, but, in addition, since all his supplies had to be brought into West Beirut from the Israeli-held environs, he had frequent occasion to cross through the IDF lines. Every time, he was stopped and searched, despite the fact that he had diplomatic licence plates, flew the Canadian flag on the automobile, had his ambassadorial credentials with him, and vehemently protested the intrusions. Such a search was in total contravention of the Vienna accords on the treatment of diplomatic personnel. The Israeli government knew that and was aware of what was going on but was either unable or unwilling to bring Sharon and the military to heel.

I protested, and the Canadian Parliament passed a resolution encouraging Ambassador Arcand to stay his ground, although by 2 August I had to order the embassy temporarily moved from Beirut to a suburban location for reasons of safety. The department eventually persuaded me that the best thing to do was to accept an insincere letter of regret from Shamir.

Though that ended the incidents officially, it did not remove the bad taste from our mouths.

* * *

On 2 August, I also had occasion to protest the renewed Israeli bombardment of Beirut, and, in a "scrum" after Question Period two days later, I denounced Israeli actions as "incomprehensible" in the context of peace. Earlier that same day, I had had a direct confrontation in caucus with dissident Liberal members from Quebec. Anti-Israel feeling ran high in the Quebec caucus on all occasions, perhaps taking courage from Trudeau's well-known attitude towards the Begin government. As so often happened in caucus, what most of the members wanted was primarily to let off steam against an adversary, in this case Israel. But the hard core demanded, in retribution for the Israeli aggression, official recognition of the PLO and Canadian sponsorship of economic sanctions against Israel.

There were only a few solo voices raised in support of Israel and a chorus on the other side. As was customary in caucus debates involving a particular minister, he or she was allowed to speak last, immediately before the prime minister's summation speech. I spoke on this occasion on the theme of balance in foreign policy, as epitomized by the Liberal tradition of Pearson and Martin. I emphasized how seeming departures from such balance had three times led to the overthrow of governments,[142] and I asked caucus members not to make the same mistake now. Then I took them through the recent history of our protests against Israeli actions to demonstrate that we were in fact being very even-handed in bestowing rebukes where they were merited. The vast majority of caucus took my admonitions to heart.[143]

Our policy was completed by Canada's strong support for President Reagan's peace initiative of 1 September, which rejected both Israeli annexation of the West Bank/Gaza and an independent Palestinian state in the occupied territories, and called for a return to the Camp David peace process, with a five-year transitional period of partial autonomy, negotiations, and a freeze on Israeli settlements. The Israelis would have none of it, however, and it was only the tragic massacres at the Sabra and Shatila refugee camps that partially broke the logjam, as a result of justifiable Israeli shame.

* * *

In a letter to the prime minister on 26 February 1982, I proposed a number of new initiatives I had been mulling over for contacts with the Arab people of the occupied territories: an invitation to the moderate Arab mayor of Bethlehem, Elias Freij, to visit Canada; mission-administered CIDA funds designated for the West Bank/Gaza; small-scale funds to NGOs for special purposes; some scholarships in Canada for Palestinian students; and increased information efforts in the territories. All of these initiatives would have been badly received in Israel, and Begin might have tried to prevent us from having such contacts with West Bank Arabs. I was also open to the endorsement of some form of Palestinian self-determination, short of the recognition of a Palestinian state.

Trudeau probably thought my suggestions did not go far enough, though he was never specific as to what he did want, and he was himself nervous for domestic political reasons about endorsing outright self-determination for the Palestinians. At one point in the spring of 1982, I received an indirect threat. Michael Pitfield informed Allan Gotlieb one day that, if the PM could not get the kind of Israeli policy he wanted from me, he would get himself someone who would do as he wanted. I never knew whether this was intended as a message for me from the PM, or whether Pitfield was supposedly "reading his mind." In any event, I paid not the slightest attention, since I had no idea anyhow what Trudeau wanted. Nor, I think, did he. Like the Quebec caucus, he wanted to lash out at Israel. With the exception of East-West relations, it was probably the area in which my views were the least close to those of the prime minister, since I did not start with an animus against the Begin government. None of this, however, had anything to do with my move to the Justice portfolio.

**Part Four
Conclusion**

Chapter 14
Retrospect and Prospect

On the evening of Thursday, 9 September 1982, I learned through a telephone call that I would be sworn in as Minister of Justice and Attorney General of Canada at Rideau Hall the next morning at nine o'clock. It would be a four-way shift, with MacEachen moving from Finance to External, Lalonde from Energy to Finance, and Chrétien from Justice to Energy. My own move to Justice completed the quadrangle.

A few days before, Trudeau had informed me that he had to shift my portfolio. We were both in Toronto for receptions and for a dinner the prime minister was giving, and at his request we met for a half hour in his hotel room. He explained that it had become politically necessary to move Allan MacEachen out of Finance, and there was nowhere but External that would be suitable for him. We discussed other portfolios in which I might be interested, but Justice had not been the focus of our discussion. I had the impression that nothing would change quickly, but inadvertently I may have had something to do with advancing the timetable.

Soon after my meeting with Trudeau, I spoke with MacEachen to assure him that I felt no resentment whatsoever at being replaced by him, since I thought he richly deserved a return to External. MacEachen was astounded at my news, as he had apparently no inkling that he was about to lose Finance, and clearly did not like the idea one bit. I was equally astonished, as I had assumed that Trudeau had spoken to him first. I suspect in retrospect that MacEachen went to the PM immediately, and that this sped up the changes over what might have been intended.

The early-morning swearing-in on 10 September did not take long, and a visibly unhappy MacEachen disappeared immediately afterwards. By 10:30 I was pressed into service to fulfill the new SSEA's schedule for the day: at 10:30 a meeting with a minister from Bhutan; at 11:00 a *tour d'horizon* with Prime Minister Robert Muldoon of New Zealand; at 12:30 a Canadian Club luncheon for Muldoon; at 4:00 a reception for former undersecretaries of state for external affairs; and at 7:30 the PM's dinner for Prime Minister Muldoon. By the next week I was settling into my new portfolio.

* * *

It was not the best of times.

After a decade of détente during the 1970s, the Cold War flamed again with the Soviet invasion of Afghanistan at the end of 1979. The West tried to counter this renewed Cold War aggression, which was accompanied by a massive Soviet nuclear warhead build-up in Eastern Europe, with an Olympic boycott and a nuclear missile modernization of its own, but was then confronted with the Soviet-induced imposition of martial law in Poland. The Second Oil Crisis, beginning in 1979, and the fundamentalism of the Ayatollah Khomeini, which swept Iran and fettered Americans and Western interests, compounded all of this.

As one might have expected, this new Soviet and Iranian belligerence led to the election of a right-wing, fire-breathing U.S. president. Ronald Reagan's zeal to bring down "the evil empire" of Soviet imperialism led to not only a new age of bipolarism in the United States, with serious consequences for the Third World, but also to a temporary fissure in the Western Alliance over European resistance to the American attempt to scuttle the Siberian natural gas pipeline.

Canada tried to lead the Western world to a new vision of the North's need to respond to the South's desperate plight, but was frustrated in the attempt to launch Global Negotiations, first by the reluctance of the Reagan Administration and ultimately by the intransigence of the Third World itself. At the same time Reagan's bipolarism frequently succumbed to the temptation to turn North-South questions into East-West ones, particularly in Latin America and southern Africa.

Progress towards a new regime on the Law of the Sea was brought to an end for a time by Western, principally American, self-interest. Negotiations on arms control made no appreciable progress, despite cautious willingness to bargain on Reagan's part, because the Soviets under Brezhnev were unprepared to negotiate in good faith. It would take a new look in Soviet leadership to create genuine possibilities of real détente.

The Middle East was in constant turmoil. Begin's over-response to Arab hostility, a misguided settlements policy, bad faith in implementing the Camp David Accord, and the destruction of the Iraqi nuclear reactor all contributed to the chaotic state of the region. The full-scale Israeli invasion of Lebanon in 1982, leading not only to the expulsion of PLO forces from Lebanon but to the massacre of Palestinians in the refugee camps, was a sombre indication of the failure to achieve peace and stability.

The large Cuban force in Angola, the South African unwillingness to free its former trusteeship territory, Namibia, and Reagan's determination to link the two, unsettled southern Africa. Cambodia was in servitude both because of the Pol Pot's determination to regain power and because of Vietnamese occupation, which reduced the country to famine and destitution.

Canadian difficulties with the United States had seldom been so widespread and deep-seated. For a time, our most serious bilateral problem in the world was the Gulf of Maine fisheries and boundary dispute. And there remained the persistence of the Garrison Diversion issue, the prevalence of American transboundary air pollution with its fallout of acid rain, and, worst of all, Washington's bruising response to Canada's National Energy Program and Foreign Investment Review Agency. Those problems were all compounded by the lack of rapport between Trudeau and Reagan, which threatened to end in a rather ugly fashion, but which we were eventually able to manage – just barely – with the prime minister's eating of some humble pie. American disaffection with Canadian policies lasted until the end of the Trudeau government's mandate. Acute environmental problems persisted until the end of the Reagan administration.

Canada internally was in disarray. The constitutional crisis, which began with the Quebec Referendum campaign in the spring of 1980, ended successfully with the proclamation of the Canadian *Charter of Rights and Freedoms* and the patriation of the constitution in the spring of 1982. While it lasted, there was a wrenching confrontation with eight of the ten provincial governments, and with a determined minority of the population, perseveringly led by Joe Clark. The combination of high interest rates resulting from the Oil Crisis, and the extreme dissension over domestic aspects of the National Energy Program, left the Canadian people badly divided on a regional basis, with considerable alienation from the government in Western Canada.

Although Canadians had little explicit interest in overall foreign policy, there was a strong constituency for foreign aid. There was also a highly vocal domestic minority in the grip of its own version of bipolarism, by which anything American-inspired was *ipso facto* suspect, and the world was seen as divided into left and right. This attitude had its outlet principally with respect to El Salvador, where I was attempting to follow a multipolar liberal policy of supporting the middle against the extremes, and with respect to disarmament, where unilateralism was the emotional response to the Western attempt to bring the Soviets to the bargaining table.

In the midst of all this, we carried on business, and better than usual. We were determined to stand up for our domestic commercial interests and to sell more abroad. The new policy of bilateralism, with its attendant emphasis on concentration of our foreign policy on selected areas and issues, was an attempt to bring us to a new age of commercial success. In my view (though some of my former colleagues would not agree with me), this led Canada ultimately and inevitably to the North American Free Trade Agreement, as well as to emphasizing our ties with the European Community, to forging new links with the Pacific Rim, to entering the Organization of American States, and generally to strengthening our relationships with Latin America.

Although the "Second Option" of closer integration with the U.S. posed its own problems for the maintenance of Canada's distinctness, it became the inevitable economic choice for Canada for a number of reasons. A major contributing factor was the undermining of the NEP, our largest instrument of independence from the United States, by Canadian provincial governments and Canadian business, and ultimately its abandonment by the Government of Canada itself after the 1984 elections. The ever-closer integration of the EC into an economic unit, now known as the European Union (EU), and the continuing imperviousness of the Japanese market as a result of its non-tariff barriers to trade, meant that the state of the world left Canada with no secure place to go for major trade expansion except the U.S. Nevertheless, I remain confident that Canadian distinctness will survive closer economic integration with our southern neighbour because of the strength of our traditions and culture. We also have the unique opportunity of somewhat taming the trade and investment practices of the American elephant through the – admittedly still very incomplete – rules of NAFTA, and perhaps those of the new World Trade Organization. I see a revised NAFTA as the best hope for our future.

The largest problem within the Western Alliance was the failure of the United States to consult adequately with its allies before taking decisions that affected them too. But more than that, we were all locked into a Cold War dance, in which steps from the one side were – usually predictably – responded to by answering steps from the other side. There was no realistic way out of this *danse macabre* until one side or the other changed choreographers.

I have the feeling that, paradoxically perhaps, Canadian influence in these issues may have been greater – or at least the influence of individual Canadian statesmen such as Lester B. Pearson, Paul Martin, and Norman Robertson may have been larger – when Canada was younger and relatively weaker than is now possible in a fully emerged post-colonialist and post-Cold-War world. The degree of networking now required to bring about change is extraordinary and the pace so glacial that it is hard for any one person to be around long enough to have a sense of significant achievement. This is obviously more true of politicians than of public servants.

Nevertheless, if policy is consistently held, one can have the feeling of contributing to the gradual evolution of progress.

As SSEA, my deepest commitment was to social justice for the Third World, but I also had strong feelings about Soviet expansionism and bipolarism. During my time in office, I became committed as well to increasing Canada's trade opportunities. My ultimate declaration was to the liberal ideal of peace through law, in which countries would respect the territorial integrity of other states as well as the human rights of their own citizens: a world of creative freedom.

* * *

There was little change in Western foreign policy as a consequence of the vagaries of election results. Clark and Trudeau in Canada, Callaghan and Thatcher in the United Kingdom, Schmidt and Kohl in the Federal Republic of Germany, Giscard and Mitterrand in France, all had the same general perception of the Soviet menace. Even in the United States there was little variation in East-West policy between the late Carter and the early Reagan regimes, the difference between which was largely one of rhetoric.

All countries have relatively permanent interests, so the broad thrust of their policies do not change greatly from administration to administration. This was as true of Canada as of other countries. What we did multilaterally was for the most part what we had to do, to be consistent with our own best interests; only cataclysmic change in the world could lead to a change in national interest. Thus, it was only the Soviet release of the Warsaw Pact countries and the tearing down of the Berlin Wall in 1989, along with the final disintegration of the Union of Soviet Socialist Republics in 1991, that brought the Cold War to an end, and ushered in a new post-Soviet era of multiple possibilities.

The new era that was made possible by Gorbachev's ending of the Cold War was given emphasis by the decisive Western victory in 1991 in the Gulf War, after which it became possible for a time to envision a new world order, where people would hammer their swords into ploughshares. The new era is ultimately more challenging, thanks to new possibilities of creative progress towards freedom, prosperity and world peace, as well as to new revelations of the dark potentialities of racism, lawlessness, poverty and environmental degradation.

As Madeleine Albright, the U.S. secretary of state, has written: "Today the labels of the past – hawk, dove, liberal, conservative – mean little. The greatest divide is between the proponents and opponents of American engagement, a divide that does not respect party lines."[144] In my view, the greatest political danger of the complex future is unipolarism, in which the whole of international affairs would revolve around Washington,[145] with its temptation to make American law apply beyond its own jurisdiction. Paradoxically, the greatest international danger after unipolarism is do-nothingism.

I wish my successors well in coping with the multidimensional agenda to come.

Acronyms

ALCMs air-launched cruise missiles
ASEAN Association of South East Asian Nations
BNA Act British North America Act, 1867
CCCB Canadian Conference of Catholic Bishops
CHOGM Commonwealth Heads of Government Meeting
CIDA Canadian International Development Agency
CSCE Conference on Security and Cooperation in Europe
CSE Communications Security Establishment
DK Democratic Kampuchea
EC European Community
FDR Democratic Revolutionary Front (El Salvador)
FMNL Farabundo Marti National Liberation Front (El Salvador)
G-7 Group of 7 (major industrial democracies)
G-77 Group of 77 (developing nations)
GATT General Agreement on Tariffs and Trade
GDU Garrison Diversion Unit
GLCMs ground-launched cruise missiles
GNP Gross National Product
FIRA Foreign Investment Review Agency
FRG Federal Republic of Germany
IAEA International Atomic Energy Agency
ICBMs intercontinental ballistic missiles
ICJ International Court of Justice
IDF Israeli Defence forces
IDRC International Development Research Centre
IJC International Joint Commission
ILO International Labour Organization
INF intermediate-range nuclear forces
LDCs less developed countries
LLDCs least developed countries
MFO Multinational Force and Observers (Middle East)
MPLA Movement for the Liberation of Angola
NAC North Atlantic Council
NAFTA North American Free Trade Agreement
NAM Non-Aligned Movement
NATO North Atlantic Treaty Organization

NDP	New Democratic Party
NEP	National Energy Program
NGOs	non-governmental organizations
NNWS	non-nuclear weapons states
NORAD	North American Air Defence Agreement
NPT	Treaty on the Non-Proliferation of Nuclear Weapons
NWS	nuclear weapons states
OAS	Organization of American States
ODA	Official Development Assistance
OECD	Organization for Economic Cooperation and Development
OPEC	Organization of Petroleum Exporting Countries
P and P	Priorities and Planning (Cabinet Committee)
PCO	Privy Council Office
PIP	petroleum incentives program
PLO	Palestine Liberation Organization
PM	Prime Minister
PMO	Prime Minister's Office
PQ	Parti Québécois
PRC	People's Republic of China
PROC	Pacific Rim Opportunities Conference
SCEAND	Standing Committee on External Affairs and National Defence
SRS	super-restricted session
SSEA	Secretary of State for External Affairs
START	Strategic Arms Reduction Talks
SWAPO	South West African People's Organization
U.K.	United Kingdom
UN	United Nations
UNGA	United Nations General Assembly
UNITA	National Union for the Total Independence of Angola
UNSSOD	United Nations Special Session on Disarmament
U.S.	United States
USSEA	Undersecretary of State for External Affairs
USSR	Union of Soviet Socialist Republics (Soviet Union)

Sources

Mark MacGuigan was the author of numerous articles for learned journals and the press. His book-length publications include *Jurisprudence: Readings and Cases* 2nd ed. (1966), *Cases and Materials on Creditor's Rights* 2nd ed. (1967), and *Abortion, Conscience & Democracy* (Toronto, 1994). His speeches and presentations as Secretary of State for External Affairs are published in the *Debates* of the House of Commons, the *Proceedings* of the Standing Committee on External Affairs and National Defence, and in the Department of External Affairs *Statements and Speeches* series.

The general, authoritative sources on Canadian foreign policy during his tenure as Secretary of State for External Affairs are Stephen Clarkson's *Canada and the Reagan Challenge: Crisis and Adjustment, 1981-1985*, 2nd ed. (Toronto, 1985) and Robert Bothwell and J.L. Granatstein's *Pirouette: Pierre Trudeau and Canadian Foreign Policy* (Toronto, 1990). The first volume of Stephen Clarkson and Christina McCall's *Trudeau and Our Times* (Toronto, 1990) centres on the prime minister's "magnificent obsession" with the constitution, and the second volume (Toronto, 1994) covers the uneasy Canadian-American relationship. All contain extensive notes and/or bibliographies to direct the reader to contemporary or more specialized studies, as does Robert Bothwell, "Foreign Relations and Defence Policy," in *Canadian History: A Reader's Guide* vol. 2 (Toronto, 1994) (see pages 79-85) and Jane Barrett, Jane Beaumont, and Lee-Anne Broadhead, *A Bibliography of Works on Canadian Foreign Relations, 1981-85* (Toronto, 1987).

There are few personal memoirs written by Canadians that deal with foreign policymaking during this era. Pierre Trudeau's *Memoirs* (Toronto, 1993) and, more specifically, *The Canadian Way: Shaping Canada's Foreign Policy, 1968-1984* (Toronto, 1995) (co-authored with Ivan Head) provide the prime ministerial perspective on key events and personalities. Mitchell Sharp's *Which Reminds Me...A Memoir* (Toronto, 1993) offers the perspective of an earlier SSEA under Trudeau (1968-74), and Allan Gotlieb's *I'll Be With You in a Minute, Mr Ambassador: The Education of a Canadian Diplomat in Washington* (Toronto, 1991) offers fascinating insights into Washington during the 1980s. The many foreign memoirs and monographs, both popular and scholarly, on the same period are too numerous to list.

The *Canadian Annual Review of Politics and Public Affairs* and the *Canada Year Book* for these years provide indispensable overviews and statistics. Three journals are of primary interest to scholars of this period (*International Journal, International Perspectives*, and *The American Review of Canadian Studies*), as well as case- and subject-specific issues covered in the Canadian Institute for International Affairs' booklet series *Behind the Headlines*.

Notes

1. I have not footnoted material I gleaned from the files, since they are something of a jumble and I know of no accurate way to cite them. Moreover, I have for the most part relied on my own notes and recollections and used the departmental files merely as confirmatory.
2. I refer not only to the daily Question Period but also to the four full days of debate on foreign policy: 9 March 1981 (El Salvador); 15 June 1981 (North-South relations); 16 June 1981 (South and Central America); and 1 June 1982 (Poland, Falklands, McDougall Report). In the term "Hansard" I also include reports of parliamentary committees, particularly the Standing Committee on External Affairs and National Defence (SCEAND).
3. Trudeau did telephone me after the 1974 election to offer me the speakership of the House, which I declined. My reasons for refusing were not only ambition, in that it was not the tradition for speakers subsequently to become ministers, but also that I felt my constituency was too political to be held on a non-partisan basis.
4. After Trudeau announced his resignation and the Clark Government was defeated on a vote of non-confidence in the House, the leaderless Liberal party arguably did not have time to elect a new leader before election day, and there was pressure for Trudeau to rescind his resignation and return as leader. The matter proved to be controversial in caucus, and one person who took a strong stand against Trudeau's return was my friend, the capable Judd Buchanan, MP for London West, and a former Trudeau minister from my region of Western Ontario. A powerful oration by the always effective Allan MacEachen carried the day for Trudeau in caucus. After the election victory, Buchanan was not invited back to cabinet, and soon resigned his seat in the House. His misfortune may have been my good fortune.
5. I had been joint chairman of two special committees on the Constitution (1970–72 and 1978), a member of the Standing Committee on Justice and

Legal Affairs from 1968 and its chairman from 1975, as well as chairman of a special committee on statutory instruments in 1968–69, and of a subcommittee on penitentiaries in 1976–77. During my party's months in opposition, I had been critic of the solicitor general, whose portfolio covered police (RCMP), parole, and penitentiaries.

6. Louis Bernard Robitaille, *La Presse*, 26 March 1980.

7. I have always had the greatest respect and admiration for Chrétien's political skills, and promised him on the eve of the Party leadership convention in 1984 that I would support him when I withdrew my own candidacy after the first ballot if I thought my votes would put him over the top. However, John Turner was so far ahead on the first ballot that the situation never arose, especially as Otto Lang, on Don Johnston's behalf, had called me to invite me to support Johnston, who intended to remain on the ballot (thus withholding his votes from Chrétien).

8. J. L. Granatstein and Robert Bothwell, *Pirouette: Pierre Trudeau and Canadian Foreign Policy* (Toronto, 1990), 382.

9. Issues of subsidization of particular industries, for example, always split the cabinet and were accordingly extremely difficult to resolve.

10. Granatstein and Bothwell, *Pirouette*, xiii.

11. Ivan L. Head and Pierre Elliott Trudeau, *The Canadian Way: Shaping Canada's Foreign Policy 1968–1984* (Toronto, 1995), 8.

12. As Secretary of State for External Affairs, I was also the minister responsible for CIDA, which had a much larger budget than External itself and in underdeveloped parts of the world was Canada's principal face. There was a certain amount of internal rivalry between CIDA and External, although no one ever explicitly challenged External's pre-eminence in the making of foreign policy or CIDA's in the distribution of Official Development Assistance (ODA). I quickly developed an excellent relationship with CIDA President Marcel Massé, and I readily agreed to his request for regular face-to-face weekly meetings in the absence of any representatives of External, so that he could make his submissions to me directly rather than through the department.

13. *Living Faith* (New York and Toronto, 1996), 139.

14. Head and Trudeau, *The Canadian Way*, x and 317.

15. Head had briefly been a junior foreign service officer before becoming a law professor at the University of Alberta. He was brought to Ottawa by Trudeau when the latter was still justice minister, and by virtue of his native brilliance soon became the PM's policy adviser and confidant. He became highly unpopular with External officials, who came to regard him as a rival power centre who owed nothing to the department and could in no way be controlled. Trudeau, to his own profit, continued to rely on

Head in foreign policy until 1978, when he was appointed president of the IDRC, the position he held during my time in office. It was considered a great victory by External when they succeeded in replacing him with one of theirs (initially this was Alan Sullivan who had served Clark in this capacity in 1979, and after the first few weeks it was Bob Fowler), although no one could ever duplicate his personal rapport with the PM.

16. The CSE did not report to me but to the minister of national defence and no doubt from time to time to the prime minister. However, tidbits from intercepted traffic found their way to my desk from time to time.

17. *Foreign Policy for Canadians* (Ottawa, 1970), 19.

18. The philosophical basis of my position is set out in my article "Law, Morals and Natural Law" (1961), 2 *Current Law and Social Problems* 89.

19. House of Commons *Debates*, 1 June 1982, 17977.

20. Marchand was a well-connected mandarin from the Privy Council Office with a strong bent towards foreign policy, who was appointed associate undersecretary shortly after I came to External.

21. Standing Committee on External Affairs and National Defence (SCEAND), 2-4-1981, 36:6.

22. SCEAND, 24-3-1982, 66:7.

23. SCEAND, 6-5-1982, 70:16.

24. There was a Canadian Press report on the address the next day, Ottawa *Citizen*, 4 June 1996, and a reproduction of excerpts a few days later, "New cabinet ministers need wisdom of Solomon," Ottawa *Citizen*, 9 June 1980. A commentary by Jack Maybee, "Minister vs. bureaucrat: Adversity or collaboration" appeared in the *Citizen*, 23 June 1980.

25. *The Department of External Affairs Act,* R.S. 1985, c. E-22, par. 10(e)(*j*).

26. That was my judgment also at the time. See SCEAND, 2-4-1981, 36:10.

27. Our most direct contribution to Afghan defence was made secretly. Afghan tribesmen were particularly partial to the Lee Enfield rifle, and the Reagan adminstration approached us under the table to ask us to collect the Lee Enfields lying around in Canadian armouries for use of the *mujahedin* in their war with the Soviets. I immediately agreed, as did Gilles Lamontagne, the Minister of National Defence, and, somewhat to my surprise, the PM. I had not taken sufficient account of his dedication to rationality and his freedom from emotional baggage when no favourite preconceptions or interests were involved. The instruction was accordingly given forthwith, without cabinet consultation. I am sure it was but a small contribution, but at least it allowed us a way of sharing in the Afghan struggle.

28. I received invaluable guidance from Canada's NATO ambassador, John Halstead, one of Canada's most perceptive envoys. In addition, I found

myself particularly indebted to Si Taylor, the assistant deputy minister for political affairs; Klaus Goldschlag, assistant deputy minister and, by the time of the Bonn Summit, the ambassador to the FRG; the late Allan McLaine, the director of Eastern European affairs and later ambassador to Poland and, ultimately, to Czechoslovakia; and Robert Cameron, the assistant undersecretary for security policy and arms control.

29. I had no involvement with Iran during my term of office, except in sponsoring Bill C-31 on 16 July 1980 to provide for the imposition of certain economic sanctions against Iran. Canada's slender involvement with the Iran-Iraq War is described by Eric B. Wang, "The Iran-Iraq War Revisited: Some Reflections on the Role of International Law," *The Canadian Yearbook of International Law 1994*, 83. Carter has recently acknowledged that "the fact that our [American] diplomats were still being held [by the Iranians] on election day was the major factor in my failure to win another term," but still defended his policy of caution and restraint. Carter, *Living Faith,* 105.

30. Canada had very little part in the Falklands War. I note in passing that the Department, in preparing its briefing notes for me frequently referred to the Falklands under their Argentine name of the "Malvinas." I believe I was once incautious enough to use the term publicly, leading to questions as to whether I was espousing the Argentine claim to sovereignty. Of course, I had no such intention, but was merely too faithfully following my text.

31. The institution was by name an "economic summit," and some of the seven, France under Giscard d'Estaing in particular, were leery of the political side of the meetings, not wanting to have their political choices constrained by collective agreement. In my experience, Canada and the United States were the strongest proponents of a political dimension at the summits.

32. I used my presence in Rome to linger for a visit to Italy. I ended the week with an official visit to the Vatican where I had a private half hour with His Holiness, and a profitable conversation with Cardinal Agostino Casaroli, the Vatican secretary of state, who was extremely well informed on Eastern Europe and a very impressive diplomat.

33. Haig had no pre-existing relationship with Reagan before becoming secretary of state. His lack of long-standing personal ties and rapport with the president and the Reaganites, however, was a source of constant unease in his relationship with the White House and ultimately brought about his downfall in mid-1982.

34. John Gray, "Mideast danger dominates economic talks," *Globe and Mail,* 21 July 1981, 1.

35. This would mean, if reciprocally accepted by the Soviets, the U.S. cancellation of its deployments of Pershing II and ground-launched cruise missiles; the USSR would have to dismantle its SS-20s and retire its SS-4s and SS-5s.

36. Alexander M. Haig, Jr., *Caveat: Realism, Reagan and Foreign Policy* (New York, 1984), 250. The best indication of Soviet responsibility is the *ex post facto* knowledge that after Polish independence Jaruzelski was allowed to live peacefully in Poland under the presidency of Lech Walesa. In a 1993 interview, he referred to the pressures that caused him to act in 1981: threatening resolutions passed by the Soviet Communist Party, the hot breath of hardline elements in his own party, tense meetings with Soviet leaders and Warsaw Pact army exercises along the Soviet and East German borders. John Darnton, "Martial law: his only real choice," *Globe and Mail*, 5 March 1993.

37. House of Commons *Debates*, 26 January 1982, 14253.

38. Ibid., 26 January 1982, 14257.

39. Ibid., 27 January 1982, 14373.

40. Ibid., 29 January 1982, 14373.

41. "Helsinki Accord Violated by Poland: MacGuigan," *Globe and Mail*, 6 March 1982, 7.

42. Reagan's proposed suspension of licences for oil and gas equipment, including pipelaying, led to a firestorm of resistance in Western Europe, since EC countries (particularly France and the FRG) had invested much political and economic capital in an agreement with the Soviets to build and pay for a 3,600-mile pipeline to bring natural gas from the Yamal Peninsula in northwest Siberia to continental western Europe. They regarded this as vital for security both of supply (in the light of OPEC crises) and of pricing.

43. Haig, *Caveat*, 309.

44. There was one lighthearted vignette in Bonn. I shared a double cottage with the prime minister, and, as I was in the shower the first morning, I could hear my door burst open and feet running. I wondered for a second if it was a terrorist attack, but, as I poked my head out cautiously around the shower curtain, I saw that the intruder was the PM's five-year old son Michel. He stayed with me while I was shaving, and when he eventually wandered out we were on the way to becoming fast friends.

45. On 25 June, the president requested and announced Haig's resignation as secretary of state. Haig had valiantly tried to act as a buffer for the Europeans and opposed the extension of the sanctions to overseas manufacturers (he also had a disagreement with the White House over American policy in the Israeli-Arab war then raging in Lebanon). I called

Haig at once to express my regret that he had been forced out because of his loyalty to the Alliance as a whole. Hormats, a highly respected assistant secretary of state who had served four administrations, also resigned in protest.

46. The natural gas pipeline was completed in 1984, much to the advantage of the Soviets. Gordon Crovitz, *Europe's Siberian Gas Pipeline: Economic Lessons and Strategic Implications*, 1984, points out that eighty per cent of the transmitted gas would be used by the Soviets themselves and that the Europeans would be paying substantially above market rates.

47. SCEAND, 25-2-1982, 65:51.

48. See, for instance, SCEAND, 25-2-1982, 65:44.

49. Peter Gizewski, "From Winning Weapon to Destroyer of Worlds: The Nuclear Taboo in International Politics" (1996) 51 *International Journal,* 297.

50. The Palme Commission's report was published as *Common Security: A Blueprint for Survival* (New York, 1982).

51. For example, members included Cyrus Vance of the U.S., former U.K. Foreign Secretary David Owen, Sonny Ramphal of the Commonwealth, Robert Ford of Canada, and Georgi Arbatov of the Soviet Union, director of the Moscow Institute of the U.S. and Canada and full member of the Central Committee of the Communist Party.

52. At the end of UNSSOD II's first week, more than 700,000 Americans (and a few Canadians) paraded in a peace march in New York City, the largest political demonstration in New York history, in an attempt to influence U.S. policy. On 14 June, 1,400 people were arrested for staging a massive civil disobedience protest at the UN missions of the five nuclear powers.

53. The Canadian government felt that it had in any event to honour contracts entered into before 1976, though with additional safeguards in lieu of adherence to the NPT.

54. For prior consent, we came to substitute advance agreement on long-term processing under agreed safeguards in place of case-by-case approval. Perhaps our additional safeguards had something to do with the fact that India had not exploded a nuclear device since 1974.

    Editor's note: On 11 May 1998, India shocked the world by conducting three underground nuclear explosions. Two days later (following two more tests), Indian External Affairs justified the tests by stating that the country required nuclear weapons to prevent "military adventurism" by neighbouring Pakistan. On 28 May, Nawaz Sharif, Pakistan's Prime Minister, announced that his country had conducted five nuclear tests of its own in response.

55. The IAEA reported that it could no longer certify that all the nuclear materials at Pakistan's KANUPP reactor were adequately accounted for in the fuel cycle. Our exports of nuclear fuel bundles to Argentina were subjected to particularly hostile scrutiny after the beginning of the Falkland Islands War in 1982. In fact, our safeguards were legally secure: the Argentines had firmly agreed not to use Canadian uranium or Canadian technology for non-peaceful purposes, although they had refused to commit themselves not to use *any* nuclear energy for non-peaceful uses. The only genuine question anyone could raise was whether the then government in Argentina could be trusted to respect them. This question was answered when Argentina soon afterwards restored democracy.

56. An ALCM was a self-guided, low-flying, highly accurate weapon with a small jet engine and wings, and a range of about 2,500 kilometres.

57. Permission for extension of such overflights was granted on 18 September 1980 for the period ending 31 December 1983.

58. President Reagan wrote Trudeau on the matter on 18 December 1981, and the PM assured him in a reply later that month that I had received authorization to negotiate and conclude the agreement.

59. I had little time for my two principal opposition critics, initially Flora MacDonald of the Conservatives and Pauline Jewett of the NDP, because I found both ritualistically against every government initiative. MacDonald was replaced in the fall of 1981 by John Crosbie, who seemed only occasionally involved in foreign affairs, but with whom I had some notable passages-at-arms. On the other hand, I had close relationships with the two secondary critics, Doug Roche of the Conservatives and Father Bob Ogle of the New Democrats. I found them able to discriminate among government programs and to judge them according to their merits as they perceived them. Although they disagreed with me on testing the cruise in Canada, we had many common areas with respect to disarmament. Roche subsequently prepared a report on UNSSOD II which was better than anything produced by the department. It thus came as no surprise to me when Roche was appointed as ambassador for disarmament after the change of government in 1984.

60. House of Commons *Debates*, 14 February 1983, 22803-4.

61. Ibid., 15 February 1982, 22851 and 16 February 1982, 22890.

62. Ibid., 16 February 1982, 22890.

63. Ibid., 18 March 1982, 23911. For subsequent discussions on the complicated decisions on testing, see the dialogue between Svend Robinson and Trudeau, SCEAND, 28 April 1982, 79:10; and my statement before SCEAND, 4 May 1982, 69:22-23.

64. Also present were Allan Gotlieb, who had been appointed the PM's personal representative for the Ottawa Summit in 1981 (as well as continuing as USSEA), Larry Smith, the assistant undersecretary for economic affairs, and Bob Fowler, the PM's foreign policy adviser. Smith was External's expert on all things North-South and was the backbone of all our initiatives in this area. He shortly became our first-and-only ambassador for North-South relations and was the principal advisor in this area through 1981–83.

65. Lewis Perinbam, the imaginative and indefatigable CIDA vice-president for special programs, was particularly helpful in setting up the Secretariat and was the initial chair of the working group on it. Perinbam was succeeded as chair by Canadian businessman Kurt Swinton (as part of a decision by those assembled that the Secretariat should not operate within CIDA as I had originally proposed). The multi-talented Iona Campagnola was also engaged by me to help organize the Secretariat, which received its charter as a non-governmental, non-profit organization on 20 March 1981.

66. The co-organizers were Algeria, Austria, Canada, the Federal Republic of Germany, France, India, Mexico, Nigeria, Sweden, Tanzania, and Yugoslavia.

67. On the economic side, energy no longer had pride of place at Ottawa as it had had in Venice. Inflation continued to be a priority, and unemployment, which was hurting all G-7 members, was much talked about. There was no division on the political issues (Afghanistan, the Middle East, and the Soviet military buildup), but no advance either. Trudeau stated in the follow-up press conference, speaking as chair for the group, that the Soviet Union must not be allowed to achieve military superiority over the West. John Gray, "Mideast danger dominates economic talks," *Globe and Mail*, 21 July 1981, 1.

68. SCEAND, 1-12-1981, 47:18.

69. House of Commons *Debates*, 16 June 1981, 10654.

70. SCEAND, 27-5-1982, 76:23.

71. House of Commons *Debates*, 16 June 1981, 10657.

72. See, for example, my comments on one project in SCEAND, 1-12-1981, 47:13-14.

73. Pym had a subsequent meeting with High Commissioner Wadds on 23 January, after he became House Leader. He then told her repeatedly, probably with some advance knowledge of the Select Committee's report, that the Canadian measure would be defeated in the House.

74. Two of the three "neutral" academic experts it heard had been retained by the provinces to fight the federal initiative.

75. *Reference re Amendment of the Constitution of Canada* (1981), 117 D.L.R. (3d) 1, 21.

76. The judicial decision of the Newfoundland Court of Appeal on 31 March 1981, was decidedly harmful to the federal cause, since all three judges agreed with the Kershaw view (without citing it) that a proper request to Westminster could not affect the powers, rights and privileges of the provinces without their consent, and that this proposed legislation would contravene that principle. *Reference re Amendment of the Constitution of Canada (No. 2)* (1981), 118 D.L.R. (3d) 1.

77. NDP leader Ed Broadbent commented that it was clear just from what the high commissioner admitted that he saw it as his function to tell Canadians what their responsibilities were and how to proceed. Investigation in fact verified the allegation. Ford had told Waddell that the constitutional amendment was "politically stupid," that it would cost the NDP seats, and that they were "crazy" to support the Liberals. Waddell, who was accompanied by NDP MP Jim Manley at the Governor General's skating party where the conversation occurred, related the whole story to interviewer Jack Webster on 9 February 1981.

78. Sonny Ramphal was one of the first people I met on the international scene and one of the most rewarding to know. He was from the Indian minority in Guyana, where he had been simultaneously foreign minister and attorney general. He was highly competent, frank in private conversation, outspoken in public, charming, and somewhat impetuous.

79. This was suggested in a meeting between Pym and Wadds on 13 March 1981.

80. *Re: Resolution To Amend the Constitution*, [1981] 1 S.C.R. 753, 807.

81. Ibid., 883 and 905.

82. Ibid., 858.

83. The account of this incident is contained in Pierre Elliott Trudeau, "Lucien Bouchard, illusionist," Montreal *Gazette,* 3 February 1996, B3. Trudeau emphasized that seventy of seventy-five members elected to the federal parliament by Quebec voted for patriating the constitution and that a CROP poll in March 1982 indicated that forty-eight per cent of Quebeckers blamed Lévesque's government for refusing to sign the accord, while only thirty-two per cent agreed with Lévesque. In June of the same year, a Gallup poll found that forty-nine per cent of Quebeckers approved of the *Constitution Act* and only sixteen per cent disapproved. Bouchard's reply, "The Problem with Pierre Trudeau," *Gazette,* 10 February 1996, B3, although filled with invective, was not able to challenge any of Trudeau's facts, as Trudeau pointed out in his rejoinder "Bouchard had no answer," *Gazette,* 17 February 1996, B5.

84. There was one important exception: after the Supreme Court's decision in *Ford v. Quebec,* [1988] 2 S.C.R. 712, striking down the Quebec public sign law as contrary both to the *Canadian Charter* and to the *Quebec Charter*, the Quebec legislature overrode the Court's decision.

85. In *Re: Objection to a Resolution to Amend the Constitution,* [1982] 2 S.C.R. 703, the Supreme Court decided on 6 December 1982 that Quebec had no right to veto.

86. The decision of the English Court of Appeal in *R. v. Secretary of State for Foreign and Commonwealth Affairs, ex parte Indian Association of Alberta,* [1982] 2 All E.R. 118 (C.A.) was handed down on 28 January 1982.

87. House of Commons *Debates*, 23 March 1981, 8519.

88. Allan Gotlieb, *I'll be with you in a minute, Mr Ambassador: The Education of a Canadian diplomat in Washington* (Toronto, University of Toronto Press, 1991), 26-28, and *passim.*

89. The chamber ultimately chosen with U.S. agreement consisted of Judge André Gros of France (Chair), Judge Roberto Ago of Italy, Judge Hermann Mosler of West Germany, Judge Stephen Schwebel of the United States, and Judge Max Cohen of Canada. This was regarded both as a strong tribunal and as a consensus court that would work well together.

90. The United Nations Conference on the Law of the Sea (UNCLOS), which ran from 1973 until 1982, was contentious at the multilateral level. By the time of UNCLOS, a consensus had emerged for recognition of a twelve-mile territorial sea if an international treaty provided for freedom of navigation in international straits, as well as for a two-hundred-mile economic zone. From Canada's point of view, pollution control was also of key importance, as we had taken groundbreaking steps in 1970 with the *Arctic Waters Pollution Prevention Act*. I did not have a great deal to do with UNCLOS, as it had been largely negotiated by our able ambassador, Alan Beesley, by the time I assumed office, and was opened for ratification after I was no longer SSEA. However, I was a passionate advocate of the provisions of the Law of the Sea Convention and I acted as an unpaid lobbyist for the cause in international corridors. For instance, a week after the final agreement on the convention's text, in an address at Mercy College in Detroit on 8 May 1982, I called on the United States "to join with Canada and most of the world in sharing the obligations, as well as the benefits, of this new international regime and the global community perspectives it involves."

91. The Air Quality Accord between the two countries was signed only on 13 March 1991 by President Bush. It was an executive agreement, rather than a treaty, and so did not require Senate advice and consent, but was

no less binding by that fact. It codified the principle that countries are responsible for the effects of their air pollution upon one another. Bruce Ackerman and David Golove, "Is NAFTA Constitutional?" 108 *Harvard Law Review* 799 (1995) argue that executive agreements have the same force as treaties in the U.S.

92. Gotlieb, *I'll be with you in a minute,* 11.

93. Mitchell Sharp, "Canada-U.S. Relations: Options for the Futures," *International Perspectives* (Autumn 1972).

94. In fact, the whole pipeline has never been built, because the American gas shortage was soon replaced by a surplus. Something like a quarter of Canada's total natural gas exports to the U.S. passes through the prebuild.

95. In 1980, for instance, Canada supplied the U.S. with $8 billion worth of natural gas, heavy oil, electricity, and uranium, whereas we imported only about $1 billion worth of coal from them. There were even American suggestions from time to time of a tripartite common market with Mexico and Canada, and a continental energy policy. Reagan, because of his inclination to trilateralism generally in American relations with Mexico and Canada, was thought to be partial to such an approach.

96. G. E. Cronkwright, "Introduction to Overview and Assessment," *The National Energy Program: Assessment and Alternatives*, Toronto, 14 April 1981, 5.

97. W.A. MacDonald, "Overview," *ibid.*, 15.

98. I have been assisted in my analysis by Jean-Paul Lacasse, "Legal Issues Relating to the Canadian National Energy Program," (1983) *16 Vanderbilt Journal of International Law*, 301.

99. The whole notion of a blended oil price in Canada at less than the world level was, it must be admitted, out of accord with the general policy thrust of our partners at the Venice Summit and led Canada to insist on carefully drawn language in the summit communiqué, by which we pledged merely to move in the direction of world market prices and so kept our options open for the forthcoming NEP.

100. I have been aided in my presentation of these events by the excellent analysis of Stephen Clarkson in *Canada and the Reagan Challenge* (Toronto, 1982).

101. This was a norm without legal obligations, but in any event the then SSEA, Allan MacEachen, had made a statement of interpretation at the time, acquiesced to by the other members, that the declaration did not prevent Canada from taking measures affecting foreign investors which we believed were necessary given our particular circumstances.

102. In his second budget, announced 12 November 1981, MacEachen did respond favourably to the American concern about further legislation.

The government formally stated that the special measures with respect to the oil and gas industry were not appropriate for other sectors. Moreover, it pledged that it would take no legislative action on expansion of FIRA coverage.

103. It was only with Gorbachev in 1985, after Trudeau's time, that it became possible to have negotiations based on reason, and even then only with some initial difficulty. And it was not sweet talk that brought the eventual transformation about, but unremitting Western pressure – political and economic, and with the promise of military retaliation for any direct aggression against the West.

104. Lubor Zink, "The Unpenetrated Problem of Pierre Trudeau," *National Review*, 25 June 1982, 751-2, 755-6.

105. Reagan evidently saw an early copy of the *National Review*, because Zink's article only appeared in the *Review* of 25 June.

106. I received considerable support in piloting the project through cabinet committee from Jean Jacques Blais, the Minister of Supply and Services, who immediately grasped the importance of the initiative.

107. SCEAND, 20-3-1981, 32:15.

108. Cuba moderated its behaviour to some extent during the 1970s, although with the fall of the Allende government in Chile in 1973 the Cubans became even further persuaded that the only way to victory was through armed struggle. In that context the Sandinista victory in Nicaragua in 1979 was for them an event of great moment.

109. The story of Sandinista-U.S. relations is imposingly related by Robert Kagan, *A Twilight Struggle: American Power and Nicaragua, 1977-1990* (New York, 1996).

110. The Canadian bishops' interpretation of events was disputed by Canadian Ambassador R. Douglas Sirrs, to whom it seemed more likely that the assassination was carried out by rogue military elements sympathetic to the right. The Salvadoran Truth Commission, set up after the end of the civil war, blamed Roberto d'Aubuisson, a swashbuckling right-wing military figure and the founder of the right-wing party Arena, for having ordered the murder.

111. The FMLN united five major guerrilla groups of Marxist orientation, numbering about 5,000 guerrillas, who were supplied through Cuba and Nicaragua, with a major operational base in Managua. The FDR included the National Revolutionary Movement (MNR) under Guillermo Ungo, a former member of the junta.

112. To do him credit, George Shultz has written that in El Salvador, "We supported a government struggling to be a democracy in the face of guerrillas on the left and generals on the right," but the general

orientation of Reaganite policy was more bipolar. Shultz, *Turmoil and Triumph: My Years as Secretary of State* (New York, 1993), 199.

113. House of Commons *Debates*, 9 March 1981, 8032.

114. Anthony Lewis, "Secrecy and Cynicism," *New York Times*, 27 December 1993, A15. See also Clifford Krauss, "Testimony in '82 on Salvador Criticized," *N.Y. Times*, 12 July 1993, A3.

115. Linda Hossie, "The ghosts of U.S. foreign policy," *Globe and Mail*, 12 November 1993, A27.

116. Nor was this clear to Monsignor Freddie Delgado, the secretary of the Catholic Bishops Conference in El Salvador. At a meeting with Ambassador Sirrs and the Canadian House Subcommittee on Relations with Latin America and the Caribbean on 23 February 1982, he said that, on a visit to Canada the previous year, he found that Canadians – he met mainly with Canadian clergy – did not understand the realities of the Salvadoran situation but, because of the distorted information they had, reflected the guerrilla point of view. I should note that this account is drawn from Ambassador Sirrs' full notes on the meeting taken at the time. Of course, the Canadian bishops may themselves have been divided. One newspaper article referred to Cardinal Emmett Carter as being of a different mind. Suzanne Fournier and Arthur Moses, "Canadians back opposing sides in tropical wars," *Globe and Mail*, 18 January 1983, 14.

117. Oakland Ross, "Killings Mar Heavy Vote in Salvador," *Globe and Mail*, 29 March 1982, 1.

118. The ostensible purpose of this visit was to plan the forthcoming visit to Canada the next month of Mexican President José Lopez-Portillo. A secondary purpose was to reassure Mexico on the opening of the Quebec trade office, of which the Mexicans were still rather leery.

119. Schultz, *Triumph and Turmoil*, 130.

120. A lot of time and energy had also gone into planning a visit to Colombia in January 1982, immediately before the one to Venezuela, but it had to be cancelled when the NATO ministerial meeting on the Polish crisis was scheduled for Brussels.

121. We were also actively promoting Telidon, the world's most advanced technology in the videotext field, and had already had one sale in Venezuela in 1981.

122. SCEAND, 27-5-1982, 76:16.

123. The sub-committee was part of the House of Commons Standing Committee on External Affairs and National Defence (SCEAND).

124. In my case, my words there and elsewhere were sufficiently strong that South African Ambassador John Becker called on E. J. Bergbusch, our director of African affairs, on 22 April 1981 to complain that I had made

a series of statements attacking South Africa. Bergbusch pointed out in reply that my attacks were in relation only to apartheid and Namibia.

125. Joseph Lelyveld, "Reagan's Views on South Africa Praised by Botha," *New York Times*, 5 March 1981, A15.

126. These issues were: the actual constitution of Namibia; the size, composition and deployment of the UN Transitional Assistance Group (UNTAG) required to implement the settlement plan; and measures to confirm the impartiality of the UN in carrying out its responsibilities in Namibia.

127. Japan was our leading trade partner after the United States: exports $4 billion, imports over $2 billion (1979); a total trade of $7.16 billion in 1980, $8.5 billion in 1981. Our trade with Australia was $568 million in exports, $466 million in imports (1979); with China $597 million in exports, $166 million in imports (1979); and with Korea $366 million in exports, $463 million in imports (1979).

128. Canada had a small aid relationship with ASEAN. Singapore (like Japan, Korea, Taiwan, and Hong Kong) was not a recipient of Canadian development assistance because of its advanced state of development. The Philippines, Malaysia, and Thailand could receive aid for occasional special projects or on an emergency basis. In my time, we had projects for fisheries and forestry development centres in those countries. Indonesia, the poorest country, was eligible for multi-year assistance, which it received in transportation, communications, agriculture, water resources, and power. We also assisted through our contributions to the World Bank and the Asian Development Bank.

129. Because of its complexity, the Asia Pacific Foundation of Canada could not be set up until June 1984. I was pleased to see it accomplished before I left cabinet.

130. The North American automotive industry was in a state of particular need at that period, but eventually, with the help of government loan guarantees to Chrysler in both Canada (in each of 1980, 1981, and 1982) and the U.S. and our temporary protectionism in both countries for the industry, it succeeded in becoming competitive again in the North American market. Needless to say, the three cabinet ministers from Windsor, one of the principal automobile-manufacturing cities in Canada, were always front and centre in those developments. It did us no harm that Ed Lumley grew up in Windsor!

131. Indeed, after merely two decades of Deng's reform, Nicholas D. Kristof wrote that "the principles governing China are not Marxist-Leninist but Market-Leninist.... Deng Xiaoping effectively transformed China from an ultra-leftist country to an ultra-rightist country and today the communist dynasty governs not by socialism but by something close to a dictatory

definition of fascism." "The Communist Dynasty Had its Run. Now What?," *New York Times*, 23 February 1997, E1.

132. Tiananmen Square made it clear that this was not a message Deng was prepared to receive.

133. I always tried to pay official visits to some of the ASEAN nations in connection with the annual meeting. I was able to have private sessions both with Prime Minister Hussein and Foreign Minister Rithaudeen of Malaysia on 28 June 1980 during the conference, and after it was over, I paid an official visit to Singapore (30 June – 1 July), meeting Prime Minister Lee Kuan Yew, Trade and Industry Minister Goh Chok Tong, and, of course, the foreign minister, 'Dhana' Dhanabalan, with whom I had developed a friendship.

134. Barbara Croissette, "Waiting for Justice in Cambodia," *New York Times*, 25 February 1996, E5. The story of Pol Pot is effectively presented by Ben Kiernan, *The Pol Pot Regime: Race, Power and Genocide in Cambodia under the Khmer Rouge 1975-79* (Yale University Press, 1996). Kiernan's estimate is that the Khmer Rouge caused the deaths of 1,671,000 people, or twenty-one per cent of the population, in less than four years of power.

135. In the long run, that is exactly what happened. The 1991 Paris accord on Cambodia led to years of contention between Prince Norodom Ranariddh and Hun Sen's Cambodian People's Party, the reincarnation of the Vietnamese-backed Communist Party that ruled the country from 1979 until the United Nations arrived to prepare for elections. Unfortunately, Hun Sen, with control over the bureaucracy, the police, and the military, ultimately became to be the real power in the country.

136. With the indispensable facilitation of President Carter, Sadat's visit led to the signing of the Camp David Accord between Egypt and Israel in 1978 and of an actual peace treaty in 1979.

137. This observation was contained in a 22 December 1981 note to file by Michael Shenstone, the assistant deputy minister for the Middle East and Africa.

138. In practice, Canada accepted Israel's control over West Jerusalem, even though it was not a *de jure* part of Israel by the terms of its 1947–48 emergence under UN auspices. East Jerusalem, seized by Israel in the Six Day War, was, on the other hand, nothing more than an occupied territory.

139. The CIC representatives informed me that the alleged Arab boycott of Jewish Canadian employees of Canadian businesses in Arab countries was a matter of concern to their organization. Stanfield had already recommended that we should consider amendments to the Canadian

Human Rights Act to counter any resignation by Canadian entrepreneurs to unreasonable foreign demands. I was sympathetic to their concern, but I had not yet found any evidence of such a practice.

140. At the controversial 1981 IAEA annual conference in Vienna, the Canadian delegation headed by Maurice Copithorne, our ambassador to Austria, maintained this position in the face of strong Saudi representations in advance of the meeting. The issue blew over at the conference, with Canada able to abstain on the Arab resolution which suspended technical assistance to Israel and referred the matter of possible Israeli suspension to the following conference.

141. See my comments to SCEAND, 26-11-1981, 46:4.

142. St. Laurent's in 1956 (vis-à-vis his ironic reference to "the supermen of Europe" in the Suez Crisis), Diefenbaker's in 1963 (with his apparently anti-U.S. defence policy), and Clark's in 1980 (in part because of his pro-Israel position).

143. I was particularly pleased to receive commendation afterwards from Keith Davey, who I regarded as the conscience as well as the 'spark plug' of the Liberal Party.

144. Madeleine Albright, "Blueprint for a Bipartisan Foreign Policy," *New York Times*, 26 January 1997, E13.

145. This was predicted by Charles Krauthammer, "The Unipolar Moment" (1991), 70 *Foreign Affairs* 23. Already, problem areas in which U.S. interests are absent, like Rwanda, are largely ignored internationally – unless some country dares to take the initiative, as Canada has done. Those where American interests are imperilled, like Haiti, are the subject of international intervention – or are not, when Washington's interests are in inaction, as in Nigeria. Other problem areas, like the former Yugoslavia, are brought under a vestige of international control only when the U.S. takes a hand.

Index